DEGAS AND THE LITTLE DANCER

DEGAS AND THE LITTLE DANCER

RICHARD KENDALL

with contributions by

DOUGLAS W. DRUICK *and* ARTHUR BEALE

YALE UNIVERSITY PRESS
NEW HAVEN AND LONDON
in association with
JOSLYN ART MUSEUM
OMAHA

To G.W.J.B. from R.K.

Published in conjunction with the exhibition
Degas and the Little Dancer, organized and circulated by
Joslyn Art Museum, with the assistance (as of November 1997)
of funds from Michael and Gail Yanney, The Douglas County
(Nebraska) Board of Commissioners, and
The National Endowment for the Arts, a federal agency.

ITINERARY

Joslyn Art Museum
Omaha, Nebraska
7 February–3 May 1998

Sterling and Francine Clark Art Institute
Williamstown, Massachusetts
30 May–8 September 1998

The Baltimore Museum of Art
Baltimore, Maryland
4 October 1998–3 January 1999

Published by Yale University Press, New Haven and London
in association with
Joslyn Art Museum, Omaha, Nebraska

THE AUTHORS

Richard Kendall is an independent scholar.

Douglas W. Druick is Prince Trust Curator of Prints and Drawings
and Searle Curator of European Painting, The Art Institute of Chicago.

Arthur Beale is Director, Objects Conservation and Scientific Research,
Textiles and Costumes Conservation, Museum of Fine Arts, Boston.

Printed in Italy

Copyright © 1998 by Joslyn Art Museum

All rights reserved.
This book may not be reproduced, in whole or in part, in any form
(beyond that copying permitted by Sections 107 and 108 of the U.S.
Copyright Law and except by reviewers for the public press), without
written permission from the publishers.

Library of Congress Catalog Card No.: 97-80502

ISBN: 0-936-36428-9

A catalogue record for this book is available from
The British Library

All works are by Edgar Degas unless otherwise indicated.

PHOTO CREDITS: © Arch. Phot./CNMHS: fig. 38; J. G. Berizzi, Paris: cat. no. 43; J. Lathion: cat. no. 38; Laurent-Sully Jaulmes: fig. 11; Lorran Meares: cat. no. 45, figs. 20, 71, 79, 82; © RMN: figs. 2 (Jean Schormans), 14 (H. Lewandowski), 42 (Chuzeville); Stuart Allen Scott: cat. no. 21a; Lee Stalsworth: cat. nos. 54, 56; Graydon Wood: cat. no. 8; Joseph Zehavi: cat. nos. 34a, 34b.

Frontispiece: *Little Dancer Aged Fourteen,* ca. 1920–21, plaster and fabric, 39 in. (99 cm), Joslyn Art Museum, Omaha, Nebraska.

COVER ILLUSTRATIONS

Front: *Little Dancer Aged Fourteen,* ca. 1920–21, plaster and fabric, 39 in. (99cm), Joslyn Art Museum, Omaha. Nebraska.

Back: *Little Dancer Aged Fourteen,* ca. 1921 or later, bronze and fabric, 38 in. (96.5 cm), The Baltimore Museum of Art, Alice Morawetz Bequest Fund (BMA 1943.1).

CONTENTS

FOREWORD AND ACKNOWLEDGMENTS

Edgar Degas is one of the best known of all the French Impressionist artists. Of his numerous subjects, his scenes of ballet dancers are perhaps the most popular, greatly appreciated by millions of viewers around the world.

Degas' statue of the *Little Dancer Aged Fourteen* is the largest, the most finished, and the most important of all his sculptures. It was the only one exhibited in his lifetime, at the 1881 Impressionist exhibition in Paris. Visitors to the show were amazed by the realistic qualities of the original wax model of this work, heightened by the addition of a real tutu, a silk hair ribbon, a wig, and ballet slippers. Some critics were appalled by the homeliness of the model, while others recognized the importance of this sculpture, which is credited with the beginning of avant-garde sculpture. Curiously, in spite of its importance and popularity, there has never been, until now, an exhibition focusing exclusively on the evolution of the *Little Dancer*. It is fitting that Joslyn Art Museum, which owns one of the two known plasters of this figure (the other is in the National Gallery of Art, Washington, D.C.), would pioneer such an exhibition.

The genesis of *Degas and the Little Dancer* began over five years ago in conversations between then Joslyn Director, Graham Beal, and English art historian Richard Kendall. I want to thank Graham for his continued support of this exhibition after he left Joslyn, and Richard Kendall for his expertise in curating such an important and beautiful show.

Degas and the Little Dancer is undoubtedly one of the most ambitious exhibitions Joslyn has ever undertaken. It could not have been done without the dedication of the Joslyn staff and the support of our sponsors, the Douglas County Board of Commissioners; the National Endowment for the Arts, a federal agency; and especially our lead sponsor for the show, Board Chairman Michael B. Yanney and his wife Gail. I express my sincere gratitude to them all.

The exhibition is the joint effort of three museums – Joslyn Art Museum, the Sterling and Francine Clark Art Institute, and The Baltimore Museum of Art. I wish to thank Michael Conforti, Director, and his staff at Williamstown, and Brenda Richardson, Deputy Director for Art, and her staff at Baltimore, for their help in the organization of the show. Additional thanks go to David Brooke, former Director of the Clark, and Arnold L. Lehman, former Director at Baltimore, for their support. Of course, without the generosity of the various public and private lenders in Europe and across the United States, who agreed to entrust us with their precious works of art for several months, there would be no show. To them we owe a great debt of gratitude for sharing their treasures with us.

An exhibition of this size requires help from virtually every member of the Joslyn staff, and I am grateful to all of them for their herculean effort. The enormous task of generating loan forms, cataloguing and recording all the works of art, and arranging for transportation to and from all venues belongs to the Collections and Exhibitions Department, and I thank Theodore W. James, Collections and Exhibitions Manager, and Penelope M. Smith, Registrar, for their accuracy and care. The exhibition installation was also carried out by Ted and his staff, including Michael Tegland and Rodney Fulton.

Special mention should go to Linda Rajcevich, Director of Marketing and Public Relations; Cindy Lee Christensen, Development Director; Steven Tlsty, Facility Manager; Katey T. Brown, Curator of Education; and Martha Lattie, Museum Shop Manager; and their staffs for their dedication and hard work. Reiko Renee Matsunami of Ballet Omaha and Audrey S. Kauders, Joslyn's Deputy Director, lent their valuable expertise to the creation of a new tutu for Joslyn's *Little Dancer Aged Fourteen*.

This catalogue is the effort of many people on two continents. I congratulate the authors – Richard Kendall, Arthur Beale, and Douglas Druick – for their excellent research and insightful essays, which make this catalogue an invaluable addition to the literature on Degas. Yale University Press in London has done a superb job of creating a handsome publication. In Omaha, Ruby C. Hagerbaumer, Curatorial Assistant, and Larry Mensching, Rights and Reproductions Department, undertook the project with diligence and good humor. Kathryn Corcoran, Head Librarian; Claudia Einecke, Associate Curator of European Art; Janet L. Farber, Associate Curator of 20th Century Art; Brandon K. Ruud, Curatorial Intern; and Marjorie Schuck, Translation Assistant in the Center for Western Studies, helped prepare the manuscript for press.

The principal author of the catalogue, Richard Kendall, joins me in expressing our warmest gratitude to Paul Mellon for kindly allowing access to his *Little Dancer Aged Fourteen;* to Jill De Vonyar-Zansky, Mollie Sayer, and Richard Thomson for their advice on the manuscript; to Jean Sutherland Boggs, Sara Campbell, William Darby, Marianne and Walter Feilchenfeldt, and George Shackelford for their generous help in tracing key works and contacting owners; and to the following individuals for their encouragement and assistance with both exhibition and catalogue: Clifford Ackley, Götz Adriani, Alexander Apsis, Daphne Barbour, Oliver Barker, David Bibby, Catherine Bridonneau, André Bromberg, Lillian Browse, Beverly Carter, Catherine Chevillot, Marjorie Cohn, Stephan Connery, Desmond Corcoran, Barbara Divver, Kate Garmeson, Thomas Gibson, Susan Ginsburg, Jack Hetherington, Colta Ives, Martine Kahane, Henri Loyrette, Laure de Margerie, Pippa Mason, Suzanne McCullagh, Mrs. Eugene McDermott, Charles S. Moffett, Marc de Montebello, Anne Pingeot, Lord Rayne, Sue Welsh Reed, Theodore Reff, Joseph Rishel, Deborah Ronen, Janet Salz, Anne Spink, Timothy Standring, Harriet Stratis, Michel Strauss, Miriam Stuart, Shelley Sturman, Martin Summers, Patricia Tang, Gary Tinterow, Mikael Wivel, Stephen Yates, Cristiane Ziegler, and Ruth Ziegler.

Douglas Druick's essay was developed from a paper given at the colloquium held at the Musée d'Orsay, Paris, in conjunction with the Degas retrospective exhibition held in Paris, Ottawa, and New York in 1988–89, and subsequently published as "La Petite Danseuse et les criminels: Degas moraliste?" in *Degas inédit: Actes du Colloque Degas,* Musée d'Orsay, 18–21 April 1988 (Paris, 1989), pp. 225–50. In that publication, he acknowledged those whose assistance and advice were critical, including Ruth Berson, Hélène Chew, Adrien Mattattia, Charles S. Moffett, Woodman Taylor, and especially Julia Sagraves, whose participation in the research was invaluable. In the rethinking of this material in the light of research on Degas and the issues surrounding this subject that have appeared since 1988, Dr. Druick also expresses his indebtedness to Richard Kendall for his encouragement, to Barbara Mirecki for her organizational assistance, and to Susan F. Rossen for her careful reading.

In regard to his catalogue contribution, Arthur Beale expresses his gratitude to all those who made his most recent research on Degas sculpture possible, especially Marsha V. Gallagher, Chief Curator of Joslyn Art Museum; Beverly Carter, Administrative Assistant of the Paul Mellon Collection; and Alison Luchs, Curator of Early European Sculpture at the National Gallery of Art, Washington, D.C. He expresses gratitude as well to the conservators whose observations and assistance were invaluable: Julie Reilly, Associate Director/Chief Conservator of the Gerald R. Ford Conservation Center, Omaha; and Shelley Sturman, Head of Object Conservation, and Daphne Barbour, Conservator of Objects, both at the National Gallery in Washington, D.C. Richard Newman, Research Scientist at the Museum of Fine Arts, Boston, ably performed the analysis on the minute samples taken from the plaster casts of the *Little Dancer Aged Fourteen.* Robert Shure of Skylight Studios in Woburn, Massachusetts, was most helpful in sharing his years of experience as mold maker. He also adds his appreciation to Henry Lie, Director of Conservation at the Strauss Center for Conservation, Harvard University, for the digitized imaging and computer assemblage of some of the X-radiographs illustrated in his text. Janet Sartor's secretarial assistance helped considerably in the production of Beale's manuscript, as did the three readers who gave such valuable comments on his text: Sara Campbell, Director of Art at the Norton Simon Museum, Daphne Barbour, and Richard Kendall, who encouraged his involvement in this project.

A special note of appreciation and gratitude goes to Marsha V. Gallagher, Joslyn's Chief Curator, who oversaw the entire project with her usual efficiency. Her enthusiasm, diligence and perseverance have brought this important exhibition and catalogue to fruition.

John E. Schloder, Ph.D.
Director
Joslyn Art Museum

INTRODUCTION

Edgar Degas' *Little Dancer Aged Fourteen*★ is among the three or four most celebrated sculptures of the modern age. Along with Rodin's *The Kiss* and the same artist's *The Thinker,* and perhaps Bartholdi's *Statue of Liberty,* Degas' statuette of a slender young ballet dancer has become recognizable to millions and admired throughout the world, the object of popular affection, scholarly debate, and the amiable disrespect of the caricaturist's pen. More than its illustrious companions, the *Little Dancer* has achieved a special kind of fame through multiplicity; made originally by Degas in wax and dressed by him in a fabric tutu, hair wig, and silk ribbon, the figure was replicated after the artist's death in some twenty-eight bronze casts that are now scattered in museums and private collections in Europe, the United States, and South America. When two early, little-studied plaster versions (one in Joslyn Art Museum, the other in the National Gallery of Art, Washington) are added to this number, a total of some thirty-one variants of the *Little Dancer Aged Fourteen* can now be accounted for. From Buenos Aires to Baltimore, and from Copenhagen to the Clark Collection in Williamstown, Degas' diminutive ballerina has become one of the defining images of our culture.

For more than a century, the prominence of the *Little Dancer Aged Fourteen* in Degas' career as an artist has also been widely acknowledged. Created between 1878 and 1881, when he was in his mid forties and at the height of his involvement with Impressionism, the *Little Dancer* was the first major sculpture associated with the movement and one of the most controversially received exhibits in its history. Regarded by some of his contemporaries as a masterpiece of realism, by others as "hideously ugly," and by yet others as a brilliant fusion of history, science, and popular culture, it was an extraordinary technical achievement for an individual with little previous experience in sculpture. For reasons that are still unclear, Degas was never again to exhibit his wax models in public, but the fame of the *Little Dancer* lived on; visible into the early years of the twentieth century in the aging artist's Montmartre apartment, Degas' sculpture entered the vocabulary of a succession of young visitors and, through first-hand contact or reputation, that of neighbors such as Suzanne Valadon, Georges Rouault, Pierre Bonnard, and Pablo Picasso (who was born in the year the *Little Dancer* was first exhibited). As a precocious venture into color, as a challenging juxtaposition of naturalism and artifice, and as a frank depiction of the commonplace, the sculpture has since been cited among the precursors of Cubism, Surrealism, and even Pop Art and its recent derivatives.

Little Dancer Aged Fourteen, 1878–81, wax and fabric, 39 in. (99 cm), Collection of Mr. and Mrs. Paul Mellon, Upperville, Virginia.

★Originally exhibited by Degas as *Petite Danseuse de quatorze ans (statuette en cire),* the title of the sculpture has been variously and confusingly translated, and has yet to find a generally accepted English form. In the present volume, the cooperation of the owners of the works in question has been granted for the use of a single title – *Little Dancer Aged Fourteen* – with the identity of individual casts indicated in the subsequent denomination of medium and location.

Despite its enormous celebrity, the *Little Dancer Aged Fourteen* has been allowed to remain curiously isolated from the rest of Degas' output and has been studied in a haphazard and partial fashion. This book – with its associated exhibition – is the first full-length consideration of the work since it was made and the first attempt to tackle certain issues that are crucial to its significance. The following pages include a unique technical examination of the sculpture in its different variants (including previously unpublished X-rays of the wax and plaster versions of the *Little Dancer*), pioneering analyses of the sculpture's reception by Degas' peers, and an unprecedented study of the figure in the sculptural context of his age. Drawing together previous research and invoking new approaches and disciplines, these studies aim to broaden our understanding of the *Little Dancer Aged Fourteen,* to correct a number of misapprehensions that have grown up around it, and to integrate the work into the high and low culture of late nineteenth-century Paris. By locating it among the drawings, pastels, prints, and oil paintings of related subjects from the artist's middle years, both book and exhibition also provide the opportunity to explore the inter-relatedness of Degas' imagery, as well as the haunting persistence of the *Little Dancer*'s form into the work of his last years. Here, too, are the key sculptures that preceded and accompanied the genesis of the *Little Dancer Aged Fourteen,* followed by a group of bronzes that show Degas' progression beyond his earlier commitment to realism. In addition, this volume brings together the most complete set of preparatory drawings for the work ever assembled, one of which – *Three Studies of a Dancer* – has been unlocated and unexhibited for more than half a century.

Something of the former neglect of the *Little Dancer Aged Fourteen* is evident in the strange history of the wax figurine itself, which was believed lost in the casting process before resurfacing in Paris in the 1950s. Already in a fragile condition at that time, the work was acquired by Paul Mellon and has remained in his private collection ever since, though it is ultimately promised – as part of a larger bequest of original waxes by the artist – to the National Gallery of Art in Washington. Known to the general public and many scholars principally through the bronze casts, the *Little Dancer* today enjoys a somewhat shadowy and ill-informed fame, especially as regards the status of the bronze and plaster variants and the original appearance of the wax statuette first exhibited in 1881. Several myths about its costume, surface coloring, and original display have gained a stubborn foothold, and – most damagingly – the world has become accustomed to Degas' young dancer in an absurdly short, entirely unhistorical tutu that distorts both the figure and its sculptural character.

For the first time since the work was exhibited by the artist, the redressed *Little Dancer Aged Fourteen* from Joslyn Art Museum – with its full, knee-length skirt – presents us with an experience of the sculpture comparable to that of Degas' earliest audiences. Sculpturally more buoyant, visually more defined, and sartorially more plausible, the figure offers new challenges to the museum visitor and specialist alike. These challenges – as well as the insights of the catalogue essays and documentation – can only intensify our engagement with this most paradoxical of sculptures. As Degas' contemporaries discovered, what at first sight seems breathtaking in its simplicity can also turn out to be subtly nuanced, contradictory, and – like the greatest works of art – provocative of new meanings for each successive generation.

1 THE WORLD OF THE LITTLE DANCER

THE SOLITARY BALLERINA

It has been the unfortunate fate of the *Little Dancer Aged Fourteen* to be singled out for its uniqueness – as the only sculpture exhibited by Degas in his lifetime, as the largest work he ever attempted in three dimensions, and as a curious, even freakish, portrait of a young ballerina in wax, hair, and fabric. In a way that is profoundly misleading, this perception has set the *Little Dancer* apart from Degas' other works of art and from most aspects of the historical context that gave it form and meaning. Though the sculpture has been endlessly cited and admired, little attention has been paid to the gradual evolution of the figure of the young ballet dancer in Degas' earlier paintings and pastels, or to the stubborn survival of the sculpture's form in his subsequent imagery. In a similar way, few attempts have been made to understand the *Little Dancer Aged Fourteen* against the background of training and rehearsal in late nineteenth-century ballet, a subject on which Degas himself was conspicuously well informed. Divorced from these circumstances, Degas' wax statuette has also remained strangely detached from the sculptural history of the period, as if it had been made in a creative vacuum and without reference to the technical concerns of other practitioners, a number of whom – it now transpires – the artist knew at first hand. Too often seen in isolation, the *Little Dancer* has been over-simplified and reduced to a near cipher, despite the widely varying responses of its first audiences, the profound ambiguity of its physical appearance, and continuing uncertainty about many of its original features.

The more closely we examine the *Little Dancer Aged Fourteen* and the visual culture to which it belonged, the more evident are its roots in current practice and in the complex development of Degas' career. During the 1870s, Degas had emerged from professional obscurity to enjoy critical acclaim as the leader of a major faction of the Impressionist group, progressively abandoning the restraint of his formative years in favor of a kind of technical and thematic bravado. Already in his mid forties when he began the sculpture, Degas was simultaneously involved in a redefinition of his realist project, pushing his skills and material resources to their limit and subverting many of the conventions that had formerly sustained his art. Now known to his peers as "the painter of dancers," Degas increasingly used the subject of the ballet to break new compositional ground or cross pictorial frontiers, such as those between pastel and printmaking or between the depiction of public spectacle and private behavior. As we move toward the end of the decade, the figure of the solitary dancer becomes the focus of much of his attention, demanding new strategies of material and psychological expression and finding its ultimate form in a one-meter-high, partly colored sculpture of a young ballet pupil. Without proposing the *Little Dancer Aged Fourteen* as a self-portrait of the artist in any but the most metaphorical sense, it is still possible to see this defiant, contained work of art as an emblem of Degas' maturity as he, too, faced a variously hostile and appreciative audience.

Few studies of the theme have taken into account the very beginnings of Degas' engagement with the dance. In the 1850s and 1860s, during his apprentice years, the artist made more than a dozen varied and separate renderings of the subject, based on classical sculptures and paintings by other artists as well as first-hand encounters with stage performances and groups of decorous or bucolic waltzers.[1] Though little more than sketches, these works announce Degas' awareness of a socially diverse tradition and perhaps his first assessment of their contemporary potential. This potential was not to be tested until about 1867, when he embarked on *Mlle Fiocre in the Ballet "La Source,"* a large and richly worked canvas showing a leading ballerina of the day posed on stage between two ornately dressed attendants and a real horse, the latter inclining its head to drink at a theatrical stream.[2] Exhibited at the Salon of 1868, when the novelist and critic Emile Zola rather surprisingly compared its palette of silvers and russets to that of a Japanese print, this picture prefigured Degas' activities at the time of the making of the *Little Dancer Aged Fourteen* in a number of curious ways.[3] Initially planned in a series of drawings, the posture of Eugénie Fiocre was also studied in the nude – presumably from a hired model – just as the *Little Dancer* was to find its earliest form in drawn and modeled studies of the naked figure. Eugénie Fiocre is shown in a setting at the Paris Opéra (where the dancer who posed for the *Little Dancer Aged Fourteen* was later to perform), where Fiocre, too, attracted the attentions of a number of painters and sculptors. Most famously, Fiocre was immortalized in a life-size bust by Jean-Baptiste Carpeaux that was cast in several materials and reduced-scale replicas; it is less well known that Degas himself expressed his appreciation of one of these models at the end of his life.[4] In a final coincidence, Degas' picture of the dancer has often been linked with his own first experiment in sculpture, a modest figurine of a drinking horse that corresponds in most respects to its painted counterpart.[5]

Within a short space of time, Degas followed these faltering experiments with a sequence of more accomplished equestrian models and a group of small, radical canvases of dance scenes, showing not just events on stage but fractured glimpses of the audience, the orchestra pit, and the theater itself. A work like the Musée d'Orsay's *Orchestra of the Opéra* of around 1870, with its looming musicians and distant view of the truncated corps de ballet, attracted both praise and patronage for the aspiring artist, initiating a life-long public association with the ballet and the appropriation of a distinctive spatial and technical vocabulary.[6] Soon the critics were on his trail; "The dance foyer is his predilection," announced Ernest Chesneau in 1874, while Etienne Carjat claimed that such scenes were "finely observed and ingeniously rendered," and Ernest d'Hervilly suggested that Degas' ballet pictures "would soon fascinate Paris."[7] Philippe Burty was more expansive: "There is as yet no-one," he wrote, "who has made such portraits of the dancer, the coryphée, made of gauze and bone, with emaciated arms, tired waist, balanced body, legs with that distinctively professional beauty whose multiple facets make up the general beauty of society."[8] Written at the time of the first Impressionist exhibition, when four of Degas' ten listed submissions were depictions of the ballet in different media and on varying scales, these observations were among the first to define the artist's professional identity. At subsequent group shows, which were held almost annually at this period, both the overall total of Degas' works and the proportion of dance subjects continued to increase, along with the fulsomeness of his admirers' prose; at the 1876 exhibition, the painting *Dance Rehearsal* (cat. 2) was saluted by Emile Zola for its "highly original character" and for the artist's "profound love of modernity, of everyday interiors and human types," while, confronted by the superb *Dance Examination* (cat. 15) in the 1880 installation, Charles Flor proposed that "Monsieur Degas deserves to be placed among the finest of today's draftsmen."[9]

From the beginning, Degas' pictures of the dance were characterized by their visual and practical daring, even a kind of brash sensationalism that reflected the sometimes lurid world the ballerinas inhabited. Delighting in the contrast between the musty gloom of the auditorium and the spectacle beyond, Degas took unprecedented liberties with the representation of the dancers themselves, plunging them into shadow or disfiguring them in the footlights, foreshortening their bodies, and showing them haphazardly from the front, the side – and most audaciously of all – with their backs to the crowd.[10] Rapidly extending his resources, he turned to pastel, *essence* (dilute oil paint on paper), pen-and-ink, gouache, and metallic pigment, and to a range of printing processes, such as etching, lithography, and monotype, as well as to bizarre combinations of these techniques that baffled his staunchest admirers.[11] Given his restlessness and near-arrogant versatility, it might be said that the only surprising feature of Degas' move into sculpture was that it took so long. Making its first, much-heralded appearance at the 1881 Impressionist exhibition, the *Little Dancer Aged Fourteen* was the latest in a series of bravura performances, here pitting the largely self-taught modeler against a two-thirds life-size statuette and all the demands of construction, elaboration, and the integration of artificial and "real" materials it entailed. Seizing yet more professional terrain, Degas asserted his originality and his dominance of an aggressively modern theme – as well as his prominence in the Impressionist enterprise – at a single stroke.

If a broad evolution can be discerned in the mass of ballet compositions from Degas' early years, it is from the image of the group to that of the individual, from the sweeping panorama of stage or rehearsal room to the predicament of the single performer. In this sense, the *Little Dancer Aged Fourteen* was the exemplification of a decade of study, of an art "made of renunciations" (as he was later to call it) that can be followed across the years.[12] With an artist as willful and unprogrammatic as Degas, there are always exceptions to any pattern of development; in this case, we can hardly overlook the fact that *Mlle Fiocre in the Ballet "La Source,"* his first dance picture, shows a single named ballerina at relatively close quarters and that certain later canvases include arrays of anonymous dancers. But the larger trend remains, as well as the sense of the *Little Dancer*'s slow emergence from the shadows – which prepared the way for, but hardly reduced the impact of, the figure's spotlit entry into the creative arena. At least seven years before the unveiling of Degas' sculpture at the sixth Impressionist exhibition, similarly posed young dancers can be found in assorted groups of drawn or painted performers, their backs erect, their arms behind them, and a single leg thrust forward. As time goes past, some of these figures detach themselves from their peers and acquire a striking separateness, achieving distinction through their deportment, their costumes, and their personal accessories. Gaining also in substance as Degas refined his mastery of light and shade, this intensely realized cast of dancers seems poised between the pictorial and the sculptural domain.

Two oil paintings shown at the first Impressionist exhibition of 1874, both of them contributing in well-documented ways to the establishment of Degas' reputation as a specialist in the dance, illustrate this progression. In *Dance Class*

Fig. 1 *Dance Class*, 1871, oil on wood, $7\frac{3}{4} \times 10\frac{5}{8}$ in. (19.7 × 27 cm), The Metropolitan Museum of Art, H.O. Havemeyer Collection, Bequest of Mrs. H.O. Havemeyer, 1929.

(fig. 1), executed in 1871, the artist arranged ten members of the corps de ballet across a tiny panel, their numbers wittily augmented by mirror reflections and a solitary, violin-playing male. Though one dancer takes a tentative step from the throng, our attention is scattered across the indolent gathering in the left foreground and their exercising companions at the distant barre, as we marvel at the compression of incident in so small a composition and perhaps agree with a contemporary English critic that "its breadth and softness of effect are first-rate."[13] Such breadth, however, precludes a lingering focus on any single performer, and in this work – and such associated canvases as the Musée d'Orsay's *Dance Class at the Opéra* – each ballerina remains contained and essentially self-effacing. Even where drawings for such figures survive, as in the refined *Ballet Dancer Adjusting Her Costume* (cat. 3), it is the posture – a generic feature common to her profession – rather than the personal distinctiveness of the model that occupies the artist. Shortly before the 1874 exhibition, Degas embarked on no less than three versions of a larger ballet subject, from which he chose the ghostly, monochrome *Ballet Rehearsal on Stage* (fig. 2) to hang in his final display.[14] Again, the emphasis is on the ensemble, here further unified by the silvery theatrical light and the dancers' shared, almost numb involvement in their routines. Exemplary as a study in pose and observation (Chesneau noted of the picture that the artist "draws all the contortions of legs and dislocations of hips and feet in a way that is precise, exact, with no purpose other than that of scrupulous fidelity"), *Ballet Rehearsal on Stage* might be a modern frieze or a superior pattern-book of theatrical behavior.[15]

Despite its early date, *Ballet Rehearsal on Stage* is also the occasion of our first meeting with an unmistakable precursor of the *Little Dancer Aged Fourteen*. Prepared in a careful chalk drawing and recurring in the two other variants of the scene, the standing dancer at the extreme left-hand edge – her hands clasped behind her back, her right leg extended – directly anticipates the pose of Degas' wax sculpture. Minor differences can be identified; here, the face tilts downward

Fig. 2 *Ballet Rehearsal on Stage*, 1874, oil on canvas, 25⅝ × 31⅞ in. (65 × 81 cm), Musée d'Orsay, Paris.

and the hair is gathered into a bun, for example, while the left hand grasps the right wrist, instead of interlacing with the fingers in the manner of the 1881 statuette. But the reposeful, matter-of-fact posture is essentially that of its three-dimensional successor, along with the air of detachment that seems to insulate the dancer from the exertions and extravagant boredom of her colleagues. As we shall discover, this pose was not chosen from the canon of standard ballet steps or exercise positions, but was a variation preferred by Degas himself, perhaps noticed in an informal gathering of "rats" – as the young dancers were colloquially known – or refined in the privacy of his studio. Even at this date, however, it is apparent that the near-symmetrical qualities of the posture answered a deep need in Degas' compositional project, allowing him to contrast a static figure with a more animated one, or to introduce a vertical note among the "contortions of legs and dislocations of hips and feet" evoked by Chesneau.

In at least a dozen finished pastels, prints, and oil paintings of this period, and many more drawings, Degas returned to variants of the monochrome dancer, until she seemed to haunt the repertoire of his middle years. Sometimes the figure is difficult to discern, as in the cropped rear view of a standing ballerina at the left of *Dance Rehearsal* (cat. 2), which is based on a study very close to that of her precursor in *Ballet Rehearsal on Stage*.[16] In other works, her stance is distinguished from the *Little Dancer* by a raised arm or a redirected glance; in both *Two Dancers* (cat. 35) and the closely related drawing from the artist's sketchbook (cat. 34a), for example, the body position is almost indistinguishable from that of the sculpture, even though the head has been turned to one side and alternative positions for the hands explored. In another subgroup, the arms come close to their distinctive arrangement in the wax figure; the brilliantly economical sketch *Dancer on Stage* (cat. 16) shows the model pushing her tutu behind her, in contrast to the rapidly brushed figure with hands on hips in the corner of *Sketches of Dancers* (cat. 1), who seems more stubbornly resigned than poised. A close cousin of this dancer recurs in another cluster of variants, now bending forward at the waist and apparently tying her sash in the small of her back. Lightly drafted in the aquatint *Two Dancers in a Rehearsal Room* (cat. 9), this character is inspected from the reverse angle in *Dancer Tying Her Scarf* (cat. 10) (where she has acquired a shawl) and from a slightly higher vantage point in *Dancer Standing* (cat. 47). The same statuesque form reappears in increasingly refined pastels and an entire series of friezelike canvases that occupied Degas into the 1880s and beyond.[17] By now spawning offshoots of its own in every medium at the artist's disposal, including further wax sculptures, this resonant image effectively carried the echo of the *Little Dancer Aged Fourteen* into the artist's last years.

As Lillian Browse noted in her pioneering volume *Degas Dancers* of 1949, another figure was similarly picked out for close attention from *Ballet Rehearsal on Stage,* as if the artist were adopting a cinematic "close-up" or allowing a detail to fill his pictorial screen.[18] This time it was the ballerina *en pointe* at the right of the composition, who (with her curtseying companion) came to dominate the canvas *Two Dancers on the Stage,* now in the Courtauld Collection.[19] If this decision gave notice of the shift from complexity to singularity in Degas' ballet scenes, it also offered an insight into the artist's motivations. In the Courtauld picture, the dancer is daringly encircled by near-emptiness, our curiosity fixed on the minutiae of her dress, silk slippers, neck ribbon, and floral headdress, as well as her dark hair and "snub-nosed and slightly simian" features, as John House has called them.[20] This is not, in other words, just another trouper from the corps de ballet, but a particular young woman with idiosyncrasies of presentation and physique, each of which necessarily contrasts with that of her more recessive attendant. As we follow Degas' work into the mid and late 1870s, such sharp characterization becomes the rule rather than the exception, often accompanied by evidence of the artist's firsthand contact with his human subjects and their theatrical world. Documented dancers, from the young and undistinguished Melina Darde, Nelly Franklin, and the Mante sisters to the more illustrious Alice Biot, Joséphine Chabot, and Rita Sangalli, appear with increasing frequency in portraits or as models for drawings, their names inscribed on the picture or recorded in titles.[21] From Degas' pastels, notebooks, and other sources we learn of his presence at a dance examination around 1880, his contacts with some of the leading choreographers, instructors, musicians and composers of the Paris Opéra, and visits to specific operas and ballets, among them Meyerbeer's *Robert le Diable,* Mozart's *Don Giovanni,* Massenet's *Le Roi de Lahore,* and Métra's *Yedda, Légende Japonaise.*[22]

The more familiar Degas became with the public face of the dance, the more inclined he was to seek out its hidden life, in penumbrous studies of the theater wings, images of backstage inertia and glimpses of dingy, conspiratorial corridors. Though ballet performances can still be seen in a limited number of works, such as the glorious flame and gold *Dancers (fan design)* from Baltimore (cat. 26) and in prints like *On Stage III* (cat. 21), *Three Ballet Dancers* (cat. 22), and *At the Theater: Woman with a Fan* (cat. 28), it was the unglamorous routines of the ballerinas' training that became the staple of his mature art. At the Opéra, access to this behind-the-scenes world was strictly regulated, confined to the wealthy or well-connected *abonnés,* or male subscribers, and to the personnel of the institution and their escorted visitors. From Henri Loyrette's studies of the records at the Paris Opéra (where both ballets and operas were performed), it appears that Degas had very limited opportunity to observe the more formal aspects of this milieu at first hand until some years after the period in question, when his pictorial vocabulary was well established. An important distinction must be made, however, between the self-conscious posturing of the Opéra *foyer de la danse,* where dancers displayed themselves to the *abonnés* before and during performances, and the day-to-day activities of the rehearsal rooms, which the artist almost certainly frequented in the company of acquaintances – such as Halévy, Mante, Dihau, and many others – who were connected to the Opéra. Degas' success in arranging his attendance at a dance examination between 1878 and 1882 is attested in two letters and a little-cited note, which make it clear that it was the young dancers of the Opéra who were under scrutiny on this occasion.[23] Working from such experiences and from reconstructions of figure groups in his studio, and from a collection of props – such as tutus, ballet shoes, fans, benches, and even a spiral staircase and conductor's rostrum he is known to have accumulated for this purpose – Degas contrived to combine plausibility with an exceptional degree of artistic freedom.[24]

In technical terms, a practice session or rehearsal scene had many advantages for a doggedly studio-based artist like Degas, allowing him to minimize the rapid movement and aerial gymnastics of a stage production and to position his dancers at will. A picture like *Dance Rehearsal* (cat. 2), the work that attracted Zola's admiration at the 1876 exhibition, was clearly contrived around a loosely re-invented exercise room at the old Opéra building, within which the artist has positioned a miscellany of individuals who stand, stretch, and gossip. Drawing each of these figures separately – or perhaps in twos and threes – in the controlled conditions of his studio, Degas then transferred his studies to the final canvas, either free-hand or by means of tracing paper or the "squaring-up" process still visible in many of his studies.[25] A selection of contemporary anecdotes allow us an insight into Degas' reliance on off-duty ballerinas for this complex, collagelike process. In 1872, the painter Evariste de Valernes noted on one of his own dance studies that it was made after "a dancer from the Opéra" in the "rue Laval studio of my friend Degas," an occasion that also produced – as Richard Thomson has shown – the russet-red canvas *Ballet Dancer with Arms Crossed* (cat. 4) by Degas himself.[26] Georges Jeanniot, another artist-acquaintance who first met Degas in 1881, recalled a number of similar events, including his introduction to a dancer-model from the Opéra who was encouraged to show her "graceful, childish back" to the visiting friend, and a drawing session with Rosita Mauri and Marie Sanlaville, both leading ballerinas of the day, who were accompanied by a group of younger dancers: "The movements were posed by the pupils of the corps de ballet," he explains, "the heads by the two stars."[27]

Many of the ballet compositions completed by Degas in the years around the *Little Dancer Aged Fourteen* bear the hallmarks of these studio encounters. In both

Dancer in Green (cat. 24) and *Dancer with a Fan* (cat. 27), we effectively share an empty, workaday space with a solitary young woman, her limbs held in positions she could sustain for long periods of time and her demeanor consistent with disciplined repose. As scenes of the ballet or of backstage existence they are hardly informative, but as records of a working relationship between the artist and a particular model they are rich in observation, physical nuance, and human immediacy. So tangible are they that such figures already seem to invite a sculptural response, a possibility made more explicit in a group of studies on paper from the late 1870s, each of which shows more than one view of a single individual. In few of the works of this period does the *Little Dancer* seem more imminent, whether in a selective analysis of limbs and features, such as *Study for Dancers at the Bar* (cat. 13) or in more ambitious spatial explorations. *Dancers* (cat. 33) not only reveals the artist rotating from one side of the woman's torso to another, but effectively records the haste of Degas' graphic procedures and an implicit sequence of movement from left to right. *Study of Three Dancers* (cat. 32) might be a preparatory gambit for the *Little Dancer* itself, the model leaning to one side and then the other, before raising her head and arriving at a state of stability that depends on her projected foot; still undecided about the position of her arms, Degas seems to toy with yet another variation in poise and energy as he readies himself for the final form of his statuette.

When Degas composed *Three Ballet Dancers* (fig. 3), he again drew the same model three times across the top of the sheet, varying her pose from the *Little Dancer*-like figure at the right to the more relaxed, open postures at left and center.[28] The result is a kind of progression, an unfinished circular tour of a largely fixed form that seems to question the constraints of picture-making. Few concessions have been made to the realities of the dance or the plausibility of the setting, the latter "filled in" almost casually to offset the implausible triplets, while a bleached and empty foreground balances their nervous physicality. In the Clark collection's *Dancing Lesson* (cat. 29), a work with an exceptional affinity with the *Little Dancer Aged Fourteen,* a comparable dialogue between mass and emptiness prevails. Here more subtly integrated into the compositional scheme, three loosely related subgroups of dancers display gentle variations on a set of postures, hinting at arrested movement and the passage of time. Returning to an image he had drawn from several angles on previous occasions, most recently in *Dancer with a Fan* (cat. 30), Degas gave particular prominence to the proud, erect figure at the center, whose slender physique and taut features have much in common with the model for the wax statuette. In the painting, Degas crisply outlines her limbs and illuminates her form with a convenient shaft of light from the window, so that she, too, seems about to step beyond the confines of her planar world.

Significantly, several of the critics who saw the *Little Dancer Aged Fourteen* in 1881 perceived it as a continuation of Degas' already familiar pictorial repertoire: Paul de Charry, for example, announced that "this time M. Degas, the painter of dancers, takes on the title of their sculptor," and Charles Ephrussi understood the work to be a natural extension of the artist's existing project, "a new endeavour, an attempt at realism in sculpture."[29] While these contemporaries would have had little or no access to Degas' notebooks, portfolios of drawings and prints, and unexhibited pastels and canvases, today we can see even more closely how accurate their assessment was. With hindsight, we can also trace the persistence of the *Little Dancer*'s form into the following decades, and beyond into Degas' paintings and sculptures of the early twentieth century. In such a process, it is impossible to exaggerate the continuing importance of the wax statuette itself,

Fig. 3 *Three Ballet Dancers*, ca. 1878–80, pastel, 31 × 19½ in. (81 × 51.5 cm), private collection, courtesy Sotheby's, London.

which remained in the artist's possession and on conspicuous, if private, display for the rest of his career. Unsold and without any known prospective buyers at the 1881 exhibition, the *Little Dancer Aged Fourteen* was a fixed presence in Degas' life, literally prominent in his studio or apartment and symbolically central to his earlier public achievement. Numerous visitors recorded their sightings of "the

Fig. 4 Suzanne Valadon, *Puberty*, pastel and charcoal, 24¼ × 13½ in. (61.3 × 34.2 cm), The Art Institute of Chicago, Gift of Carter H. Harrison.

remains of his celebrated statue of *La Danseuse,"* as the American collector Louisine Havemeyer described it, and there is some evidence that the figure acquired a cult status in Degas' circle.[30] Painter and sculptor acquaintances of these years – from Paul-Albert Bartholomé, Georges Jeanniot, and Walter Sickert to Maurice Denis and Georges Rouault – inevitably became conversant with the work, and when Suzanne Valadon made regular calls to discuss her drawings with Degas at the turn of the century, it apparently left its mark. Impressed as she was by both Degas' technique and subject matter, it is hardly fanciful to see a reflection of – or even an act of homage to – the *Little Dancer* in her forceful pastel and charcoal study *Puberty* of 1908 (fig. 4).[31]

Living and working in the shadow of the *Little Dancer Aged Fourteen* for more than three decades, Degas was repeatedly stimulated to rework its distinctive forms or respond to its sculptural potential in the idiom of the moment. Some of the waxes that followed it, such as *Dancer Ready to Dance, Right Leg Forward* (cat. 50), *Grand Arabesque, First Time* (cat. 51) and *Dancer Moving Forward* (cat. 53), take up the position of legs and body while progressively animating the model's arms and head, as the ballerina seems to gather energy for a leap from her terrestrial roots. Now appearing naked and without pretensions to topicality, these dancers also reveal a maturity of physique that distances them from the coy suggestiveness that had once been identified in their adolescent precursor. If certain drawings of this period, like the touchingly earnest *Dancer at Rest* (cat. 60), remind us of Degas' continuing attention to the niceties of the practice room, others reiterate his gathering confidence in three-dimensional structure and bodily movement. Seen together, *Dancer Adjusting Her Dress* (cat. 46) and *Dancers* (cat. 49) offer a persuasive account of a single standing figure, massively blocked in with light and shade and inventively various in the positioning of the arms in a way that recalls his first sculptural studies. But it is in a group of three related waxes from the last decades of Degas' life that the most deliberate echoes of the *Little Dancer* can be felt. In the two versions of *Dancer at Rest, Hands Behind Her Back, Right Leg Forward* (cats. 58 and 59), we confront a muscular, almost agonized variant of the solitary ballerina, now with an energetic striding posture and elbows braced to support her spine. If we resist the notion that these figures – made as much as two decades after the 1881 wax – reflect Degas' own increasing sense of mortality and physical decline, it is less easy to accommodate their strangely poignant successor, *Dressed Dancer at Rest, Hands Behind Her Back, Right Leg Forward* (cat. 61). Unquestionably a revisitation of the *Little Dancer Aged Fourteen* from the artist's later years, this work seems to unite the dense expressiveness of the final decades with a memory of his earlier literalism, its massiveness in near-tragic contrast with the lean, tensile form of his 1881 masterpiece.

THE LIFE OF THE "RAT"

"I could tell you things to make you blush or make you weep . . ."

The belief that Degas' art offers an exact, documentary account of the ballet in nineteenth-century Paris is one of the most stubborn misconceptions surrounding his achievement. In actuality, his dance pastels and paintings – and in subtly different ways, his sculptures – are pitched somewhere between fact and fiction, between his acquired expertise in the performers' world on the one hand and a curious blend of obsession, inventiveness, and shameless nostalgia on the other.

Historians of the ballet have stressed the accuracy of certain aspects of Degas' testimony: Lillian Browse, herself a trained dancer who once interviewed some of the artist's surviving models, writes of his "absolute faithfulness" to the "laws and conventions" of the classical ballet; the author of a dozen volumes on the nineteenth-century dance, Ivor Guest, salutes Degas' "miraculous precision" and "unsurpassed penetration into the mysteries of the ballet"; and Martine Kahane, an authority on the history of the Opéra, singles Degas out for his precise portrayal of the dancers' predicament and their "bodies formed by work, their features carved by exhaustion."[32] Our brief survey of Degas' dance imagery in the 1870s offers much to support these views, in evidence of visits to known performances at the Opéra, in personal and professional contact with a number of dancers, and in his documented study of their poses, costumes, and routines. Consistent with his first-hand scrutiny of laundresses, cabaret artistes, prostitutes, and hat-shop assistants during this same period, his representations of the ballet appear to emerge from the same broadly based project of realism – with its search for "the special characteristics of the modern individual," as the critic Edmond Duranty expressed it – at a defining stage of Degas' early maturity.[33]

Yet the same pictorial and archival evidence can be made to tell a different story, one that runs parallel to Degas' known engagement with realism but, in certain ways, brings us nearer to the complexity of that engagement and to the "systematic preoccupation with strangeness" that Duranty had also discerned in him.[34] For all its documentary precision and atmospheric plausibility, a painting like *Ballet Rehearsal on Stage* (fig. 2) is revealed on closer inspection to be a kind of jigsaw, a confection of postures, properties, and light effects that was almost certainly never seen in this form by Degas or any of his contemporaries. When we discover that most of its poses were repeated in other works, and that a number of its characters were entirely repainted as the picture progressed, the contrivance of Degas' method – in its way, as false and arbitrary as the theatrical spectacle itself – is definitively unmasked.[35] The more pedantic we become, the more the "artifice" (as Degas himself referred to it) of his art is paraded before us. It has often been pointed out, for example, that the costumes and ornaments worn by Degas' dancers in rehearsal are largely fanciful: in daily practice, the plainest of tutus, bodices, and stockings were insisted upon, sometimes augmented by shawls or street clothes to offset the cold for those in attendance. Witnesses of these events are emphatic on the point, describing the simple "white tutus, white underdrawers" made of muslin that were worn by pupils, an ensemble clearly visible in at least one of the artist's drawings, *Dancer Stretching at the Bar* (cat. 14) and in the misleadingly titled print, *Actresses in Their Dressing Rooms* (cat. 17), which surely shows partly costumed dancers.[36] Other accounts elaborate on the situation, as in the story of the hilarious reception that greeted one beginner when she attempted to introduce a hint of embroidery into her exercise outfit.[37] Another contemporary records the notorious appetite of the "rats" for gifts of jewelry, but there is every reason to believe that the ribbons, colored sashes, floral head-dresses, and other decorations visible in such rehearsal scenes as *Dancing Lesson* (cat. 29) and *The Ballet Class* (cat. 8) were expressions of pure artistic license on Degas' part.[38]

Less frequently analyzed are the rooms in which Degas' ballet exercises take place, which were again determined more by his tastes and painterly inclinations than by historical accuracy. When Degas made his first pictures of the dance, performances of operas and ballets were held at the Théâtre de l'Académie Royale de Musique, situated a short distance from the artist's studio in a fifty-year-old

Fig. 5 *The Opéra, Paris*, ca. 1900, postcard.

building on the rue Le Peletier. His early representations of the stage, which show a distinctive rectangular "peep-hole" at the level of the dancers' legs and an oval, latticelike pattern along the lower balcony, are unmistakably based on this rue Le Peletier theater, while many of the rehearsal scenes that accompany them are similarly set in rooms that can be identified on the same site.[39] Not long before the opening in 1875 of the new Opéra (fig. 5) – a vast and extravagantly ornamented edifice designed by Charles Garnier and located in the center of the city – the old rue Le Peletier structure was accidentally burnt to the ground, along with the bulk of its stage sets and its complex of corridors, vestibules, and practice rooms. Just as this combination of events obliged the Opéra to transform its public image and parts of its repertoire, so we might have expected Degas to reconstruct his vocabulary of the dance. Surprisingly and rather revealingly, the opposite happened. To a large extent, Degas chose to disregard the elaborate new *foyer de la danse,* in which formal rehearsals were now held, as well as Garnier's spectacular auditorium and most of the Opéra's new productions, and to continue for many years to depict his dancers in the long-vanished spaces of the rue Le Peletier. Where distinctive architecture can be seen in works of the mid and late 1870s, such as the tall windows and leafy courtyard of *Dance Rehearsal* (cat. 2), it is clearly a reminiscence of the destroyed structure, while the soiled rooms often used by Degas' rehearsal classes are manifestly not those "with fluted columns, gilded chandeliers, painted panels and ceiling medallions" described in the Palais Garnier, as the new building became known.[40]

If Degas' pictures of the dance show fictitious gatherings in defunct interiors, what can be said with certainty about the real world occupied by the model who posed for the *Little Dancer Aged Fourteen*? Through the slenderest of coincidences – the inscription of a fragmentary address and the name "Marie" on one of the preparatory drawings (cat. 43) – and some keen detective work, earlier researchers have been able to establish that the subject of the sculpture was entirely factual. She was Marie van Goethem, a dancer at the Palais Garnier who came from a Belgian family living in Paris, whose mother was a laundress and father a tailor.[41] They lived in the rue de Douai on the lower slopes of Montmartre, just a few doors from Degas' opera-loving friend Ludovic Halévy and a block or two from the studios and apartments rented by Degas in this area during the period in question.[42] Such geographical proximity may well have brought sculptor and model together, leading to a sustained professional relationship with the family that evidently lasted for several years. Marie was one of three sisters – the others were Antoinette and Louise-Joséphine – all of whom passed through the dance classes at the Opéra; a reference to "Antoinette Vangutten – aged 12" in a notebook used by Degas until about 1874 suggests that the eldest girl had posed for some of the artist's earliest ballet pictures.[43]

Given that Marie reached the age of fourteen in February 1878 and that the *Little Dancer* was almost complete in April 1880, it would appear that the extraordinary cycle of drawings related directly or obliquely to the sculpture – some ten sheets in all, incorporating around thirty complete or partial studies of the figure – were made during this two-year period, if not in a more concentrated burst of activity (see cats. 34a, 35, 36, 38, 40, 41, 42, 43, and fig. 19).[44] Marie was clearly a regular visitor to Degas' studio, posing both clothed and naked for the artist, and returning to model for other pastels and paintings well into the following decade. A slightly later notebook confirms the artist's contact with her some time between 1880 and 1884, while Browse and others have seen the echo of Marie's youthful physique, pert features, and briefly famous long hair in a number of later works.[45] Somewhat confusingly, the seated and rather comical chaperone in the magnificent canvas of *The Ballet Class* (cat. 8) was said by Mary Cassatt to be based on the young dancer, where the standing figure at the right of the same picture seems a much more likely candidate.[46] In the delicately improvised study for this individual, *Two Dancers* (cat. 7), we sense the same adolescent uncertainty that informs the *Little Dancer,* as well as such identical features as the receding chin and childishly slender arm. By the mid 1880s, the ballerina identified by Lillian Browse as the older Marie van Goethem had advanced in both stature and prominence; a pastel entitled *Dancer with Long Hair Bowing* and a series of related works show a mature performer in a starring role, now accompanied by her own attendants.[47]

In other respects, Marie van Goethem's life as a dancer appears to have remained largely undistinguished, if characteristic of many hundreds of her peers who graced the corps de ballet. She was barely noticed in the voluminous, coyly intimate journalism that occupied itself with events surrounding the Opéra, though in the early 1880s "Mademoiselle Van Goeuthen" earned a brief mention as a "model . . . for painters, who is frequently seen at the Brasserie des Martyrs, the Nouvelle Athènes café and the bar of the Rat Mort."[48] All three of these establishments were closely linked to bohemian artistic circles, and suggestions that Marie herself was often to be found there ("I could tell you things to make you blush or make you weep," continued the author) were intended to hint at a somewhat lax way of life. After this date, little is recorded of her activities, though there has been some confusion over the careers of the three van Goethem sisters; Louise-Joséphine is known to have worked as a ballet teacher, while Browse suggests that Marie became a *sujet* or middle-ranking dancer, continuing her association with the Opéra until as late as 1914.[49]

Almost none of this information, of course, would have been available to visitors at the sixth Impressionist exhibition, where Degas' sculpture was announced in the catalogue – starkly and anonymously – as *Petite Danseuse de quatorze ans (statuette en cire).*[50] Crucially, however, Degas chose to pinpoint the dancer's youthfulness, not just in her proportions and distinctive physiognomy but in his specification of the model's age, the first and last time he was to do so in the title of one of his pictures or sculptures. For Degas' audiences in 1881, such details were loaded with meaning, defining the young girl as a representative of a clearly defined stratum of her profession and of certain of the hazards, aspirations, and contradictory values of contemporary ballet. That the *Little Dancer* was seen in this way is apparent across the spectrum of the 1881 criticism, where the sculpture is reviled or revered as if it were a real, living individual and simultaneously treated as a paradigm of society's ills. In the late twentieth century, it is difficult to imagine a world where the figure of an unknown dancer could stir such passions or where the dance itself still occupied a central position in the metropolitan imagination. Far from being an esoteric activity followed by the few, ballet at the Opéra filled the gossip columns and reviews, featured in cheap illustrations and widely read novels, and supported a cult of personality that has few rivals even today. Analogies have been proposed with cinema in the golden age of Hollywood or television in our own time, but both cases fall short of the mark, missing the extraordinary fusion of the highest artistic standards with the most blatant and officially sanctioned vice, and the concentration of both in a single edifice, the Palais Garnier. It was here, at the cultural heart of Paris – "the cradle of the dance," according to the choreographer and authority on the ballet, Arthur Saint-Léon – that visiting kings and princes were entertained by the state, and here also that internationally renowned celebrities – such as Rosita Mauri, a dancer who earned 40,000 francs a year and was portrayed by Degas – were besieged by their admirers.[51] It was under this same roof that Baron Haussman, the architect of the rebuilt city, began his scandalous liaison with a young ballerina, and it was in the foyers and reception rooms that reputations were famously destroyed, fortunes were lost, and a bizarre semi-official prostitution was conducted.

Throughout much of the nineteenth century, the public spectacle and backstage cavortings of the Opéra formed part of the daily fare of Paris, finding expression in engravings and *carte-de-visite* photographs, newspaper cartoons by Daumier, Gavarni, Bertall, Cham, and many lesser talents (figs. 9 and 13), and a steady stream of booklets of instruction, solemn treatises on the dance, and publications with such suggestive titles as *Behind the Curtain* and *These Young Ladies of the Opéra*.[52] If those who saw the *Little Dancer Aged Fourteen* knew little of Marie van Goethem, they were certainly conversant with her world, whether they attended performances (several of the critics at the 1881 exhibition – among them Ephrussi, Claretie, and Silvestre – were regulars at the Palais Garnier) or followed the fortunes of its stars from a distance. Prominent in the city's folklore was the image of the "rat," the young trainee dancer who represented the lure of stardom and the rigors of professional life, as well as its vulnerability to corruption. Traditionally, Kahane tells us, these "rats" were recruited from families of dancers or from those

> of distinctly modest origin or irregular status. Around 1850, more than half the certificates of engagement at the school of dance indicate that the children had no known father and that their mothers were concierges, laundresses etc. The situation evolved between 1870 and 1900 with the arrival in the corps de ballet of young Italian dancers from more respectable backgrounds (such as Mauri, Subra, Zambelli) and young girls from good families (such as Cléo de Mérode, who became the mistress of Leopold II, King of the Belgians).[53]

In 1856, Saint-Léon could still deplore the haphazard education of the "rats," protesting that "a true school of dancing does not exist and has never existed," but

Fig. 6 Paul Renouard, *First Exercises*, lithograph, from the *Gazette des Beaux-Arts*, 1881.

by the time the van Goethem sisters took up their studies, the situation had been considerably regularized.[54] Apprentices began their instruction between the ages of five and eight, progressing to the corps de ballet and through the various stages of *coryphée, petit sujet,* and *premier sujet* and ultimately to the level of *étoile,* according to their talent, dedication, and success in attracting patronage.[55] A lithograph by Degas' admirer Paul Renouard (fig. 6), published in 1881, shows the start of this process, as a debutante struggles to master her first steps, while another illustration by the same artist (fig. 7) depicts an older group gathered around a drawing (apparently by Renouard himself) based on a sequence of dance positions.[56] In Degas' pastels, younger pupils are often shown accompanied by their mothers or a chaperone figure, as in the dramatically composed *Dance Examination* (cat. 15), allowing the artist further opportunities to contrast his mature, clothed characters with the beginners' relative fragility.

As they proved their aptitude and physical suitability, the girls embarked on an increasingly demanding regime of daily exercise and occasional subordinate appearances on the stage. "We cannot imagine the courage, patience and incessant work required to become a talented dancer," wrote Albert Vizentini in 1868, some ten years before the *Little Dancer Aged Fourteen* was begun:

> The true dancer is obsessed with her art and sacrifices everything to it. At sixteen as at thirty, she must undergo the same painful exercises; stretching at the barre, lifting oneself at the knees, *pliés, écartes,* leaning back until the limbs creak in unison, exhausting oneself, making oneself continually hoarse, accepting neither fatigue nor sluggishness, these are the daily routines of the dancer who, after attending classes from nine until one, and rehearsal from one until four, appears in the evening with a smile on her lips to perform as a sylph as if nothing had happened.[57]

As a fourteen-year-old, Marie van Goethem may not yet have arrived at this exhausting schedule, though the advancement of individuals varied dramatically with their accomplishment; the title role in Saint-Léon's *Coppélia* of 1870, for example, was created by Giuseppina Bozzacchi, an unknown from the Opéra dance school who was just sixteen, while another little dancer aged fourteen, the

Fig. 7 Paul Renouard, *The Children's Dance Class at the Opéra*, lithograph, from the *Gazette des Beaux-Arts*, 1881.

American prodigy Augusta Maywood, had made an even more sensational debut on the Paris stage some three decades earlier.[58]

There was considerable ambivalence among admirers of the ballet about the effects of this punishing routine on the physique of the young dancer. From the beginning of the century, pupils had been advised to develop "graceful and supple movements" and a "decent voluptuousness in their attitudes," in the words of the ballet instructor Charles Blasis, and were often urged to model themselves on famous works of art, such as the *Venus Belvedere* or the "nymphs of Corot."[59] Perversely, however, the very exercises that prepared the "rats" for their profession were seen to prejudice their glamour, one English writer observing that the "effects of this artificial existence . . . were painfully visible . . . their cheeks hollow and pale . . . their limbs nipped and wasted," and Ernest Chesneau deploring the "thinnesses" and "professional deformities" of the modern dancer.[60] Experts on the ballet had for some time insisted that candidates be selected with its athletic demands in mind, explaining that the appropriate bodily characteristics "promised almost certain success to those that possessed them." Georges Duval, author of an 1875 booklet called *Terpsichore: petit guide à l'usage des amateurs de ballets,* went on to enumerate the preferred qualities of arms, legs, and body in a young girl entering the profession, explaining that the "dancer should have the greatest facility in the hips, so that the movement of the thighs is free and the knees are turned out."[61]

Degas' alertness to the progressive stages of the ballet dancer's formation and subsequent career is touchingly evident in a succession of his works of art. Seen together, his dance images of the 1870s can seem documentary, almost filmic, as he traces a variety of individuals through their early steps and nervous preliminary examinations, through the rituals of the barre, the dressing room and the rehearsal, to their first stage appearances and eventual rise to stardom, and even beyond, into dignified retirement. Though the episodes of this story are scattered across several media and fill dramatically varied frames, we can also follow the maturing of the dancer's physique, beginning with the angular child and advancing to the ampler forms of executants long past their prime. In the drawing *Little Girl Practicing at the Bar* (cat. 12) we see the still-unformed ingénue at her exercise, while the same eight- or nine-year-old recovers gratefully from her labors in *Ballet Girl in Repose* (cat. 11).[62] Significantly, both drawings carry the artist's own inscriptions, such as "emphasize the elbow bone" and "battements à la seconde," as if Degas was also learning the protocols of the dance and the finer points of its execution. Now some years older, a similarly fine-limbed individual posed for *Dancer with a Fan* (cat. 30), a stockier adolescent labors awkwardly in *Dancer Stretching at the Bar* (cat. 14), and a cluster of young hopefuls train under a dancing-master in *The Ballet Class* (cat. 8). By the time they reach the *Dance Rehearsal* (cat. 2), a group of more confident and physically mature apprentices seem accustomed to their shadowy backstage life, if only as a necessary prelude to the brilliance of their solo debut. In the wonderfully exuberant *Three Ballet Dancers* (cat. 22), the moment of exposure on stage has arrived, the gymnastic preparations of the dance school triumphantly vindicated as the ballerinas display their finest *pas de chat* or most flirtatious *pas battu* in the glare of the footlights.

As with so many aspects of its identity, the place of the *Little Dancer Aged Fourteen* in this professional saga is defined only by its imprecision, the model seemingly poised between childhood and maturity, between the potential of a highly trained young body and the moment of its artistic fulfillment. Typically, a fourteen-year-old pupil would have been studying for six or seven years and making frequent if largely decorative contributions to stage productions, perhaps as one of the disheveled sprites in the background of *At the Theater: Woman with a Fan* (cat. 28), the fairy presences among the light and color of the Baltimore *Dancers (fan design)* (cat. 26) or the attendants in *Dancers in the Wings* (cat. 19). Fourteen was specified as the age when the "rat was no longer a rat" by Nestor Roqueplan, a mid-century director of the Opéra, and Martine Kahane has referred to the "transitory state" – both sexual and technical – of this phase in a dancer's career.[63] It is unlikely to have been a coincidence that Degas chose such a moment as the subject of his sculpture, rejecting the pre-pubescent innocence of the ballet pupil in *Ballet Girl in Repose* (cat. 11), on the one hand, and the ready-formed elegance of the *étoile* – which attracted so many of his successors to the theme – on the other. In his sequence of drawings of Marie van Goethem, we seem to watch as Degas negotiates her uncertain status, defining a long-limbed, flat-chested adolescent in *Three Studies of a Nude Dancer* (cat. 36), responding to the figure's slightly fuller forms in *Study of a Nude Dancer* (cat. 38) and progressing to the rounded, assertive hips and shoulders of the emergent woman in the later clothed variants. If in these latter studies her transmutation is accentuated by the curves of the dancer's costume, the possibility that Degas recorded a real evolution in the girl's body over the months and years of the sculpture's fabrication (Marie was seventeen when the *Little Dancer* finally appeared) still deserves to be taken seriously.

The indeterminate significance of this child-woman, pupil-dancer clearly threw the first critics of the wax statuette into disarray. More than one writer assumed that the model was *younger* than specified, Paul de Charry guessing that she was "thirteen or fourteen years old," Paul Mantz referring to her as "an unfortunate child," and Nina de Villard placing her in the "class of little ones at the Opéra."[64] Jules Claretie was more specific, hinting that she had "scarcely reached puberty," while Elie de Mont took the opposite point of view; "The proof that this young girl of fourteen years is not real," the critic wrote, "is that she has nothing of youth about her; her thinness is dryness, it is the thinness, the stiffness of age, not of childhood."[65] There were further doubts about Marie van Goethem's appearance, at least as depicted in Degas' sculpture. For some, she was "a skinny urchin" or a "flower of the gutter," whose doubtlessly squalid upbringing had made her "old before her time."[66] Others were more measured, appreciating that "the nervous curvature of the legs, the solid ankles enclosed in worn shoes, the bony torso – as supple as steel" were those of a pupil who was "learning her craft."[67] Both Huysmans and de Villard understood that the young dancer's body had been re-shaped by harsh training, the former noting her "legs broken by exercise" and the latter, the most informed of the critics in this respect, acknowledging that it was "necessary to suffer to arrive at the airy lightness of the sylph and the butterfly; today it is the sad reality of the discipline . . . the child is ugly, but a delightful refinement in the chin, the eyelids, the ankles, promises well for the future."[68]

"Un vieil abonné," a pseudonymous author of the day who is now identified as Paul Mahalin, gave some gruesome details of the "equipment" used in the body-shaping regime at the Opéra, listing the "boxes, rings, straps and bars . . . an entire torture apparatus" to which the young dancers submitted. "Each day," he elaborated, "the pupil imprisons her feet in one of these grooved boxes. There, her heels back-to-back and her knees turned out, she accustoms her poor martyred feet to remaining, by themselves, in a straight line."[69] The results of this "torture," which survives in a modified form even today, have been widely

Fig. 8 *The Fourth Position*, from Berthe Bernay, *La Danse au théâtre*, 1890, Victoria and Albert Picture Library, London.

misunderstood in the context of the *Little Dancer.* Far from being a poor specimen, the attitude of Marie van Goethem suggests that she would have been among the more successful products of the Opéra dance school, her proportions considered near-ideal and her limbs already well adapted to the trials ahead. Dance instructors of today still value many of the qualities she exhibits, such as the ample "turn-out" running from foot to hip, the supple back, flexible ankles, and long legs and arms, irrespective of their contribution to her glamour and poise.[70] The precise significance of the *Little Dancer*'s pose has also, it seems, been much misrepresented. It is not the case that the figure is shown in a strict "fourth position," one of the five standard dispositions of feet and legs taught to all pupils of the dance and regularly practiced in the exercise room.[71] Nineteenth-century ballet manuals defined the requirements of the fourth position, "the feet turned completely outwards in a straight line," but arranged in such a way that they "half cross each other without touching"; a plate in *La Danse au théâtre* (fig. 8) by Berthe Bernay (herself a *petit sujet* in 1881 and thus a senior colleague of Marie van Goethem) illustrates the stance and is accompanied by a recommendation that the feet should be "thirty centimeters apart."[72] A drawing by Degas in the present volume (cat. 60) is accompanied by the artist's note *"à la 5e,"* indicating that it represents the fifth position, similar to the fourth but with the feet close together.

By none of these criteria was the model for the *Little Dancer Aged Fourteen* correctly or formally posed, a fact made more conspicuous by the unorthodox arrangement of her arms and hands, which are loosely clasped behind her back. In reality, the figure is best described as being in a "relaxed fourth position," the sort of pose adopted by a well drilled pupil in a moment of respite, or perhaps as a preliminary stretching maneuver. Not for the first time, it would appear, we find ourselves confronted by visual information about the *Little Dancer* that is tantalizingly opaque; by a pupil who does not practice, a performer who is not represented on stage (such a pose would be inconceivable in a ballet production), and a tired athlete who is not fully at ease. Tangential though they may seem, such features of Marie van Goethem's position have a direct bearing on the detailed appearance of the sculpture and on its reception by Degas' contemporaries. If there is no implied audience, there is hardly a need for gorgeous costume or the continuous, simpering smile urged upon debutantes; if the model is not understood to be in class, she does not need to follow the textbook or show herself to best advantage; and if she is caught in some in-between world that is neither rehearsal nor recreation, she might well retreat into her thoughts, behind the "half-closed eyes" that were noted by one observer in 1881.[73]

If we are not to imagine our young dancer on the Opéra stage or going through her paces, what are we to read into her posture? Was this an arbitrary invention of Degas' own or an improvisation by the model, designed to allow Marie van Goethem a degree of comfort as she posed for thirty or more studies and perhaps for the sculpture itself? Everything we know about the deliberation of Degas' images makes such a view unlikely; as an artist who had studied the ballet for more than a decade, recording precise terms for dance positions on his drawings, as well as notes of correction for both himself and the ballerina, Degas would hardly have designed his first major sculpture on a mere whim. A few years after he completed the *Little Dancer,* one of the artist's friends claimed, "Degas always looks for the accidental," indicating the cut-off compositions and unexpected angles of view in his pastels that often reveal a startling new truth about the chosen theme.[74] In his wax statuette, Degas has again side-stepped the obvious, spurning the perfection of the performance and the anonymity of the rehearsal hall for a more ill-defined moment, a glimpse of the model when she is self-absorbed and somewhat off her guard. This is certainly how his contemporaries saw the figure, treating its subject as an idiosyncratic individual caught at a revealing, imperfect moment. Though the critic of the London-based *Artist* magazine insisted that the "ballet girl . . . is in the act of dancing," the majority accepted that she was tired after training, agreeing with Charles Ephrussi that we see her wearing "her working clothes, weary and exhausted, relaxing her worn-out limbs."[75] Clearly shocked that they were not presented with a stereotypical beauty from the corps de ballet, many recoiled from this vision of ordinariness. Paul Mantz complained that she was dirty, his colleagues that she was "frightful" or "odiously ugly," while the outraged Elie de Mont asked why the artist had gone out of his way to choose such a curiosity: "I don't ask that art should always be elegant, but I don't believe that its role is to champion the cause of ugliness."[76]

More explicit were the insinuations that the young dancer was already, or would soon become, sexually dissolute. Seeing in the sculpture "the savage inelegance of the schoolgirl who is turning into a woman and for whom diplomats will make fools of themselves," Mantz believed that Degas had "picked a flower of precocious depravity from the espaliers of the theater."[77] For Ephrussi, the *Little Dancer* represented "the Opéra rat in her modern form, learning her craft, with all her disposition and stock of bad instincts and licentious inclinations," just as he sensed "the intimate allures and profession of the individual."[78] Startling though these implications are for modern admirers of the work, they were commonplace in the literature surrounding the ballet in the nineteenth century and rooted in the well documented and often grim facts of the dancers' existence. As Martine Kahane explains, such individuals "were excessively badly paid," their conditions frequently turning "these precocious children into prostitutes" whose ambition was "to find themselves a titled protector who would ensure them a decent existence."[79] Some succeeded spectacularly, adding to a roll-call of legendary marriages into the nobility of Europe and the world of high finance, while many were obliged to compete for the favors of the wealthy male clientele of the Opéra.[80]

Both police and theater authorities turned a blind eye to the sexual traffic associated with the dance, which was protected by some of the most powerful male institutions in the city and effectively encouraged by certain features of the Palais Garnier itself.[81] From its inception, the *foyer de la danse* in the new building was intended to combine several functions, ranging from a formal reception room to a rehearsal hall for the corps de ballet, but its most celebrated use was that of "a place of rendezvous and for passing the time" for the privileged *abonnés*.[82] The objects of their attentions were often the more senior ballerinas (juniors and male dancers were officially excluded) and it was acknowledged by Garnier himself that the foyer had been partly designed to show off their charms, as they postured – "coquettishly and picturesquely costumed" – before, during, or after performances.[83] Along with the novelists, dramatists, caricaturists, and humorists of his day, Degas helped to make the relationship between the *abonnés* and their prey into one of the emblems of the age. In the lithographs of Lami and Daumier, the backstage studies of Forain, Renouard and Béraud, and the pastels and monotypes of Degas, the black-suited *abonné* is an ever-present, rapacious specter in the dancers' universe, loitering in the wings, invading the stage during intervals and, in prints like *Pauline and Virginie Conversing with Admirers* (cat. 6) and *In the Foyer* (cat. 5), ambushing the "rats" in corridors and reception rooms. In their turn, dancers and actresses who ruined their lovers with demands for jewels,

Fig. 9 Alfred Grévin, *The Dance Pupils*, illustration from the *Petit Journal pour rire*, no. 293.

carriages, and apartments took on near-mythical status, analyzed at length in novels like Zola's *Nana* and celebrated in countless images in the popular press. One such work, Alfred Grévin's *The Dance Pupils* (fig. 9), published on the front page of the magazine *Petit Journal pour rire,* openly signals the carnal nature of the young pupil's ambition as well as the complicity of her mother and friend in the project. Here Grévin – draftsman, theater designer, and founder of the Paris waxwork museum – seems to identify himself with another of the city's causes, saluting the aspiring "rat" as a sexual adventurer, even as a vernacular heroine, while a somewhat pun-laden caption refers frankly to her future earning power.[84]

If the physical allure of the ballet for its predominantly male followers was freely acknowledged, the reality behind the dancer's reputation was already in doubt. More than a decade before the *Little Dancer* appeared, the far-from-prudish Goncourt brothers noted that "fewer than a dozen dancers" were actually supported by the rich lovers of legend and claimed that a majority of the corps de ballet "lead a family life. Many live with their mother or have an attachment to a workman."[85] Several contemporary authors, among them the Comte de Maugny, argued that the long hours of the dancers' training left them with little time for amorous adventure, and Kahane proposes that, in practice, the "rats" could be divided into two types: the "naive, pure young girl dedicated to her art" and the "flighty kept woman, multiplying her affairs and ruining her admirers."[86] A pertinent case of the former was provided by the Mante sisters, daughters of a "respectable" professional family known socially to Degas (at one date, they lived in the same building as the artist) with a long-standing association with the Opéra, where the father, Louis-Amédée Mante, played the double-bass for almost half a century.[87] All three Mante girls embarked on the ballet and posed occasionally in Degas' studio, with Suzanne, Blanche, and their mother providing the subject for two pastel groups and – according to information given by the elderly sitter to Lillian Browse – Suzanne modeling for such drawings as *Little Girl Practicing at the Bar* (cat. 12) and *Ballet Girl in Repose* (cat. 11).[88] In contrast to Grévin's drawing, the accent in the Philadelphia version of the pastel (fig. 10) is on the vulnerability of the daughter preparing for the ballet, here accentuated by the proximity of her more securely costumed sister and the warm, enveloping presence of Madame Mante. Again contrary to the legend, both girls progressed through the hierarchies of the dance establishment and graduated to become instructors in their own right, remaining with the company for many years.[89]

In the majority of cases, of course, the private lives of individual young dancers, whether Suzanne and Blanche Mante or Marie van Goethem, remained unknown to those who saw Degas' paintings and sculpture, and thus irrelevant to the impact of specific works of art. More than such localized biographies, it was "the myth of the dancer" – as Kahane has called it – the image of "the loose woman who destroyed the fortunes of great worldly figures" that dominated the imaginations of late-nineteenth-century audiences, just as it has persisted into our own selectively informed views of the dance. When writers and journalists reported on the ballet, the sexual spectacle of performances and backstage spaces was often taken for granted, dancers attracting as much comment for their looks as for their athleticism or professional skill. Commentators like Vizentini and Mahalin referred openly to both the appearance and private behavior of individual ballerinas, their published remarks about "elegant knees," "large lips," and a dancer's "embonpoint" offering a virtual directory of available charms.[90] In such an outwardly formal society, the Opéra supplied one of few opportunities to glimpse the lightly clad female form, a fact recognized by the grandest as well as

Fig. 10 *The Mante Family*, ca. 1886, pastel, 34¾ × 19⅛ in. (88.1 × 48.5 cm), Philadelphia Museum of Art, Given by Mrs. John Wintersteen.

the most scurrilous observers of the day. In a review of the 1876 Impressionist exhibition, Stéphane Mallarmé wrote of the "semi-nakedness of the young ballet dancers" in Degas' rehearsal pictures, and in 1881 Jules Claretie could allude to the "seductive curiosities" visible in such works, while an enthusiast for the foyer admitted that many went there principally to "look closely at the legs of Miss B."[91]

Even closer to home, Degas' writer and librettist friend Ludovic Halévy gave definitive form to the sexually available "rat" in a series of widely read stories, published during the 1870s and collected under the title *La Famille Cardinal* in 1883. The first tale, *Madame Cardinal,* which appeared in 1870 and was set in that year, introduces us to the daughters Pauline and Virginie, both still in their teens but already habituated to the ways of the Opéra and well advanced – with the help of their formidable mother – along its professional and amorous paths.[92] As in Grévin's cartoon, the mother-chaperone figure of the stories is brazenly concerned with her offspring's advancement, Madame Cardinal encouraging the approaches of the wealthy and slightly improbable Marquis Cavalcanti to the thirteen-year-old Virginie while maintaining the apparent respectability of her household. Hypocrisy and misleading appearances are the unifying themes in tales that range over the double standards of their parents and the daughters' manipulation of a variety of lovers, ending with Pauline's abandonment of the ballet and of her outward propriety when she becomes *une grande cocotte.* The sisters, their mother, and Halévy himself also appear in a suite of more than thirty dazzling black-and-white monotypes made by Degas in response to these stories in the years between 1876 and 1877.[93] Though never used as illustrations in the published volume of Halévy's tales, the rapid brushwork and skittish compositions of Degas' prints, such as *Pauline and Virgine Conversing with Admirers* (cat. 6), capture the illusory forms of the young Cardinals' world, contrasting the fragile whites and silvers of the dancers with the somber, black-suited *abonnés.* With the lightest and most incisive of touches, Degas encapsulates both the comedy and the threat of this backstage choreography, *In the Foyer* (cat. 5) presenting a caricatural male voyeur as he feasts his eyes on the suddenly accessible form of a *Little Dancer*-like ballerina.

In almost every sense, it seems, Degas was complicit in the public and private experience of the dancer, attending performances, annotating her off-duty encounters, and hiring underpaid pupils to model in his Montmartre studio. For Degas, as for the frock-coated *abonnés,* the ballet was a pretext for licensed proximity to the female body, sanctioned by art and encouraged by the camaraderie of the predominantly male audience. If he lacked the means at this date to become an *abonné* himself, he was well acquainted with many stalwarts of the Opéra and knew that the apartments of some of them – such as Isaac de Camondo, Jean-Baptiste Faure, Count Ludovic Lepic, Ludovic Halévy, and Charles Ephrussi – were hung with his pictures of the dance.[94] More than is sometimes appreciated, these pastels and paintings were projected at a discerning, ballet-obsessed circle, made by an artist who knew both his subject and his clientele and their openness or otherwise to artistic experimentation. If an admirer in 1880 could hail "Degas, the painter of dancers" for his "keen and accurate observations" of life behind the proscenium, the same writer could note of *The Dance Examination,* "At first sight it is disagreeable to the eye, but one grows accustomed to it."[95] This conjunction of approval and perplexity might be said to summarize the contemporary response to Degas' ballet imagery, not least the flurry of comment that surrounded the first appearance of the *Little Dancer Aged Fourteen.* Fluent in the ways of the Opéra, few of his contemporaries questioned the precision of Degas' depiction of his chosen model, nor the details of her physique, clothing, and self-presentation; what irritated them was the artist's boldness in taking them beyond their comfortable assumptions about the dance and the conventions of sculpture. Given the models available, Elie de Mont asked, "Why did he choose this one?"; knowing the beauties to be found at the Opéra, Paul Mantz demanded, "Why is she so ugly?"; acknowledging that such individuals existed in the "depths of the dance schools," Henri Trianon inquired, "What have they to do with the business of sculpture?"; and, baffled by almost every aspect of the work, "Our Lady Correspondent" wailed, "Can anyone calling himself an artist more hopelessly degrade what he ought to reverence and love?"[96]

When we look at the *Little Dancer Aged Fourteen* today, it is only with difficulty that we decipher the facts and fantasies that have attached themselves to the work, both in our own time and in the milieu that first gave it meaning. What is overwhelmingly evident is that, from its inception, Degas chose to engage with one of the most resonant images of his day, an image that was seen by his peers to link high art with the gutter and to provoke anxiety as much as approval. More versed than we in these social semaphores, Degas' audiences were either thrilled by its novelty or exasperated by its awkwardness, while none seemed indifferent to the sculpture's presence. Those accustomed to the sparkling elegance of Garnier's auditorium were perplexed by the elevation of a mere "rat" – dressed in exercise clothes and perhaps unwashed – to such prominence, while the "adepts" of the new art (groups of "nihilist men and women," as one visitor described them) were enthralled by its audacity.[97] Experts in the dance were able to concede the "singular exactitude" of the work, while those expecting titillation were thwarted at every turn by the indifferent expression of the dancer's pinched features or by a lack of voluptuousness in her young body. And for established followers of Degas' art, here was another challenge: a colored, three-dimensional object by a painter they knew well, leading them from the familiar illusions of pictorial space to the treacherous pseudo-realities of sculpture.

2 THE MAKING OF THE SCULPTURE

"A wax dancer whose naturalism is strangely attractive, troubling, . . ."[1]

Degas was effectively the founder of a distinguished line of untaught sculptor-painters in the modern age, soon to include Paul Gauguin and, most famously, to be followed by Pablo Picasso and Henri Matisse in the early twentieth century. As an amateur embarking on the first large-scale sculpture of his career, Degas – like his successors – was obliged to confront the simplest practical matters as well as the grander pretensions of his project. Some of the former have already been touched on; the selection of a model from among the "rats" at the Opéra and the choice of her pose, for example, and the use to be made of the artist's pre-existing "stock" of drawn and painted images. At a technical level, there was the challenge of constructing the meter-high wax figure – a formidable task for a virtual beginner – and of dressing it in specially made, reduced-scale tutu, bodice, wig, and dancing shoes. Common to all these considerations was an even more fundamental question: that of the status of Degas' semi-private modeling venture in the very competitive world of nineteenth-century sculpture. Was Degas making this image of a young dancer to assist him with his picture making, in the way that his later wax horses, ballerinas, and bather-figures appear to have been conceived, or was it intended from the start for public display, as a bold intervention in the sculptural exchanges of his day? If the latter, how well acquainted was Degas with the crosscurrents of opinion in the contemporary medium, and how appropriate or otherwise was his contribution to them? In short, was the *Little Dancer Aged Fourteen* merely an eccentric studio experiment, or was it to be an informed, radical, and eye-catching work of three-dimensional art?

In his 1976 monograph on the artist, Charles Millard asserted that "Degas' sculpture is a very paradigm of the development of sculpture in nineteenth-century France, a résumé of its statements and problems, its exploratory and modern strains."[2] Among the few authors to have attempted to locate the *Little Dancer Aged Fourteen* in the era's broader sculptural concerns – which he groups together as the "monumental," the "classical," and the "romantic and contemporary" – Millard stressed the historic roots of Degas' formation and established a number of pioneering links with the technical debates of the age. The extent of Degas' participation in this milieu, however, has remained a matter of uncertainty for many, exacerbated by his reputation as an untaught modeler and – with the solitary exception of the *Little Dancer* – a reluctant exhibitor. In recent years there has been a decisive shift in our perception of Degas the amateur sculptor. If, as we increasingly believe, Degas' experiments in wax, clay, and mixed materials were openly conducted, often in the company of friends who were professionals; if certain of his finished models were proudly presented in his apartment and almost casually accessible in his studio to visiting artists, critics, and

Fig. 11 Jean-Auguste Barre, *Marie Taglioni in "La Sylphide,"* 1837, bronze, 17¾ in. (45 cm), Musée des Arts décoratifs, Paris.

dealers; if several attempts were made during Degas' lifetime to cast his wax and clay sculptures into more durable materials; and if the reputation of some of his three-dimensional achievements – most notably the *Little Dancer Aged Fourteen* – persisted throughout his career, then the image of Degas as a sculptural recluse must finally be reassessed.[3]

As our understanding of French sculpture in the second half of the nineteenth century has deepened, so Millard's claim for the paradigmatic status of Degas' work has been progressively vindicated. Whether charting the evolution of realism or studying sculpture within the Impressionist enterprise, following the arguments that raged around polychromy or the decline of the public monument, the *Little Dancer Aged Fourteen* is encountered near the center of each argument or at the threshold of innovation. In retrospect, Degas' fabrication between 1878 and 1881 of a costumed wax statuette of an ordinary Parisian adolescent seems almost prescient, anticipating and simultaneously embodying a revolution in sculpture and a radical re-evaluation of its relationship to the spectator and the material world. Far from being prophetic, of course, the making of the *Little Dancer* was a precisely calculated maneuver by an artist conversant with many of the personalities – including sculptors and critics, theorists and collectors – with whom he was engaged. While advances have been made in the integration of Degas' sculpture with the art of his fellow Impressionists, insufficient attention has been paid to his documented and sometimes enthusiastic engagement with practitioners from more conservative traditions. Not only did Degas regularly scrutinize the Salons and the International Exhibitions of these years (as late as 1891, Berthe Morisot reported that he still "stayed in the Salon from morning till night") but he could look back on first-hand acquaintance with a range of professional and occasional sculptors, from his friends Dr. Camus and Gustave Moreau to the aspiring Joseph Cuvelier and the celebrated Henri Chapu, while his awareness of the achievements of Carpeaux, Dubois, Meissonier, and Bartholomé is well attested.[4] In the present study, we can only single out a few of these strands, emphasizing those largely overlooked in earlier examinations of the *Little Dancer* and those most closely related to its manufacture. But by concentrating on prominent commentators and sculptors or works that Degas is known to have encountered, we can significantly advance Millard's claim and locate the *Little Dancer* more securely in its time.

Jean-Auguste Barre's study *Marie Taglioni in "La Sylphide"* (fig. 11) is a winsome reminder of one of the crucial precedents Degas must have consulted as he began the *Little Dancer Aged Fourteen:* that of the existing tradition of ballet sculpture. Barre was a minor figure with a modest reputation for medals and portrait busts, and his depictions of two leading ballerinas of the day, Taglioni and Fanny Elssler (fig. 12), tended to reiterate the conventional view of the dancer and her attributes. In both sculptures, the public spectacle of the ballet has provided the subject, as a daintily dressed *étoile* steps through her performance on a miniature stage and the intricacies of her costume are itemized for our delight. The figure of Elssler is conspicuous in this respect, with a finely worked silk and lace outfit appropriate to her "Spanish" role in *Le Diable boiteux* and minutely modeled bouquets of roses at her feet, and it is no surprise to find that this elegant object was also produced as a luxurious silvered bronze.[5] The two works are thought to have been unveiled at the Salon of 1837, when Taglioni and Elssler were both in their mid twenties, representing the dancers at the height of their celebrity rather than in a moment of obscure apprenticeship, like that chosen by Degas for his studies of Marie van Goethem. Despite these fundamental differences, a substantial link with Degas can

Fig. 12 Jean-Auguste Barre, *Fanny Elssler*, 1837, silvered bronze, 16⅞ in. (42.9 cm), The Fine Arts Museums of San Francisco, Gift of Mrs. Alma de Bretteville Spreckels.

be established in the case of each of Barre's sculptures, through the family of his long-established friends, the Rouarts. The brothers Alexis and Henri Rouart were collectors of wide and imaginative taste, amassing Egyptian mummies and Tanagra figurines, lithographs by Daumier and paintings by Corot, Millet, and the Impressionists, which they famously made available to visitors young and old.[6] A confirmed bachelor, Degas regarded their apartments as extensions of his home, and it was there that he would have become familiar with both Barre images, a bronze cast of the figure of Taglioni in Alexis' collection and the original plaster statuette of Elssler among Henri's extensive holdings.[7] Given that the two brothers were also ardent collectors of pictures by Degas himself, with a pronounced preference for his ballet scenes, the opportunity for direct comparison of the dance imagery of successive generations – not just for the Rouarts but for their visiting artist-friend – must have been continuous and irresistible.

Predictable though they may be, Barre's bronzes remind us that ballet and sculpture enjoyed a subtle and often reciprocal association throughout much of the nineteenth century. As we have seen, dance pupils were often urged to emulate the great pictures and sculptures of the past: in 1820, Charles Blasis had demanded that "A dancer should be able, at any moment, to provide a model for a painter or sculptor," words that were closely echoed in Georges Duval's pedagogical text published shortly before the making of the *Little Dancer*.[8] In their working lives, dancers found themselves in frequent juxtaposition with their sculptural counterparts, most obviously in the figures that ornamented the facade and interior of the rue Le Peletier theater and the Garnier Opéra, but also in certain of their everyday rehearsal rooms. An anonymous lithograph from *Charivari* of 1846 (fig. 13) shows one such encounter, where a "rat" and her companions inspect a bust by Houdon of the dancer Jacqueline Guimard, while puzzling over the practice of recording celebrated ballerinas without showing their legs.[9] Such a bust is known to have been present in the rue Le Peletier dance foyer, appearing in numerous prints of the scene and – as a curious, half-remembered variant – in a fan painting by Degas from the late 1870s.[10] Visitors to the Palais Garnier were regularly and publicly exposed to Carpeaux's larger-than-life-size *The Dance*, whose naked and very unballetic marble dancers scandalized Paris when they first appeared in 1869.[11] One consequence of the notoriety of the work was Carpeaux's decision to capitalize on his fame by supervising casts and reduced-scale replicas of *The Dance* in a variety of media. Another of Carpeaux's creations, the portrait bust of *Eugénie Fiocre* (the dancer Degas had painted in the 1860s) was similarly produced in a number of variants, including the marble shown at the 1870 Salon, a plaster now in the Musée d'Orsay, and a more popular reduction in terracotta.[12] Drawn to it perhaps by nostalgia, Degas himself apparently acquired a copy of the latter at some unspecified date, Daniel Halévy telling us that the artist would still caress it with affection in his half-blind old age.[13]

Degas' documented awareness of the existing patterns of dance sculpture, from classical prototypes to works by a wide variety of his immediate contemporaries, gives added purposefulness to his own achievement in the *Little Dancer Aged Fourteen*. Far from being overshadowed by his antecedents, Degas seems to have reversed the majority of their assumptions, from such fundamental questions as their choice of subject, medium, and finish to the means of presenting the completed object to the public. Where Barre had opted for a moment of spectacle, Degas chose the banality of the rehearsal room; where a product of Romanticism, such as Francisque-Joseph Duret's acclaimed *Dancing Neapolitan*

Fig. 13 Anon., *The Opéra in the Nineteenth Century*, lithograph, from *Charivari*, 21 February, 1846.

Boy of 1833, explored the lyrical, pantheistic energies of the dance, Degas' figure emphasized inertia; and where the mannered classicism of James Pradier's *Dancer with a Scarf* exploited the sinuousness of bronze, the *Little Dancer* stressed coarseness of surface and quotidian emotion. Closer to the historical example of Barre, Degas again rejected the "cabinet" scale and implicit decorativeness of his output, along with the cult of personality it entailed. Houdon, Barre, and Carpeaux had all – in their different registers – immortalized the celebrities of their day or aspired to embody the spirit of the dance itself (Houdon's bust in the dance foyer was named after the muse of the dance, *Terpsichore*). By contrast, the *Little Dancer* was anonymous and insignificant, modeled on a scale that was neither charmingly miniature nor grandiose, and made in materials that were defiantly resistant to most forms of replication. His image is particular, domestic, and unyielding, juxtaposing the brute facts of sculpture with the daily realities of the dance for the first time in the history of either medium. If painted representations of such subjects had become almost commonplace by this date, we search in vain for their equivalents in three dimensions, either at the Salon or in the more informal products of artists' studios.[14] Indeed, so radical was Degas' departure that it was more than a generation before other sculptors followed his lead, when the likes of Rupert Carabin, Pavel Troubetzkoi, and Leonetto Cappiello extended his examination of the less decorous world of the dance into the vernacular of their own age.[15]

A further consideration uniting the depiction of the dance with the wider issues of sculpture, and of largely overlooked significance in the case of the *Little Dancer Aged Fourteen,* was that of the depiction of infants, children, and adolescents. The mid century saw an extraordinary proliferation of such images, not just in painted family portraits and instructive prints, but in reliefs, marble carvings, cast bronzes, polished marbles, and monuments on almost every scale. Perhaps encouraged by the reception of François-Joseph Bosio's full-size *Henri IV as a Child,* shown as a plaster in 1822 and cast in silver by order of Louis XVIII, renderings of historic and exemplary youths became a regular feature at the annual state-sponsored Salon.[16] Bosio's decision to present Henri in childhood and wearing appropriate sixteenth-century doublet and hose resulted in a form that is oddly – and probably coincidentally – analogous to Degas' *Little Dancer,* despite the emphatic historicism and sumptuous finish of the earlier work. Nearer to Degas' own day in style of costume, if not in pose, was Carpeaux's marble group *The Prince Imperial and His Dog Nero* of 1865, a work commissioned by the Emperor that shows the eight-year-old prince at natural scale, clad in contemporary jacket and loose trousers.[17] During the 1870s, this trend toward informality embraced the children of the middle classes and even the picturesque poor, most controversially in works like Vincenzo Gemito's bronzes of half-naked urchins and Neapolitan fisherboys. Several of the sculptors who achieved fame with their representations of children belonged to Degas' generation or were known to him personally, like the marble carver Henri Chapu, who had been part of the same circle at the Villa Medici in Rome during Degas' Italian sojourn.[18] When Chapu's life-size *Young Boy* was exhibited at the Salon of 1879, it was widely praised for its easy naturalism, one critic claiming, "It is perfect . . . the marble is treated with extreme suppleness and beneath the folds of cloth we sense a body."[19] Given their earlier association and his own current engagement with the *Little Dancer,* Degas would surely have taken note of this confident, realistically clothed vision of precocious manhood, if only to define the technical and stylistic distance he had traveled from his former colleague.

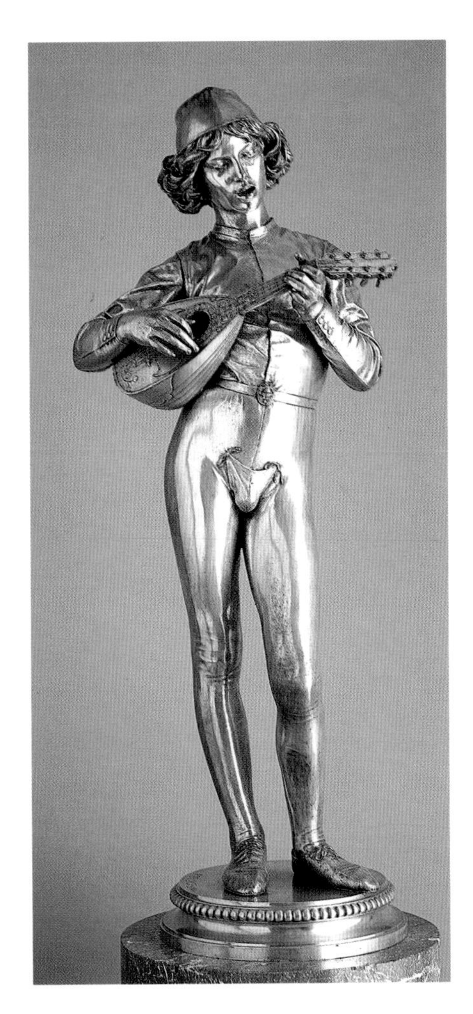

Fig. 14 Paul Dubois, *Florentine Singer of the Fifteenth Century*, 1865, silvered bronze, 61 in. (1.55 m.), Musée d'Orsay, Paris.

Arguably the most critically approved and popularly acclaimed emblem of youth in the years immediately prior to the *Little Dancer,* however, was Paul Dubois' life-size *Florentine Singer of the Fifteenth Century* (fig. 14). Awarded a medal of honor when it was presented as a plaster at the 1865 Salon (the exhibition at which Degas made his own debut as a painter), the work was translated into silvered bronze by order of the state and subsequently mass-produced in no less than six alternative sizes by the Barbedienne foundry and three reduced-scale versions in terracotta by the Manufacture de Sèvres.[20] Installed in the Musée du Luxembourg, which contained the foremost collection of modern painting and sculpture in Paris, Dubois' figure won over a range of opinion by combining a high degree of finish with a relaxed demeanor, and a picturesque theme with evident wholesomeness. This fusion of qualities was specifically welcomed by its audience, Paul Mantz (who was to become one of the harsher critics of the *Little Dancer Aged Fourteen*) claiming that "the head, a happy mingling of rusticity and finesse, is really that of a Florentine of the glorious age: the body, supple and nervous, is full of youth and elegance."[21] As with Bosio's *Henri IV as a Child,* we can hardly overlook certain superficial similarities between this icon of adolescence and Degas' wax statuette; though Dubois' subject was male, he displays a conspicuous pair of bestockinged legs and a finely detailed costume, while his broadly symmetrical pose depends on a distribution of weight that is generically akin to that of the *Little Dancer.* Separated by more than a decade, the two works nevertheless share an ambition to represent the qualities of incipient adulthood in a single, resonant image, an identity of purpose that Degas may have signaled in his witty echoes of the cadences of Dubois' title.[22]

The possibility that the *Little Dancer Aged Fourteen* was a self-conscious, even mischief-making response to the renowned *Florentine Singer of the Fifteenth Century* – and that Degas was aware of more general parallels between Dubois' career and his own – deserves consideration for a number of reasons. Paul Valéry tells us of Degas' respect in later life for Dubois' massive equestrian statue of *Joan of Arc* (a youthful heroine of another age), one of very few specific works of contemporary sculpture the artist is known to have admired.[23] Born just five years earlier than Degas into a comparable bourgeois family, Paul Dubois preceded him at the classically based Lycée Louis-le-Grand and likewise spent a brief spell at the Ecole des Beaux-Arts, then followed the younger artist in several years of independently financed study in Italy.[24] If we cannot confirm Jeanne Fevre's assertion that the two men met in Rome in 1859, when Degas is said to have mixed with "Léon Bonnat, Gustave Moreau, Georges Bizet, Dubois and Chapu," it is beyond doubt that they developed a similar passion for Italian Renaissance art and planned near-identical works – such as their variants on the theme of a striding, youthful John the Baptist – at this time.[25] As both attempted to establish themselves in Paris in the 1860s, it was Dubois who clung most stubbornly to his Italianate roots, while sharing some common ground with Degas in his descriptive portraits of contemporary musicians, painters, and scientists, such as the bust of *Louis Pasteur* exhibited in 1880.[26] Despite the divergence of their careers and public imagery, Dubois may well have represented a model of conventional technical practice of some significance for the untutored Degas, a possibility strengthened by parallels in their procedures; Dubois worked as both sculptor and painter, typically defining his three-dimensional subject in a sequence of closely related drawings; similarly, Dubois often chose to develop his forms in wax, ranging from rapidly improvised sketches that might incorporate other materials to full-scale figures;

and, predominantly, Dubois remained an instinctive modeler, rather than a carver of marble or stone.[27]

In 1881, when the *Little Dancer Aged Fourteen* was first unveiled, the memory of Dubois' *Florentine Singer* was still very much alive in the sculptural mind of Paris. Both Eugène Guillaume and Jules Buisson referred nostalgically to Dubois' figure in their Salon criticism of that year, Guillaume noting its persistent but positive influence on younger artists and Buisson approving its modest dimensions, which he believed were better suited to the economic circumstances of the present than the grand monuments to which they were accustomed.[28] His approving description of figures like those of Dubois as "cabinet sculpture" – whether in the original version installed at the Musée du Luxembourg or in its many smaller-scale offspring – represents a more positive view of the mass-production of works by Bosio, Carpeaux, Barre, and others, a pattern deplored as early as 1846 by Charles Baudelaire. Complaining that the sculptors of his day belonged to a "vast workshop" willing to reduce the great art of the past to "match-boxes, goldsmiths' motifs, busts and bas-reliefs" and "cigar- and shawl-boxes," Baudelaire argued that "there are no childish trivialities which the sculptor will not dare."[29] Part of this trend toward "a drawing-room or a bedroom art," as Baudelaire correctly predicted, was a taste for "trifling prettiness" over "grandeur," and an indulgence in extravagantly detailed carving and modeling of hair, fabrics, jewelry, and costume.[30] Not confined to figures of children and youths, this tendency undoubtedly contributed to the appeal of popular favorites like the *Florentine Singer* and Chapu's *Young Boy,* but was seen by a growing number as a blight on the seriousness of modern sculpture. Singling out examples of such virtuosity by exhibitors from Italy – who were widely associated with the practice – Anatole de Montaiglon wrote scathingly at the time of the 1878 Exposition Universelle of their "facility" and their aspirations toward sculptural "trompe l'oeil," the "triumph of the practitioner over the sculptor, craft over art, puerile execution over form and idea."[31]

When Joris-Karl Huysmans welcomed the appearance of the *Little Dancer Aged Fourteen* at such length and with such conviction, he, too, referred to such sculptural fashions, if only to dismiss them with his most haughty rhetoric. Hailing the *Little Dancer* as the "only truly modern attempt at realism in sculpture that I know," Huysmans specifically distanced it from the "once-daring efforts at peasants teaching children to read or giving them a drink, . . . Greek or Renaissance peasants, . . . [and] this abominable sculpture from contemporary Italy, these clock-decorations in wax, these mawkish women constructed from fashion engravings."[32] For Huysmans, Degas' achievement was to have turned his back on half-a-dozen contemporary traits at once; against historicism, sentiment, and implausible narrative on the one hand, and the modish delight in verisimilitude and facile contemporaneity on the other. Two years earlier, in an extended Salon review that cited Degas in its first pages, Huysmans had proclaimed that sculpture would either "adapt itself to modern life" or perish; now, with the unveiling of Degas' wax figure, he seems to have felt himself vindicated.[33] Noting the proximity of Degas and Huysmans at this time, Philip Ward-Jackson has proposed that the latter may have written his 1879 text with an awareness of Degas' current engagement on the *Little Dancer:* "the likelihood is that he knew her to be waiting in the wings," he suggests.[34] Whatever Huysmans' relationship to the work, it is clear that a number of critics shared his sense that sculptural realism and its challenges must be confronted. A leading if essentially conservative sculptor himself, Eugène Guillaume had written at length and with considerable shrewdness in 1879 on the representation of the everyday world, articulating both its appeal and its practical and psychological limitations: "To see nature without an intermediary, without prejudice of race or education . . . is something difficult, something impossible for the artist," he explained. "Each art is characterized by something incomplete and fictive, in a word, by some aspect of reality: here, it is color that must be overlooked; there, the dimensions are at fault . . . imitation is nothing but a certain appearance of reality."[35]

Fig. 15 Eugène Guillaume, *Napoleon as a Roman Emperor*, 1858, wax on a wooden base, 20¾ in. (52.5 cm), Musée d'Orsay, Paris.

Degas' challenge in making the *Little Dancer* – to negotiate the pitfalls of "imitation" and the lure of meretricious modernity – is strikingly anticipated in Guillaume's statement. Before examining its consequences, one final practical decision made by Degas the amateur sculptor in approaching his figure must be considered: that of his use of wax. Today, wax has been banished to the periphery of the sculptor's repertoire and, in our rare encounters with the material, is associated with inferior genres (such as artificial flower making) or long redundant and sometimes dubious crafts. In Degas' century, beeswax, paraffin wax, and stearin were ubiquitous substances, not just in domestic and industrial contexts but in virtually every branch of the sculptor's activity. Among the practitioners already discussed, the majority used wax to a lesser or greater extent; Carpeaux, for example, exploited its pliability in a number of small, sensuously improvised models that recall its former use by Michelangelo; the sculptor-critic Guillaume followed established procedure by first modeling his subject in wax on a reduced scale, as in his study for a monument to *Napoleon as a Roman Emperor* (fig. 15), then proceeding to a full-size marble or bronze; while Dubois almost exhausted the medium's possibilities, working at hasty miniature sketches, decorative panels, broad explorations of equestrian groups, and a highly finished, life-size female figure in wax that was later cast in plaster and bronze.[36] Many of their sculptor colleagues, such as Barye, Falguière, Gemito, Meissonier, Mène, Moreau, and Rodin, turned habitually or occasionally to wax, studies in the medium appearing as a regular feature at the annual Salon and even attracting specialist collectors. Far from being eccentric, in the latter part of the nineteenth century wax was among the most commonplace and public of all the sculptor's materials.

In his short story *The Studio*, published in 1881 and designed to enlighten the general reader on the subject of artists' techniques, Degas' close acquaintance Edmond Duranty included a guide to the procedures and materials of the sculptor. Discussing the nature of wax, Duranty explained that it was "a mixture of ordinary wax, turpentine, fat and flour, which can be colored grey, green, brown and red or left in its state of whiteness. Modelling wax costs three or four francs a pound."[37] Apart from the necessary pigments, these additives were included to extend and soften the wax so that it could be manipulated according to the sculptor's wishes, then allowed to harden with the passage of time. Such a medium had numerous advantages, not least for the beginner. As Duranty makes clear, it was cheap and freely available; in his introduction to the compendious 1987 *Sculptures en cire de l'ancienne Egypt à l'art abstrait*, Jean-René Gaborit adds that wax was relatively clean and easy to handle, comparing favorably with terracotta in terms of durability and combining readily with other materials, such as "cardboard, paper, cloth, glass, metallic ornaments, wire or hair."[38] Almost from the beginning of its use in the ancient world, as Degas' contemporaries were well aware, wax had been inseparable from certain modes of painstaking, mixed-media naturalism, notably in portraits of the recently deceased and more ambitious effigies of robed and be-jeweled kings and queens, and – in recent times – in

Fig. 16 Pierre-Jules Mène, *Toreador*, 1877, bronze, 21 in. (53 cm), courtesy Sotheby's, London.

displays of the celebrated and notorious in the manner of Madame Tussaud's. As well as its versatility, it was the surface appearance of this "lightly translucent, smooth and matte" substance, when mixed with the appropriate color, that made it ideal for the reproduction, "even the illusion, of the varied appearance of human flesh."[39]

Anatomical models, dolls and hairdressers' dummies were typically made of tinted wax in Degas' day, often in conjunction with "real" items of clothing and artificial eyes, hair wigs, and lifelike teeth, and it was standard practice to discuss such items in terms of their uncanny "realism."[40] For similar reasons, modeling with wax was regarded as more akin to painting than to the sculptural skills of carving and construction, and it is hardly a coincidence that several painters admired by Degas, among them the seventeenth-century artist Nicolas Poussin and more immediate peers like Moreau, Meissonier, Gauguin, and Pissarro, made wax figures at some point in their careers.[41] Conversely, a number of generally obscure specialists in wax sculpture tended to favor "painterly" subjects, often involving miniature narratives and the application of color. Wax was chosen by dozens of long-forgotten contributors to the Paris Salon, who annually exhibited portrait studies and groups of birds and animals, the character of many of them evident in such anecdotal titles as *The Wolf and the Stork* and *Terrier with Rats*.[42] Sullied by its association with popular crafts, its links with sentimental illusionism, and its tendency to become "an activity for amateurs," wax sculpture came heavily burdened with the values of its age.[43]

If the accessibility and painterliness of wax goes some way toward explaining its adoption by an outsider like Degas, it must be set against the equally abundant evidence that many artists of distinction, from the much-decorated Dubois to the more pedestrian Pierre-Jules Mène, proudly exhibited their wax sculptures in this same public forum. An important figure in Degas' sculptural background, Joseph Cuvelier, is a minor if typical case in point. Degas seems to have become acquainted with Cuvelier in the late 1860s, when the latter was establishing himself as a specialist in modest-scale groups of horses and riders, such as the forty-centimeter-high *Portrait of Monsieur Baude* included in its wax form at the Salon of 1869.[44] Though Cuvelier was killed while serving in the Franco-Prussian war of 1871, his technical example may already have contributed to Degas' earliest experiments with wax, a phase called to mind at the1878 Exposition Universelle, when several of Cuvelier's equestrian waxes were again displayed.[45] The previous year, the animal sculptor Mène had shown at the Salon a rather uncharacteristic statuette of a striding, richly dressed *Toreador* as a highly finished wax, prior to its translation into bronze (fig. 16), while the portraitist Jules Franceschi was to include a wax bust of the composer Charles Gounod in the exhibition of 1879.[46] Surviving sculptures of this kind, like Franceschi's wax *Portrait of the Painter Edouard-Louis Dubufe* of 1878 (fig. 17), remind us that these were not mere studies or sketches, but highly resolved works that were either preserved for their intrinsic qualities or destined for immediate translation into sophisticated bronzes. Where Mène's figure is almost overburdened by its pedantic detail, Franceschi's honey-colored wax draws much of its vivacity from the nature of the "lightly translucent" substance itself, a characteristic that would necessarily be lost in the casting process.

The widespread use of wax in the 1870s was part of a more general revival of interest in the medium at a number of levels. Pursuing its ancient origins, scholarly books and articles traced the application of wax in early Egyptian "cire perdue" metal casting, in Roman funerary portraiture, and in the tradition of the *ex-voto*

Fig. 17 Jules Franceschi, *Portrait of the Painter Edouard-Louis Dubufe*, 1878, wax, 15 in. (38.1 cm), Los Angeles County Museum of Art, Gift of Harry Kahn.

figure in the Middle Ages and Renaissance, while drawing attention to renowned wax objects which had survived from former centuries. In 1878, for example, Anatole de Montaiglon delivered a lecture on the "History of Wax Sculpture" at the Union Centrale; the following year, an article by Louis Gonse on the "Musée Wicar, objets de l'art: la tête de cire" appeared in the *Gazette des Beaux-Arts;* and in 1882 the same journal published a sequence of historical essays by Spire Blondel entitled *Wax Modellers*.[47] In less exalted contexts, wax was also enjoying a revived currency. Though temporary displays of wax figures had been popular for centuries, they finally became institutionalized in France in 1882 with the foundation of the Musée Grévin, a waxwork museum based on Madame Tussaud's in London which was opened by the entrepreneur Alfred Grévin, already encountered in this study in his capacity as a cartoonist (see fig. 9). As Theodore Reff has discovered, Degas' links with several of the personalities depicted in Grévin's first installations are striking, though a description of himself as "a frenzied Grévin" in one of the artist's letters of 1880 appears to concern Degas' draftsmanship as much as his current attempts at sculpture.[48] Reff has also pointed out the prevalence of historic battle panoramas featuring wax figures, an attraction that excited the enthusiasm of Jules Claretie some months after his review of the *Little Dancer Aged Fourteen*. Visiting one such spectacle, Claretie evoked the vivid illusion created by a combination of wax, plaster, and paint, resulting in a population of "wax mannequins" dressed in soldiers' uniforms. Judging that this mixture of "the morgue and the Musée du Luxembourg, the Salon and Madame Tussaud's" would prove successful with the public, Claretie reflected on the morbid yet essentially paradoxical nature of such representations; of one waxen corpse he wrote that it "provoked the most atrocious sensation of reality itself," adding that "if the wax panorama figures have the air of the dead, they have, conversely, the air of wax figures."[49]

When Eugène Guillaume reviewed the sculpture section of the Salon of 1879, noting that "despite its fragility" wax was producing "more and more interesting results," he was making an altogether more specific point.[50] In the course of the decade, several ambitious younger sculptors had adopted wax as their primary medium, presenting finished and sometimes life-size figures in the material at this most prestigious of contemporary exhibitions. Where Dubois' image of a standing, naked young woman – entitled *Eve* – was first executed in wax before being translated into plaster and shown in 1873, artists like Henri Cros and Dubois' associate, René de Saint-Marceaux, now displayed waxes that, by virtue of their surface coloration and painterly detail, announced themselves as complete, self-contained works.[51] Though Cros' more prominent achievements, such as the 1875 polychrome wax head of *Isabeau de Bavière* now in the Musée d'Orsay, were insistently medieval in theme and decorative in manner, he also made smaller, naturalistically tinted portrait reliefs of individuals from his circle.[52] Guillaume noted the use of color by both Saint-Marceaux and Cros, but reserved his most complete commentary for an even more confident work, Jean Désiré Ringel's *Demi-monde,* which he described as "a colored wax statue at natural scale."[53] Subsequently destroyed, the appearance of Ringel's figure can best be imagined by referring to illustrations of another lost work, the terracotta *Splendeur et misère* of 1881 that incorporated a real hat and spectacles, and such surviving waxes as his lugubriously vivid *Portrait of Maurice Rollinat* of 1892.[54] The outspokenly naturalistic *Demi-monde* excited consternation and praise in equal measure, remembered as a "charming statue" by Blondel in 1882, but evidently found provocative by the kind of audiences who recoiled from the *Little Dancer Aged*

Fourteen.[55] Struggling to articulate his discomfort, Guillaume acknowledged that Ringel's sculpture showed great skill and promise for a virtual unknown, but suggested that the application of color was inappropriate to such a lowly form; "adding color to simple reality," he argued, "gives it an indefinable quality of dullness and morbidity," reminding the critic of "galleries of anatomy" or of wax "cast in a mold."[56]

THE FIRST IMPRESSIONIST SCULPTURE

If ever the ground can be said to have been prepared for a sculpture of a young adult in contemporary costume, fashioned in wax and partially tinted, it was surely at this time and in this milieu. Such a subject spanned the gradually evolving imagery of the Salon and the world of the "Intransigents," while the choice of medium reverberated with contemporary scholarship, current studio practice, and the latest novelties of the boulevards and department stores. Critics trembled as they anticipated such objects at future exhibitions; "this is sculpture for the Chinese or for fashion houses," protested Anatole de Montaiglon, predicting that "dressed mannequins from the galleries of clothiers will soon become the last word in art."[57] For Degas, too, the moment was ripe, both technically and in terms of his advancing claims to seniority ("It is truly regrettable that this distinguished, exceptional, witty and grave artist is not represented in the Musée du Luxembourg," wrote his admirer Philippe Burty as early as 1879).[58] Sculpture was one of the few avenues that neither he nor his immediate colleagues in the Impressionist circle had explored, at least in public, and the recent successes of Henri Cros (another semi-amateur, whom Degas almost certainly knew), Ringel, and others – with works that were avowedly experimental or topical in theme – may well have spurred Degas on. At the 1880 Impressionist show, he and his current protégé, Paul Gauguin, together seized the initiative, Degas announcing his *Little Dancer Aged Fourteen* in the catalogue but failing to produce it for the display, and Gauguin showing a life-size bust of his twenty-nine-year-old wife, carved in marble but apparently begun as a wax.[59] The following year, when the *Little Dancer* finally appeared, Gauguin again showed his solidarity by submitting two studies of young women in variously colored and painted materials, both in unmistakably modish garb; the medallion of a popular performer, known as the *Singer,* made from wood and plaster touched with color; and the *Little Parisian,* a tinted carving of a woman out walking that has often been compared to Degas' statuette.[60]

As with Gauguin, it seems overwhelmingly probable that Degas made a group of exploratory studies of the human figure as he embarked on this new sculptural project, feeling his way in matters of scale, medium, and surface embellishment. Frustratingly, an unidentified number of Degas' sculptures are known to have been destroyed and those that survive have proved notoriously resistant to dating, while each of the candidates for the pre-*Little Dancer* phase have found themselves challenged for practical or stylistic reasons.[61] On the basis of the artist's notebooks and other supporting documentation, however, four very varied sculptures can be plausibly linked with the years around 1880, reinforcing the notion of a vital, opportunistic engagement with the medium at this time. The latest of these is probably the *Apple Pickers,* a modeled scene of children at the foot of a tree, dated by Reff to the summer of 1881 and further distanced from the *Little Dancer* by its relief format and construction from clay.[62] Interspersed with sketches for this work

Fig. 18 *Study for the "Schoolgirl,"* ca. 1880–81, pencil, 6½ × 4¼ in. (16.4 × 10.7 cm), Notebook 34, p. 17, Bibliothèque Nationale, Paris.

in a contemporary notebook are three pencil drawings for another figure, the *Schoolgirl* (cat. 31, bronze), a small wax statuette of an adolescent in everyday clothing that has much in common with the larger work, including the now-familiar advanced right leg and small-featured visage.[63] One of these drawings (fig. 18) shows the extent of their similarity, in the long plait of hair and angular bodily form, while the *Little Dancer*-like arm pushed abruptly into the small of the back is one of the few recurrences of this motif outside Degas' dance repertoire.

A more contentious precursor of the 1881 figure is *Dancer at Rest, Hands on Her Hips, Left Leg Forward* (cat. 37), which has been variously located between 1878 and 1895 by different authorities.[64] Though it differs in projecting the left leg and maintaining the separation of the hands, this study – as Alison Luchs and others have accepted – is perhaps the most convincing candidate for the missing link between Degas' early equestrian exercises and the extraordinary maturity of the *Little Dancer Aged Fourteen*.[65] It is instructive to find, for example, that the standing figure has none of the sinuousness or acrobatic complexity of the waxes from later years; that its surface shows extensive working with a toothed modeling implement of a kind used on the 1881 wax; and that it has a distinctive anatomical vagueness around the breast, waist, and hips that would be consistent with an early trial with reduced-scale clothing. More than one acquaintance of the artist reported the presence of *several* dressed figures, "dancing girls modelled in red wax, some dressed in muslin skirts," as George Moore recalls, raising the possibility that the *Dancer at Rest* might have been among the first to be costumed in this way.[66]

Before falling into the too-common error of assuming that artists make their work in strict, production-line sequences of paintings or sculptures, completing one before moving on to the next, it should be noted that everything we know about Degas' studio practice indicates a quite different pattern. Renowned for his procrastination, Degas would over-paint canvases and retouch pastels months or sometimes years after their inception, gathering around him hundreds of partially completed pictures and "borrowing" figures from images still in progress. Between 1879 and 1881, he was almost certainly surrounded by a variety of sculptures in progressive states of completion, as well as a scattering of drawings and sketchbook studies related to them. Encouraged by the flexibility of the medium, a step forward on one wax model could stimulate modifications to another; new drawings might be made before, during, and – as was certainly the case in later years – after the resolution of a particular figurine; and acquired skills could be applied retrospectively to an earlier effort, in a continuous, mobile process of mutual influence. Whatever its precise history, the fourth sculpture associated with this phase, the *Nude Study for the Little Dancer Aged Fourteen* (cat. 39), must have played a crucial role in such a process. The tradition of defining the naked body before advancing to its clothed successor was of considerable antiquity, along with the practice of making smaller studies for full-size or monumental works, whether in sculpture or painting. As a younger man, Degas had learned to employ both these approaches, gradually abandoning them as his mastery increased and a more direct response to his subject matter became appropriate, though occasionally reviving them as the occasion demanded in later life.

In this sense, his drawings of a nude Marie van Goethem (cats. 36 and 38) might be seen as a cautious, temporary return to the routines of his youth by an artist approaching an unfamiliar challenge. *Nude Study for the Little Dancer Aged Fourteen* has always been understood to fulfill the same preliminary role, allowing Michael

Pantazzi to claim, "There has never been any doubt that the nude version . . . is the model for the dressed version . . . and that, as such, it preceded it."[67] Following Daphne Barbour's 1995 publication of her technical examination of the sculpture, however, even this secure point of reference has lost its hold. X-ray and pigment analysis and close scrutiny of the surface of the *Nude Study* have established that the present wax (from which all the known bronzes ultimately derive) was partially cast from an earlier version at Degas' direction and may therefore post-date the *Little Dancer* itself.[68] Important though this undoubtedly is in shedding light on the artist's ingenuity and longer-term ambitions, it does not distract from the overwhelming probability that an original wax form of the *Nude Study* existed in the late 1870s and that it was intimately involved in the sculptural evolution of that moment. Barbour also puts forward an intriguing case for seeing the generalized surfaces of the known nude study as a reflection of Degas' later manner, requiring us to imagine a detailed, descriptive finish to the lost early version that would have been more consistent with the wax *Little Dancer*.

With the exception of the *Apple Pickers,* all Degas' early studies were made principally of wax, built around supporting structures of wire and metal, and attached to a haphazard variety of wooden and other bases. The latter vary from rough planks to blocks of plaster, though the heavy wooden platform chosen for the *Little Dancer Aged Fourteen* is exceptional in its sophistication, even suggesting a section of a real dance rehearsal floor to one modern author.[69] If the *Schoolgirl* is modeled on a commercially manufactured armature (a rarity in Degas' oeuvre), everything else about this group of waxes suggests enthusiastic improvisation, as the artist toyed with different scales, a palette of somber pigments and, above all, a range of finishes. In its softened state, wax can be manipulated with the hands into the desired form, then further added to or modified until the desired texture and degree of refinement have been achieved. Parts of the *Nude Study* have been left relatively coarse, while the much smaller *Schoolgirl* comes equipped with fully detailed belt, hat, shoes, and satchel, all coaxed into the surface of the wax with a fine point or blade. In Degas' later years, the marks of his fingers are often vividly apparent in his rough and expressive waxes, but in these trial studies, a more impersonal, if still uneven, treatment has been preferred. Various tools were used, including the kind of toothed scraping implement much employed by sculptors and modelers, here leaving a hatchwork of parallel abrasions in areas of the *Nude Study* and the *Little Dancer.* At least one critic was confused by this apparent carelessness, arguing that the irregularities "inscribed on the flesh" of the *Little Dancer Aged Fourteen* reduced the illusionistic effect that he assumed to be Degas' ambition.[70] In practice, Degas seems to have consciously opted for a number of contrasting finishes in the 1881 wax, from the delicately smoothed face and neck to the more insistently textured, expressive arms; even at this level, it appears, the artist wished to signal the paradoxical nature of his medium and the ambiguity of his sculptural aspirations.

At the center of these experiments, and perhaps of others now lost or destroyed, was inevitably the process of constructing the *Little Dancer Aged Fourteen* itself (frontispiece). Circumstantial evidence suggests that it was begun some time after February 1878, when Marie van Goethem celebrated her fourteenth birthday, but almost nothing else is known of the preparations Degas made, the advice he took, or the practical assistance he sought out.[71] Having only experienced wax modeling on a small scale, in perhaps half a dozen earlier studies of horses, Degas might have been expected to turn to his sculptor friends for guidance at such a critical time. Detailed examination of the *Little Dancer* undertaken by Arthur Beale, however, has revealed just the kind of unorthodox use of materials and doubtful command of technique that we might associate with an amateur.[72] As if acknowledging his limitations, Degas relied in the first instance on his skills as a draftsman, testing out a series of poses for the model and exploring several possibilities before making his choice. On each of a pair of very similar sheets – so alike that they must have been executed side by side – the artist drew the nude model three times, her right foot extended and only the position of her arms varying from sheet to sheet. One of these compositions, known only in an old photograph, shows the young dancer with both arms across her chest and her right hand reaching toward her left shoulder, a gesture repeated in a lively, almost caricatural sketchbook drawing of a clothed dancer seen from behind (cat. 34a), also made about this time.[73] The sketchbook is of considerable significance in the evolution of the *Little Dancer*, containing studies for another of Degas' sculptures, the *Apple Pickers,* various dance motifs, and several pages of often-quoted notes for future projects. In one such list, the artist proposed "drawing a profile which wouldn't move, moving myself, going up or down, the same for a whole figure . . . draw a series of arm movements of the dance, or of legs which wouldn't move, turning around them oneself."[74] Especially valuable in an artist who rarely committed his mental processes to paper, this combined record of visual strategies and works in progress gives us a rare insight into Degas' creative activity in the years around 1880.

The same source provides a specific key to some of the studies under review, such as the handsome charcoal and pastel *Two Dancers* (cat. 35), a virtual reworking of the notebook drawing from two contrasted points of view. Here we can vividly imagine the artist "turning around" the standing figure as he drew the two poses, "going up or down" to select his vantage point, and opting for a position well above the dancer's shoulders and widely splayed feet. The sheet is noticeably artful in its composition, an examination of its surface revealing that the nearer of the two figures was added over the beginnings of a scenery background, as if the artist has hesitated between picture making and sculptural research. Had he extended the use of color (it was begun on green paper and touched with white highlights), such a study might have been developed into a backstage scene like that of *Dancer Resting* (fig. 23), another superb pastel with the closest possible links to the making of the *Little Dancer Aged Fourteen.* Beneath the refined detail of the newspaper-reading ballerina (the same height as the figure in *Two Dancers* and several other studies for the sculpture), a similarly vigorous depiction in charcoal of an adolescent body can be discerned, again seen from a conspicuously high angle against a sharply tilted floor. In both cases, it seems, Degas decided to pursue the image's pictorial potential, recoiling from the sculptural complexities of the pose and settling for a less ambitious, more symmetrical stance in his final choice for the wax sculpture.

By returning to the second of the two initial sheets, *Three Studies of a Nude Dancer* (cat. 36), Degas effectively determined the future course of his project.[75] With strokes of charcoal on gray paper, the long-limbed ease and supercilious erectness of the *Little Dancer* has been anticipated in almost every particular, the entire figure documented from front, back, and side as if it were a scientific specimen. A sign that Degas may have moved directly into sculpture at this early stage, perhaps beginning work on the preliminary version of the *Nude Study for the Little Dancer Aged Fourteen,* is incorporated on the same sheet in a scribbled diagram at top right that resembles a primitive wire armature. Further evidence of his three-dimensional thinking may be implicit in the only other known drawing of the naked figure, the *Study of a Nude Dancer* (cat. 38) now in Oslo, which tackles Marie van Goethem's form from a more complex, three-quarter view. Struggling a little with her wayward legs and omitting her left arm, perhaps for greater spatial clarity, the artist proceeded to block out the masses of the girl's torso in broad swathes of charcoal. Already, it seems, the passage of time may be spelled out in the transition from the waiflike thinness of the first studies to the fuller curves and rudimentary breasts of the Oslo study, while the possibility that the freer, more urgent drawing manner may represent a return to the model at a critical point in the execution of the *Nude Study* should perhaps be entertained.

Much ingenuity has been expended on the group of masterful drawings of Marie van Goethem in full dancer's costume; more than one commentator has proposed that they were made after – rather than in preparation for – the *Little Dancer Aged Fourteen,* as a self-imposed exercise of the kind indicated in the artist's notebook, as a draftsmanly tour de force, or simply as gifts for friends and admirers. Others have suggested that more than one model was involved, while a recent study has detected a visible transformation of Marie's features, from relative neutrality to atavistic decline, as the sequence advanced.[76] If some of these interpretations lay a greater burden on the drawings than they can bear and overlook the visual license an artist might naturally be allowed, all of them recognize the exceptional nature of the pictorial project. More than in any other of his works of art, Degas has attempted to comprehend, even to achieve complete mastery over, a single three-dimensional form in all its palpability and space-occupying complexity, using only the conventional means of line and tone on a succession of sheets of paper. Slowly circling around his stationary model, not just once but several times, Degas became the moon to his subject's earth, moving through the surrounding space and implicitly and provocatively through time.

Stopping to record no less than seventeen angles of view or details, some only a few degrees removed from their neighbors, the artist embraced the entire standing figure and isolated recalcitrant features. *Two Studies of a Dancer* (fig. 19) reveals how minutely the subject was scrutinized and highlights some of the problems encountered. Beginning with the left-hand dancer, Degas sketched in the head, hair, and tutu rather broadly, then concentrated his attention on the girl's strangely tensed, caliper-like arms and crossed feet. Shifting very slightly to the right, he then repeated the body even more peremptorily, but returned to the legs with his charcoal, pastels, and – more unexpectedly – his watercolors to tackle their now separated, steeply angled juxtaposition.[77] This disposition of arms and legs continued to exert him, as we can see from two further attempts at the former in *Four Studies of a Dancer* (cat. 43) and *Three Studies of a Dancer* (cat. 41), and an entire sheet devoted to the latter, *Studies for Little Dancer Aged Fourteen* (cat. 42). Though he eventually mastered them, the forms of the ballet dancer's limbs have a complex spatial as well as linear life, presenting the artist with unfamiliar demands that evidently strained at his previous accomplishments.

In the same way that Degas omitted the left-hand arm in *Study of a Nude Dancer* (cat. 38) in order to articulate the figure, so he allowed himself considerable license in his efforts to define the costumed model. In *Four Studies of a Dancer* (cat. 43), each view of the subject focuses on a challenging element, such as the face, the profile, or the still-elusive arms, while ruthlessly excluding the remainder of the body.[78] The recently rediscovered *Three Studies of a Dancer* (cat. 41) shows the artist disregarding details like the buttons and lace trimming on the girl's bodice and, even more drastically, lifting the long hair of the left-hand figure into a bun

Fig. 19 *Two Studies of a Dancer*, ca. 1878–80, chalk and pastel, 18⅝ × 23 in. (47.2 × 58.5 cm), Lord Rayne, London.

in order to explore her shoulders and collar bone. Similar liberties are taken in *Three Studies of a Dancer in Fourth Position* (cat. 40), where bodices are variously complete and hair bunched or lowered according to the artist's localized interest. In all three of these sheets, stray lines on the surrounding paper and abandoned or partly erased contours persuade us that these are working drawings, made in the first instance to assist the process of observation rather than as marketable works of art. By contrast with the elegant *Two Dancers* (cat. 35) and the boldly asymmetrical *Dancer Resting* (fig. 23), the figures in the working sheets are arranged schematically, their strokes of pastel on tutus, hair, and stockings included as much for visual coherence as documentary accuracy. The fact that two of the drawings were acquired by contemporary admirers of Degas, the collector Jacques Doucet and the critic Roger Marx (who illustrated the study he owned in an article of 1897), can be seen to reflect a growing taste for the artist's more uninhibited draftsmanship, though it remains conceivable that he added further touches of color before selling or presenting them to his acquaintances.[79]

Fig. 20 *Little Dancer Aged Fourteen* (without skirt), ca. 1920–21, plaster, 39 in. (99 cm), Joslyn Art Museum, Omaha.

It is often forgotten that when he moved from his drawings to the making of the wax *Little Dancer Aged Fourteen,* Degas progressed from studies of a clothed model to the construction of an effectively nude figure. More accurately, knowing that the dancer's tutu, bodice, and wig could only be attached to the sculpture at a later stage, most of Degas' time was spent in the presence of a curious hybrid, neither clothed nor truly naked, anatomically incomplete and probably bald. Even today, the figure is disconcerting when seen without its skirt (fig. 20), revealing areas of approximate modeling around the thighs and waist that must formerly have extended to the dancer's torso, feet, and head. Requiring even more of the artist's imagination, the need to envisage the sculpture's final costumed form at every turn must have considerably heightened his need for a comprehensive set of drawings. Given the complexity of the project, it is also highly probable that Marie van Goethem continued to pose on occasion for the wax statuette itself, though once again the drawings would have provided the best possible substitute when the young apprentice was engaged in her relentless routines at the Opéra. Even the finest sheets of studies would hardly provide sufficient detail in areas such as her head and face, for example, or for the interlaced fingers that are barely indicated in the surviving studies. Most importantly, the ballerina, in her billowing tutu and decorative accessories, would have reminded Degas of the visual ensemble he had initially envisaged, and its distinctive balance of lightness and insubstantiality with hard contours, dense color, and emphatic mass.

More misunderstandings continue to exist about the costume and accessories of the *Little Dancer* than about any other aspect of the sculpture. As recently as 1988 it was asserted – in an otherwise exemplary summary of the figure's history – that the wax was first shown "dressed in a real bodice, tutu, stockings and ballet shoes: on her head was a wig with a pigtail tied with a leek-green ribbon, and she wore a similar ribbon around her neck. The wax body was tinted to simulate flesh."[80] Almost all these statements are partially accurate or misleading, a situation exacerbated by the ahistorical presentation of many of the bronze casts of the *Little Dancer* in the world's major museums. In the first place, of course, the wax statuette is a study on a *reduced scale,* at ninety-nine centimeters high some two-thirds the size of an average fourteen-year-old. For this reason, few of the items of costume could have been "real," but were miniaturized versions made especially for this somewhat doll-like creation: it is surely significant, as Theodore Reff has pointed out, that a Degas notebook records a visit to a supplier of hair for dolls or puppets at this time.[81] While it is conceivable that the bodice and skirt were those intended for a younger child, the probability remains that they, like the wig (which has a loosely bunched plait rather than a "pigtail") were devised especially for Degas' sculpture. Now covered with a layer of colored wax, the dancing shoes seem likewise to be contrived, evidently made of a canvaslike material (not the "pink satin" noted by one critic) yet insufficiently substantial to be in any sense "real."[82] More serious still is the confusion over the *Little Dancer*'s stockings or tights. Though one of the dozen or so accounts of the figure's first appearance refers to its legs in "silk tights with slight creases," this was almost certainly a misreading of the work: a more careful examination of the sculpture shows that creases, folds, and even the indentations in the legs caused by the shoe-ribbons have been modeled in wax by the artist, details that would hardly have been included if they were soon to be obliterated by a pair of tights.[83]

In the early criticism of the *Little Dancer,* ribbons of various kinds were described on the 1881 figurine, though it is again unlikely that all the reports are reliable; Paul Mantz noted a "blue ribbon at the belt," Nina de Villard the "heavy hair tied with a green ribbon," Joris-Karl Huysmans a "leek-green ribbon" at either waist or neck, and Our Lady Correspondent the "emerald green ribbons" tying the dancer's hair.[84] A useful reminder of the fallibility of the critical record, it seems improbable that all these adornments were in place at the same time, and even clearer that the gold, pink, and white ribbons seen on variants of the *Little Dancer* today lack the simplest justification. There was greater consistency among visitors to the 1881 exhibition over the model's wig, which was understood to be of "real hair" and was observed to "fall almost to her small, half-closed eyes" by Ephrussi and "in a chignon . . . to her shoulders" by Huysmans.[85] The indication in Huysmans' essay that the wig was made of horse or animal hair has been much reported, though glimpses of the original fibers seen through the broken wax today show it to be both fine and near-blonde.[86]

What is also unclear is the extent to which this hairpiece was already covered in wax when the figure was first exhibited. Both Ephrussi's and Huysmans' texts imply a certain fullness and profusion in the dancer's locks, and the description by Louisine Havemeyer of the dust-covered statue in later years ("How woolly the dark hair appeared," she remembered) encourages the conjecture that the wig may originally have been used in its normal, uncoated state.[87] Certainly the wax has been applied rather broadly and perhaps hastily over the hair, and we might again ask why Degas went to the trouble of incorporating a miniature wig into his statuette if he had always intended to conceal it. It is beyond question, however, that the delicately made fabric bodice was first eased over the dancer's torso and buttoned, then somewhat unevenly covered with wax that had apparently been tinted pale yellow.[88] In this case, the application of wax was noted by a critic, and the translucency of the added layer allowed the texture and detailing of the garment to show through, even as it established some unity between body and costume. In the same way that Degas had spread a film of reddish wax over the dancer's shoes to provide continuity with the legs, so the addition of colored coatings of wax to bodice and hair may have introduced an important element of unity into an otherwise disparate collection of materials.

Two further features of Degas' embellishment of the *Little Dancer* have given rise to widespread confusion. The first is the question of the color of the wax body, a primary factor in its first appearance and in any claims to visual realism the sculpture may have had. Despite the assertions of several modern authors that the head and limbs were painted to resemble flesh – a bold departure even in the polychromy-obsessed sculptural circles of the early 1880s, and one that would surely have provoked attention – only one commentator, the irate Lady Correspondent of the London *Artist* magazine, claimed that "her hair and skin are colored to life."[89] Ephrussi's often-cited wish that "the color of the wax" had been better mixed or blended "in the dirty areas which spoil the general appearance" corresponds exactly with variations in the wax itself – still visible today – which fades from red-brown and near-black in the legs and thighs to a deep honey in parts of the face.[90] If some of these shifts of hue were the result of Degas' technical inexperience, others were evidently intended to differentiate areas of the body, most notably in a sharp transition from warmer to cooler brown at the hairline near the dancer's temples. Even more conclusively, Arthur Beale's study of the surface of the wax has led him to believe that it was "never painted or tinted" in any way.[91] No particles or traces of applied color survive on the surface of the wax in its present state, and we are obliged to visualize the sculpture at the sixth Impressionist exhibition in its bronze- or mahogany-like hues. Far from resembling human skin, an option that was open to Degas and widely exploited in the wax sculptures of the day, the body of the *Little Dancer Aged Fourteen* looked for all the world like an antique statue.

In perhaps the last ironical twist to this most convoluted of sculptures, toward the end of its construction Degas dressed his partly naked wax structure in a simple fabric tutu, as close to its "real" counterpart as any element of the work. Outrageously travestied in the various limp and stained, or coquettish and bristlingly short skirts seen on bronze casts throughout the world today, this tutu would unquestionably have been almost knee-length and full, as shown in every one of the preparatory drawings for the sculpture and in the countless pastels and paintings of dancers in Degas' repertoire. Inexplicably, when the newly minted bronzes were first "dressed" in the early 1920s, they were equipped with minuscule skirts that barely covered their hips, an anachronistic pattern that has persisted into our own times and profoundly distorted the perception of Degas' sculpture.[92] Witnesses of the original *Little Dancer* leave no doubt that the outfit on the wax figure was entirely conventional, even if their mastery of fabric terminology was somewhat uncertain; Mantz, for example, described the costume as a "dress of gauze," Huysmans spoke of its "muslin skirts," and Our Lady Correspondent noted the "real tulle petticoats" worn by the young ballerina.[93]

Degas' contemporaries were also unanimous in their accounts of ballet dancers' dresses, evoking their voluminous, enveloping clouds of fine material that sometimes reached the ankles but never rose significantly above the knee. Writing of Degas' pictures in 1876, Stéphane Mallarmé had described how the "muslin drapery forms a luminous, ever-moving atmosphere" around the bodies of the ballerinas, while Ludovic Halévy recorded the way dancers would "puff out their gauze skirts" prior to going on stage.[94] Several sources indicate that a typical beginner would be allocated "five metres of muslin" with which to make her first tutu, enough to account for the substantial bulk and length of Marie van Goethem's dress in images like *Three Studies of a Dancer in Fourth Position* (cat. 40) and *Three Studies of a Dancer* (cat. 41).[95] In both these drawings, the skirt clearly billows upward and outward around the hips, "lifting" the figure in such a way that, when applied to the sculpture, would necessarily have transformed its apparent mass and radically altered its initial impact on viewers of the day. Significantly, too, the length of this original dress concealed much of the dancer's lower body, drastically reducing the prominence of the legs and obviating the need for the artist to model the wax in detail above the knees.[96] Even the childish tutus worn by novices at practice, such as those visible in Renouard's lithographs (figs. 6 and 7) are substantial by the standards of most of today's dressed bronzes, and we must look forward to the time when museums and collectors follow the brave lead of the Baltimore Museum of Art, the Museum Boijmans Van Beuningen and, most immediate to the present project, the Joslyn Art Museum, in returning the *Little Dancer* to its historic propriety.[97]

In the spring of 1880, Degas had sufficient confidence in the progress of his dressed wax dancer to announce its imminent appearance at the forthcoming exhibition of Impressionist art, the fifth in the group's history. Listed in the printed catalogue, the sculpture was still not in place, however, when the installation was opened on 1 April. Five days later, the critic Gustave Goetschy revealed that the work had yet to appear, but told his readers he had heard "marvellous things" of the promised "ballerina aged fourteen modelled from life, dressed in a genuine 'bouffant' skirt and wearing real dancing shoes."[98] Other critics mentioned it briefly, losing interest when the work failed to materialize by the exhibition's closing date, 30 April. Though the cause of the delay is not known, we might reasonably surmise that the exceptional practical challenges the artist had set himself, and so formidably surmounted through most of the sculpture's gestation, were to blame, along with his notorious fastidiousness in matters of display. Stories that were circulated subsequently, telling of the need for last-minute reinforcement to the wax and of Degas' drastic remodeling of the mouth, turn out to be without apparent foundation, though such technical factors as the integration of the wig and the wax coating of the bodice and shoes seem once again to have delayed the figure's unveiling at the following year's exhibition.[99] Apparently for reasons of presentation as much as a need for security, Degas had ordered a glass cabinet and now installed it in the galleries chosen for the 1881 show, where critics had fun at his expense by admiring the "luxurious simplicity" of the empty vitrine.[100] On 8 April 1881 Auguste Dalligny could still observe that the "wax statuette" was missing, but a week later Louis Enault became the first critic to respond to the newly installed work. In two brisk phrases, Enault announced to the world that the "*Petite Danseuse* by M. Degas, a half-life-size wax statuette, is simply frightful. Never has the misfortune of adolescence been more sadly represented."[101] Soon other critics followed, but within three weeks the exhibition had closed, after one of the briefest and – at least initially – most inglorious public appearances by any of Degas' works of art.

3 "CAN ART DESCEND LOWER?"

LOW ART, HIGH ART, AND THE *LITTLE DANCER AGED FOURTEEN*

When Degas' *Little Dancer Aged Fourteen* was first exhibited in public in 1881, it provoked a barrage of criticism that was exceptional even in the turbulent history of Impressionist art. Most remarkable of all was the sheer range and diversity of this response. There was extravagant praise and frank hostility; an essay-length eulogy from the brilliant young novelist Joris-Karl Huysmans and a number of withering asides from obscure journalists ("Have you ever seen a model so horrible, so repugnant?" wrote one); while the American-born painter James McNeill Whistler was so enthralled that he could only utter "short cries, gesticulating in front of the glass case that held the wax figurine."[1] Even broader than this range of personal taste, however, was the spectrum of the critics' language and their vocabulary of association, as writer after writer searched for the apposite analogy or the finely barbed insult with which to address the sculpture. Citing ancient and exotic cultures, the art of the Middle Ages and the Renaissance, popular crafts and the artifacts of the industrial age, as well as images from the modern novel and contemporary science, Degas' peers ranged high and low in their attempts to articulate the "troubling spectacle" of his sculpture.[2]

Despite, or perhaps because of, this confusion, the reception of the *Little Dancer* was unusually well documented. Announced in the catalogue of the sixth Impressionist exhibition, the sculpture was anticipated with interest before its delayed appearance, then discussed by commentators of many persuasions as the show unfolded; several distinguished art critics of the day treated the work at length, while some almost inadvertently recorded the views of the general public – that least-reported of all Impressionist audiences. More recently, two collections of published criticism associated with the event have appeared, to which can be added the observations of a number of British correspondents, a cluster of references from the months and years immediately after the exhibition, and a series of recollections by those who knew the work at first hand.[3] In all, almost thirty responses to the *Little Dancer* from Degas' lifetime can now be assembled, varying not just in length and literary distinction but in almost every aspect of their critical judgment. A significant proportion express distaste, finding the figure "frightful" or "ugly," while a reviewer for the English journal *Artist* (who signed herself "Our Lady Correspondent") wrote disgustedly of the dancer as a "semi-idiot" with "the head and expression of an Aztec" – "Can art descend lower?" she asked her readers.[4] At the other extreme, several writers heralded its "singular truthfulness," Paul de Charry claiming "the model is perfect," Huysmans announcing that it was "the first truly modern attempt at sculpture I know," and Nina de Villard predicting that it would become "the leading expression of a new art."[5]

Moments of apparent consensus could conceal a conflict of meaning; when the

Little Dancer Aged Fourteen, ca. 1920–21, plaster and fabric, 39 in. (99 cm), Joslyn Art Museum, Omaha, Nebraska (cat.45).

Fig. 21 William Rothenstein, *Degas*, ink, 8¼ × 5¼ in. (20.9 × 13.5 cm), The Art Institute of Chicago, Gift of Albert Roullier Memorial Collection.

critic of the *National Observer,* Charles Whibley, recalled the "extreme originality" of the sculpture, it was in tones of lofty disdain, whereas Huysmans' earlier use of the same term had been entirely approving.[6] Even accounts of the *Little Dancer*'s physical attributes could be at odds with each other: for Charles Ephrussi the meter-high statue was "half life-size," while for Comtesse Louise it was "life-size"; Paul Mantz saw it adorned with a blue ribbon, rather than the "leek-green" ribbon recorded by Huysmans and de Villard; and, uniquely, the cartoonist and occasional critic Bertall announced that the statuette – which was constructed from wax, human or animal hair, and textiles of several kinds – was made of "terracotta."[7] Withdrawn from public view at the close of the 1881 exhibition, the *Little Dancer Aged Fourteen* continued to be remembered with varying degrees of accuracy. A passing remark by Jules Claretie in the *Gazette des Beaux-Arts* of 1881 referred to Degas' recent sculptural activity, and in 1882 Emile Soldi mentioned the "real fabrics" used on the *Little Dancer* in his Salon review, while Félix Fénéon listed the artist's "living painted waxes" among his defining achievements in 1886.[8] By 1890, George Moore could remember the "dancing girls modelled in red wax, some dressed in muslin skirts" he had seen in Degas' studio, and in the same year Henri de Regnier and Paul Helleu discussed "the dressed dancer" when they met in the apartment of Stéphane Mallarmé; about this time, William Rothenstein made a caricature of Degas posed in the attitude of the *Little Dancer* (fig. 21), a conceit repeated by Michel Manzi in a more elaborate and little-known etching; in 1897 Roger Marx still enthused about the "incomparable wax" and chose to illustrate one of the studies for the work in a current article; and in 1904 the English writer Wynford Dewhurst evoked the 1881 exhibition as the moment when Degas had "commenced to model figures of dancers in wax."[9]

If Degas' sculpture made a lasting impact, nothing quite prepares us for the inventive and sometimes bizarre attempts by his critics to locate the work in more familiar genres, to link it with well-defined artistic and extra-artistic modes of representation, or to find parallels for its appearance in remote traditions.[10] Faced with a costumed and partially tinted *Little Dancer,* one writer looked back across the centuries to gothic France, with its "village churches, their virgins, their saints in colored wood, covered with ornaments, fabrics and jewels."[11] Venturing further afield, another recalled "the realism of multi-colored Spanish sculptures," and yet another was reminded of medieval Spain, and specifically of "the Christ from the cathedral of Burgos, on which the hair is real, the thorns are real thorns, the drapery genuine fabric."[12] Charles Whibley preferred a comparison with late Hellenistic art, suggesting a resemblance between the *Little Dancer* and the colored Tanagra figurines that had caused such a stir in the Paris of the 1870s.[13] At least two observers described the young girl's features as "Aztec," though their use of the word may have had other, more colloquial meanings.[14] Finally and most exotically, a succession of Degas' acquaintances sensed a kinship between the wax figure and the sculpture of ancient Egypt, remembering it as "a kind of hallucinating mummy" or, in Louisine Havemeyer's phrase, boasting that the *Little Dancer Aged Fourteen* was "one of the greatest works of art since the dynasties of the Nile."[15]

At the other extreme of this baffling catalogue, certain analogies *were* proposed between Degas' sculpture and the products of his own culture, but largely with objects *outside* the artistic domain. Predictably, waxwork exhibitions and "the manipulations of Mme. Tussaud's" were cited, along with such related items as "dummies in hairdressers' windows," puppets, and children's dolls: "strange dolls

– dolls if you will, but dolls modelled by a man of genius," in the words of George Moore.[16] Paul Mantz apparently had toys or automata in mind when he wrote of the sculpture's "almost mechanical movement," adding that the figure showed the "perfect truth of the pantomime" as well as the "savage inelegance of a schoolgirl."[17] Certain of his peers were reminded of a scientific specimen in a glass case, arguing that the *Little Dancer Aged Fourteen* had no place in an art gallery and should be exiled to a "museum of zoology, anthropology, physiology."[18] One critic suggested that it should be taken to the Musée Dupuytren, a celebrated collection of anatomical specimens belonging to the Faculté de Médecine and exhibited at the Couvent des Cordeliers; another recommended the Jardin des Plantes, where skeletons, fossils, and wild animals were displayed to the public; and a third speculated that, if the sculpture had been smaller, attempts could be made to "seal it in a flask of spirits of wine."[19]

Other links of a topical kind, though equally disparate and contradictory in nature, were made with contemporary literature, notably with the school of Naturalism represented by Zola and his followers, among whom Huysmans could still be counted. Claiming that the *Little Dancer Aged Fourteen* was imbued with "the spirit of a philosopher *à la Baudelaire,*" the conservative critic Paul Mantz detected in the sculpture the work of an "observant artist" who operated under "the supreme law of naturalism," achieving "a singular truthfulness of movement" and "an extreme realism."[20] Most of his colleagues acknowledged the modernity and precision of the figure: some with approval, as in Huysmans' salute to the "terrible reality of this statuette" or de Charry's acknowledgment of its "extraordinary reality . . . a real masterpiece"; one or two facetiously, as in Bertall's observation that "it appeared to open new horizons for costumiers and milliners"; while at least one expressed contempt, announcing, "This is 'Realism' so called: this is in art what M. Zola is in literature. Such being the case, let us make a big hole and bury all our ideals; do not let us drag them through the mire until they become sufficiently soiled to meet the new schools."[21] The more circumspect Charles Ephrussi was able to concede that, "despite her dreadful ugliness," the *Little Dancer* struck an "original accent," proposing – in a very Zola-esque phrase – that the work was the outcome of "exact science."[22] By this date, the novels of Zola were widely associated with the "science" of evolutionism and with the belief that behavioral traits and the propensity to vice were largely inherited, more than one critic hinting at a similar context for Degas' sculpture. The reactionary Henry Trianon, for example, claimed that the artist's model was "the type of horror and bestiality," and several visitors noted the proximity of Degas' wax figure in the exhibition to two of his drawings of notorious murderers.[23] Using much the same language as Zola's opponents, who had recently savaged both *L'Assommoir* and *Nana* as examples of depravity, some of Ephrussi's colleagues were less constrained.[24] Jules Claretie, himself a minor novelist, observed that "the depraved muzzle of this barely pubescent girl, a flower of the gutter, is unforgettable," while Comtesse Louise claimed that Degas had used the *Little Dancer* to perpetrate a joke, offering "a little Nana of fifteen years, dressed as a dancer, in front of which imbeciles are in ecstasy."[25]

How can we begin to understand the critical and popular confusion that first greeted the *Little Dancer Aged Fourteen*? Violent controversy in sculptural matters was by no means unknown, of course, in Degas' Paris; the furor that surrounded the installation of Carpeaux's bucolic *The Dance* on the facade of the Opéra in 1869, for example, had been both more public and more persistent, while claims in 1877 that Rodin had cast his life-size *Age of Bronze* from a living model were arguably more damning. Memories of both these events may have resurfaced in 1881, but the circumstances of Degas' wax figure remain quite distinct. Exhibited in the relative obscurity of an Impressionist group show, in a sequence of anonymous first-floor rooms on the boulevard des Capucines, the *Little Dancer* shared neither the scale nor the rhetorical pretension of Carpeaux's and Rodin's statues. Unlike them, it made no claims on the time-honored subject of the nude, nor did it aspire to the immortal languages of bronze or marble. Yet within its modest constraints, Degas' diminutive ballerina proved as disorienting to its audiences as the grandest projects of the day, overturning assumptions, crossing frontiers of propriety, and apparently threatening the identity of sculpture itself.

At its simplest, of course, it was precisely *because* Degas stepped aside from the dominant modes of nineteenth-century statuary that his sculpture caused such disruption. Tellingly and somewhat surprisingly, very few critics of the *Little Dancer* mentioned the work of other sculptors in their texts, their primary response being – as we have seen – to look beyond the confines of the modern medium to historic, mass-produced, or documentary genres. Many aspects of Degas' figurine and its presentation seem to encourage such an approach. Displayed at a distance from the Salon, it was identified with the marginal world of the *Indépendants*, as the Impressionists still preferred to call themselves, but, just as importantly, with a rejection of the grand public statement in favor of the private – and perhaps therefore more suspect – dialogue between spectator and art object. As one of the first three-dimensional items in an Impressionist exhibition ("They are beginning to assert their independence in sculptural form," warned Jules Claretie. "We're going to have – good God – *Impressionist sculptors!*"), the *Little Dancer* also stood for doubtful innovation and an expansion of the newcomers' territory.[26] Even the materials of Degas' statuette were compromising; wax and fabric were widely used in preparatory studies, but here the artist seemed to be passing them off as a finished work: "It is barely a maquette!" protested one critic; "If Monsieur Degas can recreate it in plaster or stone, this would be a masterpiece," condescended another.[27] Most provocative of all, however, was the identity of Degas' modeled figure. In contrast to *The Dance* and the *Age of Bronze,* and to the vast majority of exhibited sculptures of the day, the *Little Dancer Aged Fourteen* represented a contemporary individual, dressed in modern clothes and engaged with – or even more impertinently, casually disengaged from – an activity that was both topical and commonplace. That young ballet dancers had a reputation for sexual license further aggravated the situation, blurring boundaries of taste and behavior and reducing a number of critics to near apoplexy.

A further destabilizing factor in the reception of the *Little Dancer Aged Fourteen* was Degas' reputation as an exhibiting artist. For more than a decade, he had intervened conspicuously in the public arena, publishing a letter critical of the Salon Jury in 1870, for example, playing off dealers, collectors, and critics as he advanced his own career, and becoming sufficiently dominant in the machinations behind the Impressionist group shows for one recent scholar to conclude that, in effect, "Degas organized the 1881 exhibition."[28] Degas had already imposed himself on these events in matters of presentation, taking a lead in the selection of rooms and concerning himself with questions of lighting, publicity, and the use of novel, eye-catching picture frames. The selection of Degas' own works was also unusually deliberated, drawing maximum attention to his current activities and advertising his claims to leadership. Representative groups of pictures – portraits, scenes of the racetrack, and the ballet – were chosen to mark out his professional terrain, while experiments with new materials or subject matter signaled his technical and thematic originality. Several images singled out in this way were defiantly strange or equivocal, fusing the skills of the printmaker and the pastelist in a single composition, for example, or boldly introducing themes from the streets – such as the laundress and the café-concert singer – into the elevated world of the gallery. Much in evidence was Degas' fluency in contemporary modes, from his abrasive mastery of lithography to his skills as a fan painter, from the quasi-photographic qualities of the black-and-white monotype to the graphic economy of the popular illustration. Such displays seem to presuppose a dialogue of a particularly modern kind between the artist and his public (whom he described as "stupid and wise at the same time" in his letter to the Salon jury), offering reassurance and a measure of continuity on the one hand, confrontation on the other.[29] At the 1881 exhibition this dialogue was strikingly apparent, a number of critics referring knowledgeably to Degas' earlier achievements as a draftsman (the pastels on display "would not increase his fame," Mantz observed haughtily), one regretting that he had temporarily "succumbed to fashion," and several exclaiming at the "novelty" of his latest creation, the *Little Dancer Aged Fourteen*.[30]

Familiar with the artist's past achievements as well as his teasing, self-conscious sense of occasion, Degas' audiences in 1881 were prepared for – perhaps demanded – innovation. In this sense, the unveiling of the *Little Dancer Aged Fourteen* can be seen as the latest in a series of carefully orchestrated events, though the vehemence and exhilaration of the public response may well have exceeded the artist's expectations.[31] From our late twentieth-century standpoint, however, it is still salutary to note the wider implications of the sculpture's appearance, at least as perceived by Degas' contemporaries. Far from confining themselves to sculptural matters, Degas' critics – like so many critics of the age – moved unquestioningly from the values of art to the values of the wider world, from the demands of realism to the imperatives of sexual decorum, from a single wax figure to the moral health of the French nation. Extreme though such claims may sound, they were implicit in the long roll-call of reactions to the *Little Dancer* in 1881; when writers noted its tinted ribbons and colored wax, they assumed a familiarity with an international debate about polychromy in ancient and modern statuary, which in turn touched on taste and respect for the past; when they invoked the "abominable sculpture" of contemporary Italy, it was to locate Degas in another feud over excessive verisimilitude, even as they asserted the pre-eminence of French culture; when references were made to ethnography and anatomical specimens, they were directed at a generation obsessed by science and its application to social problems; and when writers addressed the sculpture as if it were a depraved child, they voiced widespread bourgeois concern over the supposed viciousness of the lower classes.

At more than one level, it seems, the *Little Dancer Aged Fourteen* was regarded as exemplary, not just of Degas' art or the challenge to sculptural tradition that it represented, but of the uneasy society to which it belonged. If some critics were excited by the work, many clearly felt threatened by it in their roles as guardians of the nation's ethics, as parents of young children ("Pray heaven that my daughter doesn't become a *sauteuse* [a dancer or loose woman]," wrote Paul Mantz on seeing the wax figure) or as guarantors of the probity of art.[32] Confronted by an object that seemed "bestial" and yet reminiscent of carvings in "village churches," that recalled the toy shop as much as the museum, Degas' peers found themselves – either pleasurably or alarmingly – *unsettled*. Though they agreed about little else, critics and public sensed that the sculpture was in some way elusive, defiant, or transitional, that it represented a step forward in the progress of art or backward into childishness, a move outside the confines of good behavior or uncomfortably close to materiality. For some, this instability was proof of the *Little Dancer*'s lack of resolution, for others, its most compelling quality; Mantz spoke of the inherent technical "contradiction" in the work, and Elie de Mont of its opposing claims to both "age" and "youth"; Huysmans, on the other hand, thrilled to the fact that it was "refined and barbarous at the same time," and Mrs. Havemeyer boasted that the statue could be simultaneously "classic" *and* "modern."[33] If the *Little Dancer Aged Fourteen* was to be defined, in other words, it would only be in a new and demanding way, as an object that not only escaped easy classification but seemed to engage its audiences precisely through this resistance to assimilation, prompting responses only to deflect them and stimulating a dozen different readings while attaching itself to none.

The challenge for those approaching the *Little Dancer Aged Fourteen* today, then, is twofold. First, to extend our grasp of its shifting, multi-layered significance for Degas and his contemporaries, not just as a work of sculpture but as one artifact among many in a conspicuously materialistic culture; and second, to characterize the work in terms of this multiplicity, not just as the singular expression of a body of dogma, of a unique engagement with realism, or an obsessive technical virtuosity. Such an approach must inevitably draw on a number of groundbreaking studies published in recent decades, several of them stimulated in part by the critical response to the 1881 exhibition. In a remarkable pioneering essay on Degas' sculpture written in 1970, Theodore Reff was among the first to broaden the context of the *Little Dancer* and its fabrication, associating the work with displays of wax figures in a popular context, such as the battle panoramas of Detaille and de Neuville, Neapolitan nativity groups, and waxwork exhibitions of contemporary celebrities.[34] Charles Millard, Lois Relin, and Michael Pantazzi extended this exploration, pointing to a wider relationship with polychrome sculpture and noting the prevalence of wax portraiture in both historic and contemporary practice.[35] In their essay *Scientific Realism: 1873–1881,* included in the catalogue of the 1988 *Degas* retrospective exhibition, Douglas Druick and Peter Zegers opened a new and productive line of inquiry that pursued links between the *Little Dancer* and the *Criminal Physiognomies* shown in the 1881 installation, relating both to current interests in physiology, evolution, and criminality.[36] Amplifying this study in a subsequent essay, as well as in the important chapter in the present catalogue, Douglas Druick has been followed by Anthea Callen, Tommaso Cassini, and others in a now widely adopted association of the wax figure with attitudes deriving from contemporary science.[37]

More recently, substantial accounts of the *Little Dancer*'s technical and historical significance by Anne Pingeot and Catherine Chevillot have added considerably to our understanding of the work's genesis, while Sara Campbell's study of the bronze casts has extended our grasp of this sensitive subject.[38] Almost by default, the publication accompanying the 1996–97 exhibition *The Colour of Sculpture* offered a summary of the current predicament of the *Little Dancer Aged Fourteen.* Absent from the installation yet referred to by most of the essayists and reproduced twice in the catalogue, Degas' wax figure emerged as a haunting presence at the technical and conceptual banquet of early modernism. For Andreas Blühm, it constituted "an aesthetic revolution," which "broke any number of taboos"; Wolfgang Drost notes the fundamental "tension between the objective reality of clothing and hair on the one hand, and the artistic *facture* in the formation of the body and face on the other"; and Alison Yarrington encapsulates many of the issues when she locates the *Little Dancer* among the "'high' and 'low' art of the period" and sets out to explore the "well-policed boundaries between them."[39]

LOW ART: DURANTY IN THE TUILERIES GARDENS

Few individuals from Degas' circle sum up the culturally unstable world of the *Little Dancer Aged Fourteen* as vividly as the writer Edmond Duranty. Not only did Duranty's wide-ranging interests coincide to a remarkable degree with those of the critics who discussed the sculpture, but many of his views evolved in close proximity to Degas' art and a number in collusion with Degas himself. Though Duranty's untimely death in 1880 denied him the opportunity to comment formally on the *Little Dancer,* his friendship with Degas reached a peak during the work's inception and realization, as a number of poignant documents and images reveal. It was in 1879, when he was much occupied with the sculpture, that Degas painted his unforgettable pastel-and-distemper-on-canvas *Portrait of Monsieur Duranty* (fig. 22), a work shown at the Impressionist exhibition of that year and later admired at length by Huysmans. The following year, the same picture was hastily reintroduced into the subsequent group exhibition as an act of respect to

Fig. 22 *Portrait of Monsieur Duranty*, 1879, distemper, watercolor and pastel on linen, 39$\frac{3}{8}$ × 40$\frac{1}{8}$ in. (100 × 102 cm), Glasgow Museums: The Burrell Collection.

their departed colleague, appearing in the same installation as the *Little Dancer's* still unoccupied vitrine.[40] More explicit still was the gift to the writer of the superb *Dancer Resting* (fig. 23), inscribed by Degas in 1879 "to my friend Duranty" and evidently based on the identical model – Marie van Goethem – who was currently posing for the *Little Dancer Aged Fourteen*.[41] Strikingly similar to the sculpture in posture and bearing, the off-duty ballerina in Degas' pastel can be seen as a droll, two-dimensional counterpart of his wax statuette, here portrayed in the act of reading a newspaper in wry homage to Degas' journalist friend. Just as importantly, the *Little Dancer* itself seems to have emerged from a cluster of initiatives and enthusiasms shared by Duranty and Degas in the late 1870s, embracing sculpture both ancient and modern, popular arts of all kinds, and an engagement with realism in all its complexity. Previously unexplored in this context, Duranty's involvement in the visual arts takes us across the decades and into some unlikely backwaters, yet eventually returns us to the wax figurine with a sharpened sense of the fundamental – perhaps terminal – challenge it presented to realism itself.

Known principally to art history as the author of a single essay, *The New Painting* published in 1876, Edmond Duranty was a man of wide interests but uncertain achievement. Critic and author, contributor to popular newspapers and learned journals, puppeteer, amateur artist, and celebrated advocate of Realism, Duranty ended his career (in his own estimation) as an unread novelist and behaving like "a defeated man," as George Moore recalls.[42] But for more than a quarter of a century, Duranty moved at many levels of artistic and literary society, from the bohemian to the elevated (he was known to be the illegitimate son of Prosper Mérimée, and his mother had friends in court circles), earning much of his living with his pen and sometimes lending it to public causes.[43] In 1856, for example, as a mere twenty-three-year-old, he had produced the short-lived journal, *Réalisme,* which championed the ideas of Champfleury. In 1864, Duranty was sufficiently renowned to be painted by Fantin-Latour alongside Whistler, Manet, and Baudelaire; during the same decade he was befriended by Zola and saw his own first novels and stories published; a habitué of the Café Guerbois, he supported several of the Impressionist artists and reviewed their shows; and, throughout these years, Duranty wrote articles, essays, and reviews on an encyclopedic variety of subjects.[44]

The company kept by Duranty during this period and the circumstances in which Degas first encountered him are of some significance. Paul-André Lemoisne tells us that the two men were already friendly by 1861, their mutual acquaintance with artists like Alphonse Legros, Fantin-Latour, Whistler, Evariste de Valernes, and Manet, and their shared interest in the work of Baudelaire, Flaubert, and Zola, ensuring regular contact in circles broadly associated with Realism. Writing to Degas in 1868, Manet sent "regards to Duranty, Fantin, Zola if you see them," and in the same year Duranty told Manet (who reported the remark to Fantin-Latour) that "Degas was on the way to becoming the painter of high life."[45] A similar phrase occurred in a Duranty short story composed about this time, *Le Simple Vie du peintre Louis Martin,* where the fictional hero meets the real Degas in the galleries of the Louvre, once again in the company of Fantin-Latour and Legros.[46] Now describing him as "the inventor of social chiaroscuro," Duranty gives a further clue to his interest in Degas when he characterizes him as "an artist of rare intelligence, preoccupied with *ideas* in a way that seems strange to most of his colleagues."[47] A shared commitment to "ideas" and to the observation of society at large runs throughout their sporadic friendship, along

Fig. 23 *Dancer Resting*, 1878–80, pastel, 30⅛ × 21⅞ in. (76.5 × 55.5 cm), private collection.

à mon ami Duranty
Degas

with a notably combative attitude toward the artistic establishment. In April 1870, for instance, one of the newspapers to which Duranty contributed most frequently at this time, the *Paris journal*, published a list of proposals addressed to the "Gentlemen of the Salon Jury," signed by the virtually unknown Degas but prefaced by Duranty himself.[48] Of considerable interest in the pre-history of Impressionism, the letter reflects the artist's "lively, constantly bubbling mind" (in Duranty's words) as well as his precocious concern for the display of drawings, paintings, and sculpture.[49] Within weeks, the clash of "ideas" was rejoined in an unexpected manner, when the same journal published Duranty's own review of the Salon exhibition, which that year included Degas' painting *Madame Camus in Red.* Clearly disconcerted by the originality of this asymmetrical, crimson-and-pink canvas, Duranty gently mocked his friend's "systematic preoccupation with strangeness" and suggested that the picture would make a "useful frontispiece for a treatise on color by Monsieur Chevreul."[50]

In the 1870s, the public and private interaction between Degas and Duranty took on a variety of forms, from a number of portrait-painting sessions (Duranty has been proposed as the subject of at least three canvases by the artist) and the espousal by Degas of Duranty's cause ("There must be a salon of *realists!*" Degas wrote in a much-cited note of 1874) to Duranty's endorsement of the artist in reviews and essays, and finally to Degas' solemn duty as one of the signatories to Duranty's death certificate in 1880 and his subsequent attempts to help the writer's mistress.[51] Their most well-known point of contact, of course, was *The New Painting,* a long and somewhat rambling defense of the group of artists exhibiting at the 1876 Impressionist exhibition, published as a pamphlet that was rumored to have been "dictated by Degas to Duranty."[52] Though the text is now accepted as the work of Duranty alone, its phraseology and emphasis clearly reflect the intimacy of the two men; here is their shared concern with urban, rather than rural, themes; a stress on draftsmanship rather than color, following Degas' well-known predilection; the surprise inclusion of Ingres, Degas' artistic hero, among Duranty's precursors of Realism; the advocacy of "a gamut of original points of view," a pronounced feature of Degas' current art; and a number of coded references to Degas himself ("a man of uncommon talent and exceedingly rare spirit," as Duranty describes him).[53] Boldly appropriating the new school for the tradition of Courbet, Millet, and Corot, Duranty proclaimed: "Like literature, current serious art criticism is Realist. . . . Painting, too, must enter this movement."[54] "The very first idea was to eliminate the partition separating the artist's studio from everyday life and to introduce the reality of the street," Duranty continued, proposing a new source of imagery in "railways, novelty stores, scaffolding, lines of gas lamps, benches on boulevards and newspaper kiosks."[55] Elsewhere Duranty demanded attention to the "special characteristics of the modern individual – in his clothing, in social situations, at home, or on the street," urging the study of physiognomy and deportment, clothing, and the language of hands.[56] Remorselessly up-to-date, Duranty also invoked physics and the possibilities of color photography, ending with a rallying cry from Zola's defense of Manet: "Science requires solid foundations and it has returned to the precise observation of facts . . . art itself strives towards certainty."[57]

Duranty's vision of a "wholly modern art, an art imbued with our surroundings, our sentiment and the things of our age" offered a virtual blueprint for the *Little Dancer Aged Fourteen,* anticipating not just its contemporaneity and the "precise observation of facts" it entailed, but the exceptional density of its visual and social signification.[58] When *The New Painting* is read alongside the scores of less well-known texts on the visual arts produced by Duranty during these years, the coincidence of his interests with those of Degas – and especially with the concerns that formed the *Little Dancer* – seems almost complete. In periodicals from the *Paris journal* to the *Gazette des Beaux-Arts,* Duranty reviewed exhibitions of current painting and displays at the Louvre, and wrote articles on drawing, printmaking, and the decoration of fans. Aspiring to a more scholarly role, he compiled a substantial series of essays on the history of sculpture, most notably that of Assyria, ancient Egypt, and Tanagra. Following in the footsteps of Champfleury and Baudelaire, Duranty emerged as a champion of the applied and vernacular arts, publishing several accounts of caricature as well as studies – of varying lengths and degrees of seriousness – on playing cards, ceramics, seaside fashions, and the circus. As we might expect from the author of *The New Painting,* there are pieces with such titles as "On Physiognomy," "Vulgar Science," and "The Gesture in Certain Paintings," while from the Realist novelist and critic there are responses to contemporary literature, from the works of Charles Dickens and Gustave Flaubert to those of Emile Zola.[59]

Duranty's visual and literary vocabulary, which scaled the heights of western culture and plunged to the depths of boulevard ephemera, presents the most forceful parallels with the language used to describe and vilify the *Little Dancer Aged Fourteen.* Two specific and largely overlooked preoccupations of the writer, however, take us even closer to Degas' sculpture. The first is that of dolls and puppets – and such associated forms as the tailor's dummy and the fashion mannequin – which together make up one of the most underestimated factors in the history of Degas' wax figurine. While certain writers have touched briefly on the question, none have explored Duranty's and Degas' documented interest in these items, and none have fully acknowledged the ubiquity and complex significance of dolls, puppets, and their derivatives at all levels of mid nineteenth-century French society.[60] Yet echoes of this theme resound around the *Little Dancer,* not just at the time of the sixth Impressionist exhibition but in succeeding accounts of the work's impact. Arguably the most fascinating of such responses is also the briefest: that of the anonymous members of the public at the 1881 show who, according to Nina de Villard, exclaimed in front of Degas' wax statuette, "c'est une poupée!" Signifying both doll and puppet, the word *poupée* opens up a universe that is at once childish and fantastic, emotionally potent yet removed from the conventional world of art. Remarks by de Villard's colleagues were almost as startling, among them Paul Mantz's recollections of "the shiny pink cleanliness" of the wax figures that were found in "hairdressers' windows" and the echo of mechanical dolls in his description of the *Little Dancer*'s posture.[61] Charles Ephrussi used the comparison only to invert it, claiming that "a vulgar artist would have made a doll of this dancer, M. Degas has made a work of strong character, of exact science, in a truly original form."[62] And in a shrewd juxtaposition of both the toylike and artistic qualities of the *Little Dancer,* George Moore spoke of it as a doll "modelled by a man of genius."[63]

The resonance of many of these phrases was even greater in their original context. If *poupée* generally meant "doll," it could also be applied to puppets (more commonly, *marionnettes*), to hair stylists' demonstration models, and to "hat-makers' and tailors' dummies . . . and plaster figures in a shooting range," as the *Petite Larousse* expressed it.[64] Eccentric though some of these forms seem today, they were visible at every turn in the industrialized world that Degas and Duranty knew, where a single factory could turn out more than 20,000 dolls in a week, and elaborate displays at the Paris and London international exhibitions were devoted

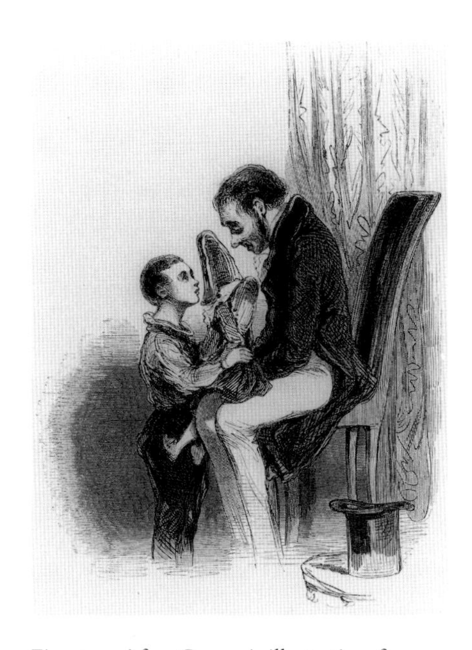

Fig. 24 After Gavarni, illustration from *Les Enfants terribles*, engraved by Caqué.

to novelties and luxury toys.[65] For our present purpose, nothing better demonstrates their currency than the interest shown in these apparently trivial articles by Degas and his friends, who admired, collected, and sometimes referred to them in their works of art. Paul Lafond, Degas' first biographer, recounts how the artist displayed a number of Neapolitan puppets or dolls *(des poupées napolitaines)* in his dining room, pointedly placing them beside more orthodox bronze and marble sculptures in a glass cabinet. Though several authors have associated these figures with Neapolitan nativity groups, Lafond gives us no further details, and they are as likely to have been locally produced dolls, marionettes, or other wax models.[66] In the same room, Lafond tells us, Degas set aside a table for "a child's toy, a large papier-mâché elephant," perhaps the one originally bought with a "basket full of toys" for the children of Georges Jeanniot and unpacked in front of Ambroise Vollard:

> "Isn't that a magnificent soldier?" Degas asked him, "And what do you think of the doll? The elephant is for me. They assured me it was real skin. It was the trunk that tickled me most: see how it lifts up when I pull the string?"[67]

Degas' personal contact with doll makers is confirmed in one of his notebooks, where he wrote down the address of a Madame Cusset who supplied *cheveux des poupées* (hair for dolls or puppets) around the time he was completing the *Little Dancer Aged Fourteen*.[68] The Paris doll-making industry also gave employment to one of Berthe Morisot's models and provided the rich variety of wooden, wax, and fabric dolls that appear in the graphic and pictorial repertoire of the day.[69] Among the printmakers admired by both Duranty and Degas – such as Daumier, Gavarni, and Manet – extensive use was made of dolls, puppets, and tailors' dummies in a number of satirical contexts, such as the image by Gavarni from *Les Enfants terribles* (fig. 24), which embodies two of these forms in a single Pulcinello-like toy. Paintings from these years by Morisot, Renoir, Astruc, Gauguin, Pissarro, and Cézanne also depict dolls of various kinds, while several of Degas' own pictures show a mischievous engagement with doll-like creations. The carved hat stand or dummy with human features in his pastel *The Milliner,* for example, is wryly juxtaposed with the face of a wide-eyed shop assistant, who has also been seen as a portrait of Marie van Goethem, the model for the *Little Dancer Aged Fourteen*.[70] In his portrait of the painter Henri Michel-Lévy, a "lay figure" – a life-size body made of wood and canvas, here fully dressed – performs a comparable function, interposing itself between the "real" figure of Michel-Lévy (which is, of course, painted) and the works of art on the fictive studio walls, one of which includes a character resembling the lifeless surrogate model.[71] Listed in the catalogue of the 1879 Impressionist exhibition (along with the portrait of Duranty), this picture makes public sport of two- and three-dimensional representation, while a number of later pastels introduce tailors' dummies and clothes stands to similar, if less comic, effect.[72]

Unsurprisingly, perhaps, Degas' delight in the more playful aspects of visual language extended to puppetry, as his letters and the recollections of his friends reveal. On vacation in the spa town of Cauterets, where he went regularly for his health, Degas later wrote:

> Preferable to everything is the real Punch and Judy show on the Esplanade this evening, I attach myself to it but I dare not answer and speak to Punch like the children sitting on the benches, whose advice Punch takes or scorns according

> to his mood. It is one of the best things for the mind at Cauterets, perhaps the only thing.[73]

On another occasion, Degas was accompanied by Jeanniot to a fun-fair in the Place Pigalle, not far from his studio, where "surrounded by the engines, the wooden horses and the roar of the animals," Jeanniot reflected on the essentially "child-like" nature of his friend.[74] Though he remained a bachelor, Degas was clearly at ease with children and their sense of humor, playing charades with younger members of the Jeanniot family and writing comic verse for their evening entertainments.[75] In later life, Jeanne Raunay tells us, Degas developed a passion for the marionette theater created by Madame Jeanniot in her Paris home, where string puppets in antique costumes were accompanied by "discreet music from another age." Remembering the contrast between the grand passions acted out by the puppets and the "puerile immobility of their faces," Raunay insists that Degas "never missed a performance."[76]

Such a taste may originally have been formed in the company of Edmond Duranty, who was once as famous for his puppetry as for his achievements as a writer. Throughout the 1860s, in the heyday of his association with Realism and during his early acquaintance with Degas, Duranty masterminded an ambitious Théâtre des Marionnettes in the public gardens of the Tuileries, near to the Orangerie and within sight of the Louvre. This was one of the cultural crossroads of the city, a meeting place for painters, writers, musicians, and socialites that was given definitive form in Manet's *Music in the Tuileries Gardens,* painted in 1862.[77] Initially advertised as entertainment for children, Duranty's theater soon attracted "Tout-Paris," from passers-by and fellow artists to members of the highest society, among them the Empress Eugénie and the Princess de Metternich, the latter coincidentally portrayed by Degas about this time.[78] Those who were consulted or gave their help included Baudelaire, Champfleury, Sardou (also the subject of a Degas portrait), Banville, and Théophile Gautier, and both Courbet and Daumier were asked to contribute to the décor, though both declined.[79] Already advanced in versatility, Duranty supervised the building of the structure, designed some of the publicity, made the prototypes of the *commedia dell'arte*-style puppets and wrote many of the plays, though he employed professionals to manipulate the characters themselves.[80] Originally fashioned in clay, the puppets were translated into wood by the sculptor Leboeuf and painted in bright colors, before receiving the attentions of a "couturier who dressed them from scraps of ancient fabric."[81] In the subsequent publications of Duranty's play texts, we can still follow Pulcinello, Pierrot, and the ballet dancer Columbine at their antics, joined by a motley cast of soldiers, gendarmes, shopkeepers, and other stock figures, while surviving illustrations of the *mise-en-scène* recall their costumes and accessories (figs. 25 and 26).

If the Théâtre des Marionnettes can be seen as an early experiment – more than a decade before *The New Painting* – in the introduction of art to the "reality of the street," we might still ask why Duranty, adult novelist and "Apostle of Realism," became involved for several years in such an apparently frivolous project. No doubt for his younger customers the puppet show provided simple amusement, but from the nature of his intended collaborators and from his own statements, it is clear that Duranty had more complex aspirations. Critics took pleasure in this paradox, imagining an audience of "babies" applauding a piece by Gautier and urging their readers to "go to the Tuileries gardens . . . serious art is hiding there,

Fig. 25 Duranty, Coindre, and Gillot, *Le Miroir de Columbine*, illustration from *Théâtre des Marionnettes du jardin des Tuileries*, 1880.

in this wooden hut, on this marionette stage."[82] As so often with Duranty, the rationale behind his actions remains curiously unresolved, even in those state-ments designed to elucidate them. Claiming that his plays dealt with "simple, everyday life, with its incidents and commonplace accidents," Duranty appeared to identify himself with the most fundamental tenets of Realism, aspiring to "hold up a mirror to the nineteenth century" in his own restatement of the well-worn contemporary phrase.[83] Consistent with such aims were the largely banal puppet narratives, with their farcical tales of housewives and neighbors, lovers and tradesmen, typically set against street scenes and humble domestic interiors. In the same pronouncements, however, Duranty acknowledged the teasing, preposterous nature of the theatrical world he had created, accepting that his *marionnettes réalistes* were acting out "a collection of comedies . . . embracing mystery and reality at the same time."[84] On his highly stylized stage, characters from the streets of Paris found themselves surrounded by "large things that have shrunk, small objects grown large, uninhabitable houses, dwarf trees . . . giant bottles, colossal pots, monumental casseroles . . .," con-fronting the mundane and the transient with the "eternal, fantastic depths."[85]

This duality becomes the virtual subject of the play *Le Miroir de Columbine,* when the dancer-puppet Columbine asks her father, Cassandre, to arrange for her portrait to be painted. At first, Cassandre resists, claiming that a portrait would be too expensive and demanding that she make do with her reflection in a mirror (fig. 25). There then follows a series of escapades and conceits that revolve around the nature of representation and the rival claims of the real and the ideal, but culminating in Cassandre's agreement to summon a painter. There is much wit at the expense of artists (including, perhaps, those present in the audience) and their studio talk, followed by the entrance of Pierrot in full painter's regalia, who proceeds to portray Columbine in the form of a brightly colored parrot.[86] Other plays reveal a similar self-consciousness, featuring marionettes with miniature dolls in place of children, for example, or presenting a "puppet-show-within-a-puppet-show," but in his most cerebral invention,

Fig. 26 Duranty, Coindre, and Gillot, *Polichinelle Précepteur*, illustration from *Théâtre des Marionettes du jardin des Tuileries*, 1880.

La Grand'Main, Duranty carried the conventions of the genre into proto-Surrealist territory.[87] In this story a real human hand is introduced into the drama alongside the puppet actors, creating an extraordinarily potent image of the arbitrariness of Duranty's marionettes and the conventional nature of theater, perhaps of art itself. Stretching the rules to their limit, or even beyond, Duranty demanded that his audience confront the artifice before them, using anomalies of scale and shifts of register to draw attention to, rather than conceal, the mechanisms of illusion.

Duranty's fascination with varied and sometimes contradictory modes of realism is further evident in the illustrations to his 1864 publication *Théâtre des Marionnettes du jardin des Tuileries.*[88] Conceding that the volume was "not in any way intended for children," Duranty recorded for posterity not only his own prose but his skills as a draftsman, the title page crediting him for both "text and composition of the drawings."[89] In the frontispiece to the play *Polichinelle Précepteur* (fig. 26), two separate worlds are memorably juxtaposed; below, a quasi-Rococo scene of contemporary children enjoying their games in the deeply wooded spaces of the Tuileries gardens, while above, an impossibly large puppet stage is occupied by wooden grotesques acting out their drama against the flimsiest of backcloths. Similarly, in the design for *Le Miroir de Columbine* (fig. 25), a seemingly innocent composition contrasts the huge figure of Polchinello with the diminutive young dancer, her naturalistic daintiness opposed to his theatrical enormity. In both cases, Duranty's color scheme is complicit in the confrontation, with primary reds, yellows, and greens reserved for the hand-painted puppets and paler tints for more orthodox figures, despite their occupation of the same pictorial frame. However modest the context, Duranty seems to imply, each codification of reality has its own patterns and claims to validity, and each – from the most childish to the most self-consciously sophisticated – may gain in force by proximity with the rest.

Celebrated throughout the 1860s, Duranty's puppet theater was forced to close at the end of the decade after a scandalous encounter between his mistress and his socially aspirant mother, who met at one of the performances.[90] Its fame lived on, however, in a world fascinated by puppetry in its many forms. Armand Silvestre, one of the critics at the sixth Impressionist exhibition, later recalled the "delicious puppets" he had seen in the Tuileries as a young man, and Jules Claretie, another of the 1881 commentators, contributed a preface to a *Histoire anecdotique des marionnettes modernes* that included one of Duranty's texts as late as 1892.[91] Appropriately, the Tuileries theater was recorded in an article by Duranty himself, in his published edition of the plays and in an illustrated memorial volume produced by Charpentier in 1880.[92] Images of puppets also continued to resonate in the work of Duranty's acquaintances, from the elderly Daumier to the generation of Astruc and Manet. In one of his 1878 articles on Daumier, Duranty remarked on the caricaturist's use of "marionettes" as being among the "traditional accessories" of his craft, and about the same time he would have seen the somewhat puppetlike sculptures of politicians – made of clay and then colored – at Daumier's retrospective exhibition.[93] Manet's 1874 lithograph *Polichinelle*, which has been distantly linked to Duranty's Tuileries theater, perpetuated a similar blend of the facetious and the topical in its depiction of the President of the Republic, Marshal MacMahon, as a hump-backed puppet, an image that appealed sufficiently to Degas to encourage him to keep the work on his apartment wall into his old age.[94]

Set against the background of Duranty's activities at the Théâtre des Marionnettes, the comparisons made by visitors to the 1881 exhibition between the *Little Dancer Aged Fourteen* and images of dolls or puppets seem both more coherent and more paradoxical. At the simplest level, by exclaiming "c'est une poupée!," some of Degas' audience effectively consigned the sculpture to the street, along with Punch and Judy shows, fun-fairs in the Place Pigalle, and toys bought in Parisian stores. Their response was one of recognition, followed by the immediate classification of an apparently familiar object and the suspicion – even the certainty – that such objects had no place in the hallowed precincts of an art gallery. Writers like Ephrussi, Huysmans, and de Villard, on the other hand, hinted that a more adult game was being played out in Degas' vitrine, just as earlier critics at the Théâtre des Marionnettes had sensed that "serious art is hiding there." In the Tuileries gardens, Duranty had taken the medium of puppetry and reshaped it for more challenging purposes, undermining the very conventions he had initially adopted as he appealed to "very naive spirits and very wise spirits" in the same performance.[95] Turning this process on its head, Degas began with a solemn, historic mode – that of sculpture – and opened it up to the expectations of an inferior genre, or perhaps half-a-dozen inferior genres at once. As with Duranty's *marionnettes réalistes,* Degas opted for breadth rather than constraint, for a kind of superior playfulness that did not preclude the highest ambition and the utmost originality. If such license delighted some of his admirers – among them perhaps the "imbeciles" who "went into ecstasy" in front of the *Little Dancer* – it seems to have disoriented or disturbed others.[96] In its early days, the Théâtre des Marionnettes had been threatened by the government authorities, who suspected that this interweaving of spectacle and intellectual pretension was subversive in intent.[97] Now it was Degas' turn to arouse doubts, as he, too, appeared to juxtapose the frivolous and the revered, dissolving the very categories that gave coherence to cultural life. When certain members of the public likened the *Little Dancer* to dolls or puppets, they were clearly shocked by their discovery, while a critic like Ephrussi was able to resolve his encounter only by arguing, with evident relief, that Degas had narrowly managed to *avoid* the resemblance to anything as vulgar as a doll.

Beyond these immediate responses, there is a further paradox, or rather a series of linked and overlapping paradoxes that lurk beneath the language of dolls in the nineteenth century. At their center is the question of likeness, of the doll as a carefully miniaturized facsimile of a living child or baby, and of related forms – such as puppets, mannequins, and wax models – as substitutes for the human figure. Then as now, a superior doll or puppet would be admired for its "lifelike" qualities and spoken of – and often spoken to – as if it were "real." A member of the audience at one of Duranty's performances, for example, reported his pleasure in the "almost living being" of one of the characters portrayed, and a visitor to an exhibition of dolls in 1878 described a particularly fine specimen "occupied by her toilette, surrounded by all the accessories which she uses to enhance her natural beauty."[98] Even shop window dummies were subject to the same excess; in Zola's novel *Au Bonheur des Dames,* a group of new arrivals from the provinces stand spellbound in front of a vast department store, as the light and color of its displays reveal "mannequins who take on a living soul."[99] By this token, we might expect the description of the *Little Dancer* as "doll-like" to be essentially complimentary, as part of the wider chorus of approval for its "extreme realism" that prompted Huysmans to claim that, as with Pygmalion's statue of Galatea, it "seemed ready to step from its base."[100] The opposite, however, was apparently the case; on a site reserved for art, a comparison with a puppet or a figure associated with "hairdressers' windows" was almost invariably derogatory, made to dismiss the object in question or draw attention to its life-*less* qualities. Surveying the halls of marble figures at the 1859 Salon, Charles Baudelaire had complained of the "monotonous whiteness of all these great dolls, exact in all their proportions of height and breadth," and denigrated certain smaller sculptures in the exhibition by comparing them to items in "toy-sellers' shops."[101] Courbet, Manet, Caillebotte, and others suffered the indignity of seeing their paintings likened to arrangements of wooden dolls by caricaturists of the day, and even writers sympathetic to their art would use such imagery to castigate their peers. Commenting on the dramas of a rival naturalist author, Zola dismissed them as mere "puppet-plays," while Gustave Geffroy was to criticize the pedestrian antics of real ballerinas as those of "puerile marionettes."[102]

In this ill-defined and contradictory situation, it is perhaps unsurprising that Degas' sculpture found so few champions, its doll-like aura out of place in a work of art, its artistic presentation inappropriate to a mere toy. Before pursuing these attitudes further, it is necessary to spell out more precisely the nature of dolls and their rapidly changing manufacture in Degas' day. Several prominent features of the sculpture would immediately have suggested a doll to the 1881 audience; its fabrication from wax, at this date still one of the principal materials for making the visible components of a doll's body; the use of actual fabric in the figure's clothing; the head of human or animal hair, a characteristic of superior classes of doll; and, of course, the youthfulness of the subject and its reduced scale. The doll historian Mary Hillier has observed that "the middle years of the nineteenth century" were the "heyday of wax doll production," describing the extent and the sophistication of the doll-making industry in both France and England during the period the *Little Dancer* was created.[103] Mass-produced but still assembled by hand, the more expensive dolls were carefully tinted to resemble human skin, had "hair inserted into the head, eyelashes and eyebrows" (as one contemporary noted), and came equipped with colored glass eyes.[104] Competition was fierce between companies like Montanari of England and Schmitt and Jumeau of France, leading to ever more elaborate costumes and subtleties of finish, to the introduction of partly

Fig. 27 Anon., *Dolls: Madame Montanari* (detail), wood engraving from *An Illustrated Cyclopædia of the Great Exhibition of 1851.*

mechanized variants and primitive voice boxes, and to the manufacture of dolls on every scale from the minuscule to the life-size. The vigor of the industry can be gauged from its representation at successive international exhibitions, where large glass cases revealed the latest dolls with their accessories, always "a great attraction . . . among the ladies and juvenile visitors," according to one visitor (fig. 27).[105]

Most of the advances in the making of dolls in Degas' lifetime were directed to one end, that of making them ever more naturalistic. As they gazed at the displays in the 1878 Paris Exposition Universelle, crowds marveled at the completeness of the illusion: "All the things of life are there, in graceful and tasteful miniature, so well done that, in looking at the vitrines that contain them, we believe we are looking at humanity itself, seen through the wrong end of opera glasses," wrote one devotee.[106] Remarking that dolls were now made of "wax flesh, painted muslin, waxed canvas" – a description that fits the *Little Dancer Aged Fourteen* rather uncannily – critics were also impressed by their modernity:

> They are all great ladies or *cocottes* with yellow hair, dressed with an extreme elegance that is inspired by the most recent fashion engravings. They are often presented enthroned in their salons, surrounded by friends and busily engaged in ordinary conversation, with charming attitudes, rolling their blue or brown eyes, waving a tightly gloved hand.[107]

Even more "lifelike" were the mechanized figures, such as the swimming dolls demonstrated to great acclaim in 1878; dolls that walked and cried (fig. 28); and animated characters of various kinds, such as the colorful *Gypsy,* who both danced and moved her arms (fig. 29). Characteristically, observers were quick to point out that these automatons represented "the application of science to the amusement and instruction of children," while other voices questioned whether such playthings would be better displayed in "the window of a fashion-shop or perfumer."[108] Yet more opinion insisted – in a telling refrain – that the finest dolls approached the status of works of art. In one tableau, the minute attention to detail was said "to reveal the *artist,"* and of a group of music-making dolls it was claimed, "These are not truly toys, but musical paintings."[109]

If the refined examples in the 1878 Exposition Universelle represented the peak of the industry, more modest wax dolls and similar objects were part of the currency of the age – as we have seen in the circles around Degas – and attracted similar responses. In a popular children's book of 1872, *Les Malheurs de Sophie,* several tales revolve around the young heroine's doll, with its "pink lips . . . brilliant blue eyes, its neck, bust and arms of wax" (fig. 30).[110] In the story *La Poupée de cire,* Sophie learns that the doll's body is hollow and that it melts when she tries to bathe it, while in a sequel she buries her damaged toy as if it had once been alive (fig. 31).[111] Producers of such dolls would sometimes make wax tailors' dummies and milliners' models as well, while the doll-making Montanari family of London confused the issue further by creating historical wax tableaux for the edification and entertainment of the public. Following its huge popular success at previous exhibitions, in1878 Richard Montanari treated Paris to his

> collection of very beautiful, life-like and spirited figures, modelled in wax, with most surprising minuteness and artistic feeling, both in the position and grouping. They represented the natives of Mexico, and also the American Indians habited in their proper costume, and displaying their characteristic customs in the several phases of civilized and savage life, with a truthfulness, in

Fig. 29 *(facing page bottom)* Musical automation of a gypsy by Gustave Vichy, ca. 1890, French, 30 in. (76 cm), courtesy Sotheby's, London.

Fig. 28 "Walking, Crying Doll" by Jules Steiner, ca. 1860, wax over composition, French, 20 in. (51 cm), courtesy Sotheby's, London.

the varied expressions and anatomical development of their different effigies, which was most remarkable.[112]

This strangely hybrid phenomenon combined the popular taste for anthropology with aspirations toward "artistic feeling," the tradition of doll making with something approaching voyeurism. Now lost, but recorded in a series of detailed engravings (fig. 32), the Montanari wax "effigies" may have lingered in the minds of their Parisian audience as exemplars of South American "civilized and savage life" and conceivably surfaced again in references to the "Aztec" appearance of the *Little Dancer* at the time of the 1881 Impressionist exhibition.

If we finally return to the *Little Dancer Aged Fourteen,* we are made forcibly aware of the sheer *familiarity* – as opposed to the strangeness or exoticism – of most of its material qualities for spectators of the day. Not only were large, elaborately dressed dolls and other wax figures everywhere in evidence, but a number were presented in glass cabinets and on public occasions, and some frankly acclaimed in the terms of art. A single exhibit from the 1878 Exposition Universelle summarizes the dilemma; the vitrine devoted to the fashion house of Madame Demarest (fig. 33) is precisely like a museum display, yet it contains several life-size dummies (in all probability made of wax) in the very latest and most glamorous outfits.[113] With such figures becoming ever more "life-like and spirited," confusion across the entire register of three-dimensional representation – from the childlike to the commercial and "artistic" – could only be intensified, threatening a breakdown in meaning and a collapse of moral distinctions. As we have seen, a crisis of precisely this kind was identified by the conservative critic Anatole de Montaiglon in his review of the sculpture section of the 1878 Salon. Exasperated by the obsessively detailed depiction of figures in modern dress, Montaiglon pronounced it "only fit for fashion houses" and observed, in a phrase that seems to foreshadow the *Little Dancer Aged Fourteen,* that "dressed mannequins from the galleries of clothiers will soon become the last word in art."[114]

Implicit in such remarks is a deep sense of unease, not just with the demise of the old sculptural order but with the potency of realism itself. If a wax model could be modern, individual, and almost as animated as the spectator looking at it, it might become the object of the same desires and passions, to say nothing of the dangerous fantasies once aroused by Duranty's wooden puppets. The roots of this dilemma, as Alex Potts has argued, go back several decades to an increasing sense of the "petty materiality" of sculpture, on the one hand, and the almost impossible task of imbuing it with "spirit," or the "auratic charge of the true work of art," on the other.[115] Citing Baudelaire's "radically perverse" analysis of contemporary sculpture at the time of the 1846 Salon, Potts explores the obsession with finely wrought detail and physical sumptuousness in such works, which effectively reduced them to "objects" on the same level as manufactured commodities, in turn attracting consumerist lust and "fetishistic" desires. Though concerning himself principally with Rilke's writings on Rodin, Potts describes a shifting intellectual context that we can now identify – if in a less articulated form – in the earlier reception of the *Little Dancer Aged Fourteen.* When Rilke compares his feelings about sculpture with those toward a child's doll, an experience "that ends up repelling rather than seducing us," we are offered a further insight into the disequilibrium surrounding Degas' wax statuette.[116] In Huysmans' 1880 reference to the strange appeal of shop window dummies, and in the 1883 poem by Maurice Rollinat (a friend of Nina de Villard, who was himself sculpted in wax by Jean Désiré Ringel) on the seductive charms of an unspecified "woman of

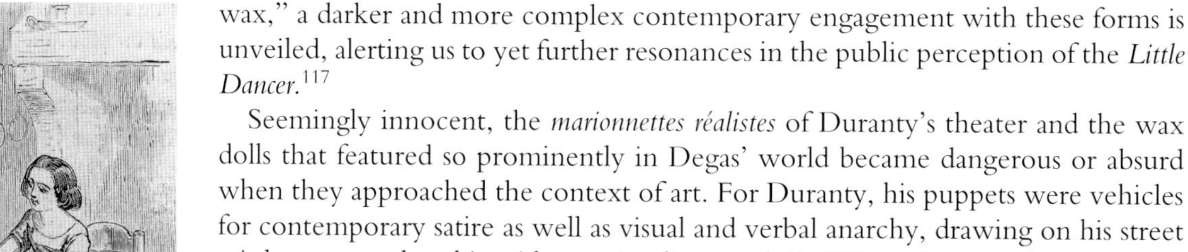

Fig. 30 H. Castelli, illustration from *Les Malheurs de Sophie*, 1872.

wax," a darker and more complex contemporary engagement with these forms is unveiled, alerting us to yet further resonances in the public perception of the *Little Dancer*.[117]

Seemingly innocent, the *marionnettes réalistes* of Duranty's theater and the wax dolls that featured so prominently in Degas' world became dangerous or absurd when they approached the context of art. For Duranty, his puppets were vehicles for contemporary satire as well as visual and verbal anarchy, drawing on his street wisdom as much as his wide-ranging literary skills. When the crowds at the 1881 Impressionist exhibition saw the *Little Dancer Aged Fourteen* as "a doll," they were thrown into a kind of cultural panic, believing that Degas had perpetrated a joke or that they should abandon propriety and "bury all our ideals." In both cases, the crime was that of destabilization, of undermining a familiar recreational edifice or subverting the conventions of form. As surrogates for ourselves, puppets and dolls are the most sensitive of subjects, revered in the proper circumstances but of uncertain status in the emerging languages of realism in painting and sculpture. In their different ways, Duranty and Degas clearly reveled in this imprecision, Degas' "preoccupation with ideas" and his "lively, constantly bubbling mind" delighting in the artifice of the theater and the shop window, even as he declared his allegiance to tradition. Among the most complex products of his maturity, the playful yet sinister, "real" yet manifestly bogus *Little Dancer Aged Fourteen* caused consternation among Degas' peers because it confronted them with the dissolving verities of their age.

Fig. 31 H. Castelli, illustration from *Les Malheurs de Sophie*, 1872.

HIGH ART: DURANTY AT THE LOUVRE

The second route leading from Edmond Duranty to the *Little Dancer Aged Fourteen* is considerably less circuitous, but equally picturesque and instructive. Where the subject of dolls and puppets took us to the Tuileries gardens, via the department stores, shop windows, and doll-making workshops of central Paris, we now travel directly to the Louvre, within sight of the former location of the Théâtre des Marionnettes, but now on quite different cultural terrain. Here we are unquestionably in the presence of High Art, among awe-inspiring collections of the great paintings and statuary of the western tradition and gallery after gallery of artifacts from past civilizations. In the twenty-or-so years of his career as a writer, Duranty journeyed frequently between these two extremes; the puppet theater of the 1860s was an unexpected amalgam of literary and visual refinement with frivolous spectacle, while some of his plays, such as *Le Miroir de Columbine,* audaciously played off the erudite against the trivial. By the end of the decade, Duranty's publications ranged freely across the spectrum; between 1870 and 1872, for example, he produced an article entitled "L'Ouverture de la galerie Lacaze au Louvre" alongside other pieces on "Le Samedi Soir au cirque" and "Méditations sur les voitures," while his novel *La Simple Vie du peintre Louis Martin* – with its encounter between Degas and the fictional painter in the Louvre's picture galleries – appeared at the same time as studies on caricature and fashion.[118]

This tendency became even more marked in the later 1870s, when the rallying cry of *The New Painting* for an art based on "railways, novelty stores, scaffolding, lines of gas lamps" was followed in rapid succession by a series of essays on the historic holdings of the Louvre. The first, published in 1877, was entitled "Promenades au Louvre: Remarques sur le geste dans quelques tableaux," while subsequent articles dealt with the museum's collections of Assyrian and Egyptian

Fig. 32 Anon., *Models of Mexican Indian Traders &c., by M. Montanari*, illustration from *Tallis's History and Description of the Crystal Palace and the Exhibition of the World's Industry in 1851*.

Fig. 33 Anon., *Madame Demarest's Exhibition*, illustration from *The Paris Exhibition of 1878*, Victoria and Albert Picture Library, London.

art, dominated by the four-part "Promenades au Louvre: Remarques à propos de l'art égyptien."[119] Appearing between 1878 and 1879 in the *Gazette des Beaux-Arts* (which carried a remarkable number of articles on Egyptian art during this period), these latter studies reveal Duranty not only in the role of aspiring scholar, but also as a contemporary critic with a new and passionate concern for sculpture.[120] Concentrating much of his attention on the stone and wood figures, the reliefs, and the smaller carvings of ancient Egypt, Duranty progressed from sweeping historical generalization to incisive comparisons with the art of his own day, often referring to issues – such as polychromy and realism – with an urgent significance for his sculptor-colleagues. Written during the period of his closest documented association with Degas, and coinciding with the formative phases of the *Little Dancer Aged Fourteen*, Duranty's "Promenades au Louvre" illustrate again the convergence of the two men's interests and their sympathy, even their collaborative effort, at a crucial moment in Degas' creative history.

Fig. 34 *Five Partial Copies after the Egyptian mural "Theban Party,"* ca. 1859–64, pencil, 10 × 7½ in. (25.4 × 19.2 cm), Notebook 18, p. 86, Bibliothèque Nationale, Paris.

Duranty's very public identification with Egyptian art had a more personal significance in his relationship with Degas. From his student days, Degas had shown a marked interest in the culture and history of ancient Egypt, making studies in his notebooks of Egyptian wall paintings and architecture, planning pictures with Egyptian themes, and executing two ambitious early oil paintings, *Young Woman and Ibis* and *Semiramis Building Babylon,* with Egyptian or Assyrian subjects.[121] An ardent copyist in the collections of the Louvre, Degas also turned to such learned sources as J.G. Wilkinson's three-volume *Manners and Customs of the Ancient Egyptians* of 1837 for certain of his studies, among them a page of drawings of young male and female Egyptian figures – many wearing the traditional wig and short skirt or tunic – in a sketchbook of the early 1860s (fig. 34).[122] A similar relieflike conception may lie behind a series of pastels made more than a decade later, when a work like *Portraits in a Frieze* seemed to offer a modern restatement of an Egyptian decorative scheme, now ironically depicting visitors to a museum.[123] In his maturity, we are told (in the somewhat fulsome prose of his niece), "Degas interested himself in everything concerning Egyptian life at the time of the Pharaohs . . . there was nothing he didn't know about this fantastic civilisation."[124] This appetite was evidently shared by his life-long friend Henri Rouart, part of whose collection of Egyptian antiquities was lovingly recorded in Degas' portrait of his daughter, *Hélène Rouart in Her Father's Study* (fig. 35), where several painted carvings and mummylike figures take up the left-hand side of the canvas.[125] Writing to another close acquaintance, the sculptor Paul-Albert Bartholomé, Degas tried to interest him in a visit to the mountains, where the artist was on vacation; "Why are you not fonder of gray marble?" he inquired; "You would come here to hew on the spot and through simple inclined planes we should make Egyptian purity descend to the verge of glory."[126]

Fig. 35 *Hélène Rouart in Her Father's Study*, ca. 1886–95, oil on canvas, 63⅜ × 47¼ in. (1.61 × 1.20 m.), National Gallery, London.

Degas, Duranty, and Rouart were not alone, of course, in the second half of the nineteenth century in their enthusiasm for all things Egyptian. As a number of recent publications have shown, "Egyptomania" had swept through the worlds of fashion and jewelry, architecture and interior design, even opera and ballet, the latter most spectacularly in a production of Verdi's *Aïda* that was compared to "an immense Egyptian frieze" by Jules Claretie in 1881.[127] Further stimulated by the cycle of international exhibitions in Paris, London, and elsewhere – when vast pavilions were built in the Egyptian style, embellished with colorful murals, and furnished with gigantic replica sculptures – the age of the Pharaohs had seized the popular imagination and made inroads into the grandest art forms. A caricature by Daumier of the 1867 Exposition Universelle, published in the widely read periodical *Le Monde illustré,* captures this encounter between ordinary Parisians and the imagery of the Egyptian past (fig. 36).[128] Combining the fashionable study of physiognomy with his own brand of realism, Daumier contrasts the mundane profiles of his French family with the absurdly exaggerated animal visages they admire, which fill them with awe and a little incredulity. In more elevated

Fig. 36 After Honoré Daumier, *At the Exposition Universelle*, 1867, wood engraving by Julien Peulot.

contexts, artists as different as Gérôme, Alma-Tadema, and Seurat catered to the Egyptian taste or absorbed its new repertoire of forms, while a British painter like Edwin Long could become renowned as a specialist in the genre. Long's grandiose canvas *Love's Labours Lost* (fig. 37) weaves together sentiment and archaeological exactitude, coincidentally using the same source – Wilkinson's *Manners and Customs of the Ancient Egyptians* – that Degas had consulted two decades previously.[129] Faithfully copying the wall paintings and architectural ornament, the hair styles, costumes, and accessories of courtly life, Long also included the kind of colored, hand-carved objects – such as Egyptian children's toys and a small, clothed wooden doll – that had recently become familiar from great exhibitions and museum displays alike.

In her autobiography, *Sixteen to Sixty: Memoirs of a Collector,* Louisine Havemeyer recalled the appearance of the *Little Dancer Aged Fourteen* at the sixth Impressionist exhibition, when she was a young woman of twenty-five:

> To some it was a revelation, to others an enigma. The graceful figure was as classic as an Egyptian statue and as modern as Degas! . . . Here was a problem! All Paris said: "Has the soul of some Egyptian come to our western world? Who has achieved this wonderful creation? Whoever he is, he is modern to his finger tips and as ancient as the pyramids!"[130]

Hyperbole aside, this is a vivid and highly specific recollection, made even more plausible by Mrs. Havemeyer's documented presence in Paris in 1881, at a time when her friend Mary Cassatt was also participating in the sixth Impressionist exhibition.[131] When her personal acquaintance with Degas and her detailed knowledge of the *Little Dancer Aged Fourteen* are taken into account (she later saw the work again in Degas' studio and tried to buy it), we must conclude that an important perception of the sculpture has hitherto been overlooked. Such a view is reinforced by the memories of others who knew the wax figure at first hand, if only in Degas' later years, when its deteriorated condition lent itself to a variety of interpretations. The pioneer cinematographer Sacha Guitry, for example, who

Fig. 37 Edwin Long, *Love's Labours Lost*, 1885, oil on canvas, 50 × 15¼ in. (127 × 191 cm), Dahesh Museum, New York.

in 1915 recorded a glimpse of the aging artist on film, called the *Little Dancer* "a kind of hallucinating mummy . . . you would have to go a long way, a very long way, right to Egypt and its ancient past to discover a work of art to equal her."[132] In a conversation with Vollard, Renoir praised a number of Degas' pictures and sculptures for their "antique" qualities, singling out the *Little Dancer* for special admiration and explaining how Degas could "combine a certain joyousness" with "the rhythm of an Egyptian bas-relief."[133] Seeing the decayed fabric on the wax figure, Paul Gsell, the intimate of Auguste Rodin, was reminded of the "yellowed rags which adorn certain mummies of Alexandria," while the journalist and bronze founder Adrien Hébrard, who was entrusted with the casting of the *Little Dancer,* remarked that it seemed "both macabre and Egyptian."[134]

Why did certain of Degas' contemporaries see the *Little Dancer,* as "Egyptian," just as others had perceived it as "Aztec," Greek, or Spanish, as puppetlike or doll-like? As in these instances, it was the physical attributes of the sculpture – its materials, colors, and manner of presentation – that appear to have suggested such links, rather than its subject matter, though the historic origins of the dance were often traced to ancient Egypt in contemporary texts.[135] Most tangibly, the wax used to make the figure was widely associated with Egyptian craft; standard histories described the introduction of the *cire perdue* technique by Egyptian bronze casters, and a two-part history of wax modeling by Spire Blondel, published in the *Gazette des Beaux-Arts* in 1882, spelled out the applications of wax in such centers as ancient Alexandria, noting an early tendency to choose the medium for trompe l'oeil sculpture and decoration.[136] Egyptian wax figures could also be found in vitrines at the Louvre, though these tended to be small and of limited sophistication.[137] More generally visible in the Louvre displays were carvings of figures wearing wigs, a standard feature of Egyptian formal attire that was often given exaggerated prominence in their sculptural effigies, and further heightened by the application of paint, gold, and ornament. The prevalence of hairpieces of various kinds in ancient Egypt was discussed in popular guides to the national collections, such as that of Emanuel Rougé, where it was explained that the shaven heads of certain portraits would "originally have been completed by a wig."[138] Though the *Little Dancer*'s hairstyle was more naturalistic than its Egyptian counterparts, several critics commented on the appearance of her hair, one claiming that Degas' "ballet-girls of wax are be-painted, be-wigged and be-flounced by himself."[139] Huysmans observed that the figure was crowned with "real hair," while Our Lady Correspondent noted (with questionable accuracy) that "her hair and skin are colored to life, and her feet are shod in pink satin shoes and sandals."[140]

In combination with its wax body, artificial headpiece, and miniature accessories, the conspicuous coloring of several elements of the sculpture seems to have confirmed its Egyptian ancestry for the likes of Louisine Havemeyer. As well as the "pink satin shoes," there was the "leek-green" ribbon in the dancer's hair, the pale yellow bodice, the white tutu, and the subtle shifts of hue from one area of the dancer's physique to another. Though it still awaits a detailed analysis, the deep brown wax surface of the *Little Dancer* – ranging from warm honey to the darkest mahogany – appears to be broadly consistent with its appearance in 1881, if somewhat "blackened" in places, as Degas himself claimed in 1903.[141] Direct examination of the wax figure also reveals passages of differentiated hue, for instance at the junction of the face and hairline, which might well have encouraged the idea that it had been "painted" for some of Degas' audience.[142] Such coloration was one of the most well known characteristics of Egyptian

Fig. 38 The Salle du Scribe in the Egyptian Galleries of the Louvre, Paris.

sculpture, from the partial painting of details of a wooden carving – where the body would be left in its natural tones – to the complete, "life-like" enhancement of skin, hair, and clothing over an entire figure. Often associated with the historic development of realism, this application of color could be seen at its most spectacular in some of the masterpieces of the Louvre's collections, such as the painted stone sculpture of the *Seated Scribe*. Referring to this image, Rougé's handbook of 1879 again deals with the subject, explaining how the dryness of the "desert sands" had "preserved the original colors" in this outstanding portrait, resulting in an image that "almost seems to speak."[143]

When Duranty was preparing his "Promenades au Louvre," he would have found the *Seated Scribe* in its own vitrine at the center of the so-called Salle du Scribe in a much-visited room at the heart of the Egyptian collections. Around it, clustered in a variety of other display cases, were dozens of carvings of standing and seated figures on various scales, many of them painted, dressed, or equipped according to their status or profession and some identifiable through inscriptions as named individuals. As archival photographs and other records show (fig. 38), such works were typically displayed in severe, almost minimal glass cases, ranging from wooden wall cabinets to free-standing vitrines with only the slenderest bronze frames to support the glass.[144] Comparable in design to the cabinets at the 1878 Exposition Universelle, though on a much reduced scale, the Louvre vitrines were inevitably engaged in a similar process of selection and emphasis, orchestrating the spectators' responses to the objects on view and singling out certain items for special attention. Wall-mounted displays tended to be more crowded and less well illuminated than free-standing vitrines, while celebrated works like the *Seated Scribe* (visible at the right of fig. 38) could be seen from all four sides, in ample space and at optimum viewing height. That such privileges were sometimes granted to less renowned items is also apparent in the installation photograph, in the exquisite carving of a striding female figure appearing at the left, resplendent on a marble column and occupying her own spacious glass

Fig. 39 *At the Louvre: The Etruscan Sarcophagus*, ca. 1879–80, pencil, 4¼ × 6¼ in. (10.8 × 16.5 cm), Sterling and Francine Clark Art Institute, Williamstown, Massachusetts.

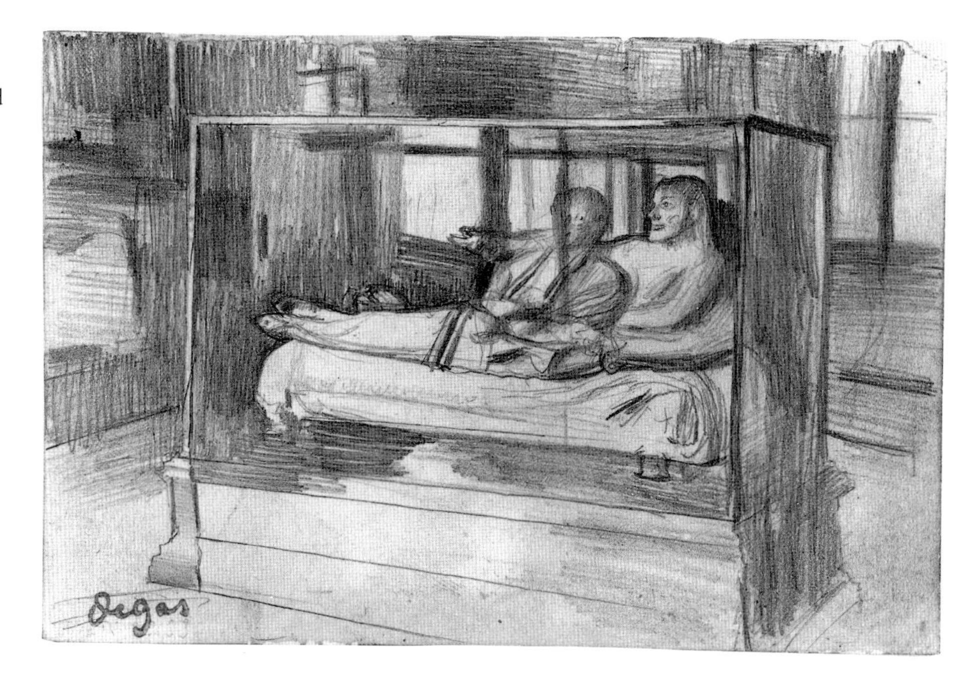

enclosure. Both confining and revealing its contents, vitrines like these enticed the viewer and raised their expectations, even as they erected a barrier between the world of flesh and blood outside and the precious objects – with their varying degrees of verisimilitude – within.

That Degas was familiar with these conventions and perhaps intrigued by their consequences we know from a drawing made in a nearby gallery in about 1879, *At the Louvre: The Etruscan Sarcophagus* (fig. 39). Here Degas has carefully recorded the fine metal frame of the vitrine and its simple pediment, as well as the effects of reflected light – partially breaking up the forms beyond – on the surface of the glass. Retaining most of these features in his magnificent etching *Mary Cassatt at the Louvre: The Etruscan Gallery* (fig. 40), the artist has juxtaposed them with the living forms of two visitors, posed for the occasion by Mary Cassatt and her sister Lydia. Slyly contrasting the celibate young women with the married Etruscan couple, Degas also defined the timeless relationship of the museum visitor to the displayed object, the former animate and free, the latter forever remote behind its pane of glass. Though we have no visual record of the vitrine originally used for the *Little Dancer Aged Fourteen*, there is every reason to believe that it conformed to such patterns and that it, too, became complicit in similar exchanges. One visitor to the 1881 exhibition mentioned the "luxurious simplicity" of Degas' glass case, and the writer Bertall commented that the sculpture was shown "in prime position at the center of one of the galleries," while de Villard clearly acknowledged its pretensions when she wrote of the *Little Dancer* that "one day it will be looked at with respect in a museum."[145] By installing his wax figure behind glass, Degas may well have chosen to protect it, as Jules Claretie assumed in his review, in the same way that wax dolls were guarded from exhibition visitors and small wax models from Salon crowds.[146] But by placing the *Little Dancer* in a vitrine at the center of his display, Degas also separated it definitively from its surroundings, situated it in its own privileged space, and gave it a museum-like prominence, like that of the *Seated Scribe* and the *Etruscan Sarcophagus* in their respective galleries. More than the vast cabinets at the Exposition Universelle or

Fig. 40 *Mary Cassatt at the Louvre: The Etruscan Gallery*, ca. 1879–80, etching and aquatint, 14 × 10⅝ in. (35.7 × 26.9 cm), The Art Institute of Chicago, Albert Rouillier Memorial Collection.

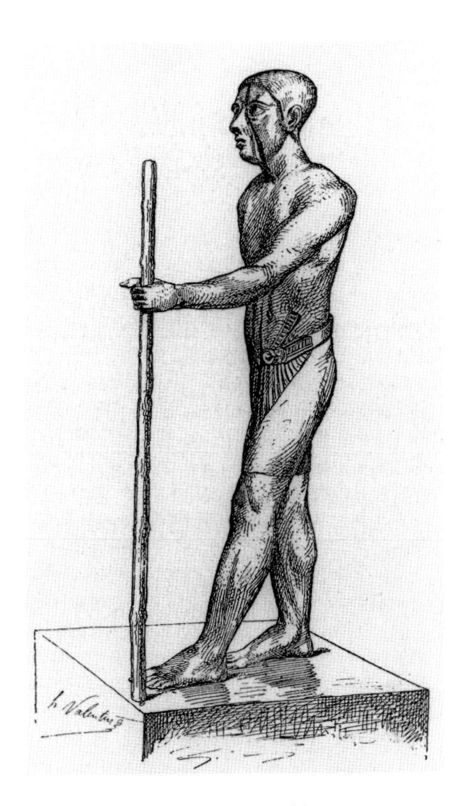

Fig. 41 *Wooden Statue, Old Empire*, illustration from Edmond Duranty, "Promenades au Louvre," 1879.

the brash displays in department-store windows, more even than the didactic presentations in museums of anthropology and ethnography, the *Little Dancer*'s vitrine marked it out as remote, exceptional, and – inescapably – a work of art.

In the pages of his "Promenades au Louvre," Duranty escorted his readers from room to room as he recounted the story of Egyptian sculpture, stopping to single out individual objects as they caught his attention. Initially stressing the subordination of sculpture to the needs of architecture and the timeless, hieratic nature of much Egyptian imagery, Duranty made increasing use of terms appropriate to the art of his own times. Writing of the "decadent" renaissance of the Saïte dynasty, the writer stopped to admire the "nervous refinement of Saïte art" with its "wealth of observation, of science," delighting in the "study of hands, feet, heads, arms, which take on an expressive quality that is firm, tight, sharply observed."[147] Later, he discussed the masterful handling of hair and the "partial or complete painting" of Egyptian statues and enthused over the "tautening of flesh in the crossed legs of the seated scribe," which he found to be "*studied* and executed with realism."[148] Warming to his theme, the journalist-critic explained that in comparison with the Egyptians, "No other people were as preoccupied with representing scenes of ordinary life, of the life of the people and the bourgeoisie," describing

> the *bas-reliefs*, the illustrated newspapers of Egypt . . . frankly realistic in keeping with their subjects, they recorded the existence of workers, sailors, labourers, house-holders, children's games, feasts, amusements, bodily exercises and a host of other things.[149]

Recalling his lists of approved subjects and his calls for topicality in *The New Painting,* Duranty's determination to see such imagery in contemporary terms was by no means orthodox, contrasting, for example, with Charles Blanc's insistence that Egyptian art was "majestic, strictly formulaic" and characterized by the "non-imitation of real life."[150] As he gained in confidence, Duranty was moved to discover even more explicit similarities; of one particular carving he claimed "the right leg . . . is almost the equal, in its truth and careful expression, of a modern sculpture."[151] But it was in his assessment of a group of wooden figures in movement that Duranty brought the argument closest to home; arguing that wood allowed the Egyptian artist greater "animation, freedom and naturalism," he observed of a standing male dignitary (fig. 41) that the free articulation of its legs might be compared with those of "une moderne poupée" – a modern puppet or doll.[152]

When Louisine Havemeyer and her peers admired the *Little Dancer Aged Fourteen* in its glass case, imagining its creator as "modern to his finger tips and as ancient as the pyramids," they seemed to share Duranty's sense of the interchangeability of genres, the continuity of techniques and materials, and the echoing sensibilities of two epochs. It is still surprising, however, to find the ease with which these transitions could be effected and the readiness of one culture to apply its values to those of another. This is nowhere more apparent in Duranty's "Promenades au Louvre" than in his treatment of another renowned sculpture, known as *La Dame Nay* (fig. 42), which was exhibited in a cabinet of varied objects in the same room as the *Seated Scribe*. Less than a foot high, this carving was sufficiently celebrated to be noted in Rougé's narrative, while Duranty chose it as one of the illustrations to his text (fig. 43).[153] Duranty was unashamed in his partiality for the work, explaining to his readers in 1879 that "The wooden statuette of la dame Nay is truly ravishing, with her pretty muzzle like a savage,

Fig. 42 *La Dame Nay*, XXVIII–XXIX dynasty, painted and gilt wood, 10½ in. (26.5 cm), Musée du Louvre, Paris.

naïve animal, her wig with its gold headband, her raw-boned, supple, cat-like allure and her traditional tight-fitting dress," before reprimanding himself for straying from his educational tour.[154] Written two years before the unveiling of the *Little Dancer Aged Fourteen*, these phrases offer the most extraordinary pre-figuration of many of the assumptions – even the specific terminology – of visitors to the sixth Impressionist exhibition. Here we find Duranty, like many of the male critics at the 1881 show, approaching the statuette as if it were a sensuous, living woman; here, too, is the suggestion of abnormal sexuality, linking *La Dame Nay*'s "ravishing" physique with her imagined animal-like behavior; even more surprisingly, there are hints of coarseness in her "raw-boned" appearance and muzzlelike face; and most unexpected of all, we find aspects of this delicately polished, finely detailed figure described as both "savage" and "naïve."

Behind Duranty's prose there is clearly a morass of contemporary prejudice and presumption, as well as a number of specific attitudes to sculpture that deserve further analysis. Most immediately, we are brought up against the currency of certain terms in critical parlance in the years immediately before the appearance of the *Little Dancer Aged Fourteen,* specifically those related to a popular understanding of anthropology and physiognomy, and to assumptions about the sexual roles of model and viewer. In a broader sense, we encounter again Duranty's willingness to step across boundaries and engage in verbal and visual ingenuity, leaping from one genre or mode of reality to another, even across the millennia. When he likened the bas-reliefs of the Egyptians to the newspapers of his own day and compared their wooden carvings to "modern dolls," Duranty was boldly – and not without irony – welcoming these objects to his realist project; when he evoked the "ravishing," "cat-like," and "savage" *La Dame Nay* in the phraseology used by fellow critics, he went further, arguing for a community of interest between the ancient craftsmen and their nineteenth-century counterparts. Not only were certain Egyptian carvings "almost the equal . . . of a modern sculpture," but they were based on modern principles, he tells us, the outcome "of observation, of science," that had been "executed with realism." Here in the galleries of the Louvre, in other words, his artist friends could find sympathetic forms and admirable exemplars in works that might engage their passions, invigorate their techniques, and inspire their most novel preoccupations.

An inscription on a drawing made by Degas for his *Portrait of Monsieur Duranty* – which shows the writer at his desk, surrounded by current manuscripts and papers – specifies that the study was made at Duranty's apartment on 25 March 1879.[155] Just three weeks earlier, the *Gazette des Beaux-Arts* had published the second of Duranty's sequence of essays on Egyptian art, to be followed four months later by the third in the series. When we consider that it was during this very period that Degas was occupied by the *Little Dancer Aged Fourteen,* the probability that an artist with such a pronounced taste for Egyptian culture would have shared, discussed, and absorbed Duranty's researches becomes overwhelming. Like Duranty, however, Degas was predominantly drawn to the past as a man attached to the present, taking from it what he could reinvent in the vernacular of his own times, if acknowledging and sometimes relishing the anachronism of his borrowings. Degas' engagement with Egyptian art was not, of

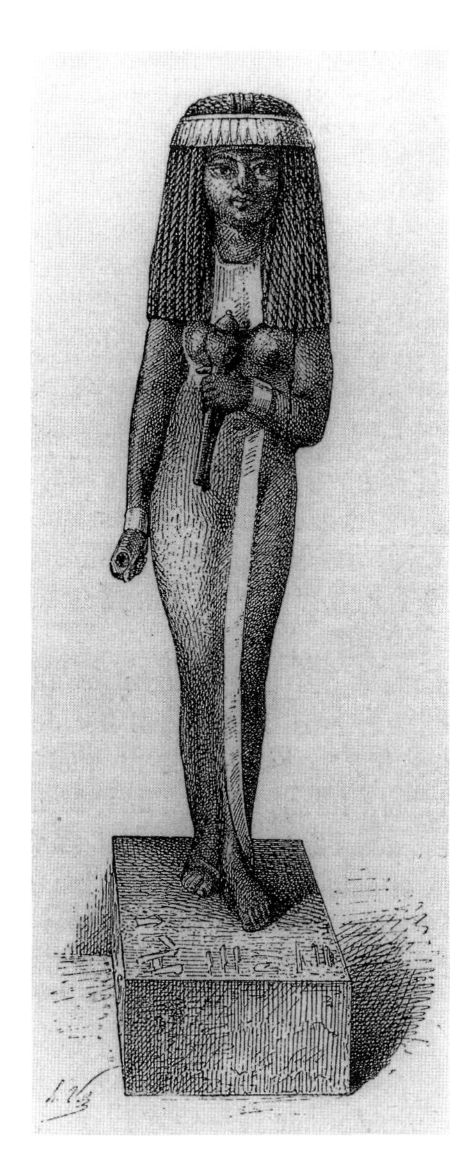

Fig. 43 *La Dame Nay*, illustration from Edmond Duranty, "Promenades au Louvre," 1879.

course, an exclusive one, any more than his recorded interest in dolls and toys or his known fascination with the science of physiognomy; nor was it a cosmetic exercise of the kind that brought wealth to Gérôme and passing success to Edwin Long. In *The New Painting,* Duranty had inveighed at some length against precisely such quaintness, this "mummification, this sickening embalming of the spirit . . . this negative and muddled art. . . . Do these artists of the Ecole really believe that they have created great art because they have rendered helmets, footstools, polychrome columns, boats, and bordered robes according to the latest archaeological decrees?" he asked in 1876.[156] Degas, too, was notorious for mocking the exoticism of his peers, on one occasion asking Gérôme, as they stood in front of his own *Young Spartans,* "I suppose it's not Turkish enough for you?"[157]

If the costume, wig, and colored materials of the *Little Dancer Aged Fourteen,* presented in a museum-like cabinet, recalled the sculptures of ancient Egypt for some of Degas' contemporaries, none of these features could be described as "archaeological" in the sense used by Duranty. For all its naïveté, Long's painting *Love's Labours Lost* recorded something of Egyptian life and art, whereas Degas' sculpture tells us nothing about either. Rather, Degas might be said to respond to "Egyptian purity" (as he called it in his letter to Bartholomé) or, more precisely, to a tantalizing combination of that "purity" with the impure engagement with daily life so freely admired in the "Promenades au Louvre." This attitude is forcefully summarized in the pose of the *Little Dancer,* a distinctive stance that is at once timeless and immediate, bordering on the casual yet strangely grand. Rooted to the spot by its broad wooden base, Degas' figure has much of the impassivity of Egyptian granite and wood carvings, a characteristic that is expressed in the deep socle of *La Dame Nay* and the massive pediments of larger monuments. Almost symmetrical when seen from the front, the *Little Dancer* also shares with the paradigmatic Egyptian figure its solemn verticality and single, projected leg; but, as Duranty observed, in the Egyptian tradition "the invariable attitude adopted for the standing statue was to advance the left leg," while in Degas' figure it is the right leg that is extended.[158]

Such broad, rather than archaeologically exact, affinities continue in the much discussed head of the *Little Dancer Aged Fourteen.* Reflecting on the physiognomies of Egyptian carved figures, Duranty commented on their absence of "moral expression," their faces that are "always impersonal. They do not look, or listen, or express delight, neither cry nor become angered."[159] A fragmentary head in pink granite from the Louvre's displays, illustrated in Duranty's text (fig. 44), exemplifies this extraordinary inwardness, as well as the emotional neutrality of the facial features he describes.[160] Set beside it, the contained expression of the *Little Dancer* – with its aloof, upturned profile and its gaze that appears distant and inward-turning at the same time – suddenly seems at home. So, too, do the observations of some of its critics, who accused Degas' model of being "empty-headed" and of expressing neither the innocence of youth nor the rectitude of ideal womanhood.[161] Whether or not it was directly affected by the Egyptian prototype it strikingly resembles, the face of Degas' sculpture shares with the granite head a resistance to the standard vocabulary of grimaces, coquettish smiles, and precociously thoughtful frowns, and it was this inscrutability – challenging in any context, but unforgivable in the representation of a child – that seemed most to have provoked the 1881 audience.

But complete solemnity was a rare feature of Degas' revisitations of the past, more commonly counterbalanced as it was by his commitment to what Duranty had called "the special characteristics of the modern individual." In *Mary Cassatt*

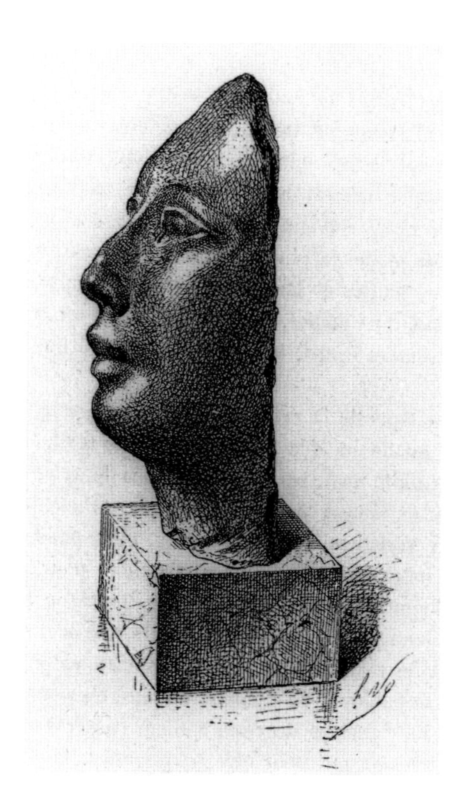

Fig. 44 *Head Fragment in Pink Granite,* illustration from Edmond Duranty, "Promenades au Louvre," 1879.

at the Louvre: The Etruscan Gallery, it was the clash of the old and the new, of the stylized and the jauntily stylish, that attracted the artist to his subject, here made doubly poignant by the direct encounter of the sculpted and the living. When audiences confronted the *Little Dancer Aged Fourteen,* they effectively took the place of the Cassatt sisters, finding themselves bemused or embarrassed by their echo within the vitrine, intrigued or threatened by its similarities to – and reassured by its differences from – their own temporal being. Like their reflected image, the wax figure was highly particularized, its clothing and posture eloquent of age, occupation, and social deportment, its character suggestive enough to provoke moral condemnation. As with a doll or puppet or ethnographic specimen, the audience felt themselves authorized to pass judgment, to compare this example with others they had seen and relate it to their quotidian experience. At the same time, the statuette clung stubbornly to its identity as a piece of sculpture, its configuration fixed and unyielding, its echoes of the cathedral and the museum disconcerting to its lay audience.

If our discursive tour of certain overlooked aspects of the reception of the *Little Dancer Aged Fourteen* – in particular its association with dolls and puppets and with Egyptian art – leads to a coherent destination, it is surely that of a broader and more generous grasp of Degas the realist, going well beyond, or even inverting, our familiar understanding of that term. Too often seen as the outcome of the artist's social and visual attentiveness, the *Little Dancer* was manifestly perceived by his contemporaries in a gamut of diverging and openly contradictory ways. As Douglas Druick, Anthea Callen, and others have convincingly shown, some of these responses claimed the *Little Dancer* for the new science of criminology, while Andreas Blühm and his colleagues have located the work in debates about the coloring of sculpture and the use of innovatory materials. What is overwhelmingly apparent is that the figure displayed at the sixth Impressionist exhibition was not uniquely circumscribed by any one of these associations, prompting some of the audience to recall visits to the Louvre and others to remember the playthings of their childhood, and yet others to resort to the rhetoric of confusion. In the same way that Duranty learned to vary the bill of fare at the Tuileries gardens, catering to the tastes of "very naïve spirits and very wise spirits," so Degas had chosen to leaven the idioms of realism and season his modernity with flavors old and still undefined. Where his choice of subject was socially specific, and perhaps knowingly provocative, the pose selected for his model was studiedly neutral, echoing figures that were several thousand years old; where the youthfulness of the dancer might have encouraged mawkishness, pity, coarseness, or outrage, the wax figurine provoked all these emotions at once; and where certain elements of the sculpture, such as the authentic bodice and tutu, seemed to propel it toward the everyday world, others pushed it firmly back into the museum cabinet.

But the most startling discovery – which emerges slowly from our long investigation – is the insistent, fundamental *unreality* of the *Little Dancer Aged Fourteen.* Literally unavoidable, the glass-and-bronze vitrine – so often omitted in photographs and even in gallery installations – corrals the figure away from everyday spaces and sensations, consigning it to an unnatural, nonillusionistic limbo and, in the words of Catherine Chevillot, audaciously "interposing between the wax figure and the spectator a conceptual level in the reading of a work of art."[162] Almost as definitively, the deep brown color of the *Little Dancer's* body is inconsistent with any reading of the subject as a typical Parisian ballerina, only becoming coherent when related to bronze casts or ancient artifacts in museum displays.[163] Arguably most critical, however, is the scale of the object, at two-thirds life-size as large as the grandest doll and more ambitious than any study or ornament, yet emphatically too small to be mistaken for a living, breathing model. At a stroke, and from the very beginning of his project, Degas chose to separate the sculpture from any possible association with direct casting from the human body, from Tussaud-like replications of appearances and from anatomical specimens, as well as from every kind of meretriciously "real" sculpture. Though enough remained of all these possibilities to trouble or excite his audience, the adoption of a reduced scale for the statuette suppressed an entire range of interpretative options, while inevitably reinforcing – and perhaps determining – others. Seemingly an expression of "extreme realism" and "exact science," the meter-high *Little Dancer Aged Fourteen* is ultimately none of these things. It is, on the contrary, a knowing contrivance, a piece of fanciful invention that grew out of Degas' vulgar appetites as much as his erudition and skill, out of his fascination with the clash of visual, sexual, and historical signals as much as his dedication to a single creed. Too close to ourselves to be entirely comfortable, the *Little Dancer* remains clamorously implausible: in characteristically provocative mode some years later, Degas confided to Walter Sickert, "One gives the idea of the true by means of the false."[164]

FRAMING *THE LITTLE DANCER AGED FOURTEEN*

Douglas W. Druick

The *Little Dancer Aged Fourteen* (p. viii) was a milestone in Edgar Degas' career, and its first exhibition in the Impressionist show of 1881 marked an important turning point in the artist's critical reputation. To be sure, by 1881 Degas was recognized as a leader of the artists who had been baptized the Impressionists at the time of their first joint exhibition in 1874. Over the course of the exhibitions the group mounted between 1874 and 1880, Degas distinguished himself for his unique ability to put powerful draftsmanship and innovative compositional skill in the service of distinctive, penetrating observations of modern life. His portrayals of laundresses, jockeys, and milliners; performers at the theater, circus, and café-concert; and especially dancers on stage and backstage (cat. 5) at the Opéra were viewed as quintessentially Parisian, amusing but with a caricaturesque edge that prompted comparisons with the satiric vision of the work of Honoré Daumier.

However, repeated exposure to Degas' work at the Impressionist exhibitions had convinced some that his was a somewhat cynical view of modernity. As one reviewer noted in 1879, the artist "resigns himself [to contemporary life]. . . with a cheerful philosophy and tries to console us through art."[1] But not everyone was as enchanted. The same year, the critic Albert Wolff declared that Degas had failed to fulfill his potential; he had reached mid-career (he was about to turn forty-five) "without having taken a step further, always making promises and nothing more." Conservative and generally hostile to the Impressionists, Wolff was venting his usual spleen. But there was some truth to his accusation that Degas promised more than he delivered. The artist had the annoying habit of listing works in the catalogues for the various Impressionist exhibitions that he would then not put on view. In 1879 there were a number of such instances, and the following year the artist appeared to carry this habit to an extreme.[2]

The catalogue for the fifth group show announced, in addition to several portraits that never materialized, the opportunity to see one of Degas' very early paintings, *Petites Filles spartiates provoquant des garçons* (1860), as well as to consider a brand new departure, a sculpture the painter listed as *Petite Danseuse de quatorze ans (statuette en cire)*. But as one disappointed reviewer grumbled in print, "We shall see neither his *Dancer*, nor his *Young Spartan Girls*, nor still other works that he had promised us." The presence in the exhibition rooms of the empty vitrine destined to house the *Little Dancer* made palpable Degas' failure to produce. And while what Degas did exhibit delighted some, it was insufficient to convince others – even supporters – that the artist was not stuck. One reviewer implied that Degas was in a rut when he remarked that his "dancers are always the dancers we know." Picking up on this, Philippe Burty, a champion of Degas, who had hailed

See p. viii. Detail of *Little Dancer Aged Fourteen*, 1878–81, wax and fabric, 39 in. (99 cm), Collection of Mr. and Mrs. Paul Mellon, Upperville, Virginia.

his originality and "genius" as early as 1874, sounded a more explicit warning. Linking Degas to Daumier, while noting he lacked the latter's generosity of spirit, Burty predicted that the younger artist's "ironic wit will diminish him if he continues to waste his time on the dance classes at the Opéra." Evidently, the tone of Degas' work, as much as the subject matter, had begun to appear limited. Attentive to signs of growth, Burty noted simply that Degas was essaying sculpture.[3]

When Degas finally put the *Little Dancer Aged Fourteen* on display the following year, at the sixth Impressionist exhibition, he effectively silenced the critics who were accusing him of stagnation and superficiality. Indeed, never before had a single work by him been so extensively reviewed or excited so much comment. The 1881 exhibition of the *Little Dancer* would take on canonical status when, in 1890, Degas' career to date was summarized in a supplement to a publication that is one of the great barometers of achievement in nineteenth-century France: the *Grand Dictionnaire universel du XIXème siècle.* Recognizing Degas' talents as a draftsman and the "truth" of his observations of modern life, the entry on the artist mentions some of his early submissions to the Salon, passes over the specifics of the work he showed in the first five Impressionist exhibitions, and focuses on his submissions of 1881. Here, the unnamed author implied, Degas had revealed himself to be a "philosopher à la Baudelaire" by exhibiting "besides some *Portraits of criminals*, such as Kirail, Knobloch, [and] Abadie, a wax statuette, *Little Dancer Aged Fourteen."* A work of "instructive ugliness," as the contemporary review the *Dictionnaire* cites declared, it seemed "troubling," "almost frightening."[4]

To twentieth-century observers familiar with Degas' oeuvre, the *Dictionnaire*'s acknowledgment of this celebrated sculpture's importance is as expected as the references used to qualify it are obscure. That Degas' contemporaries found the sculpture ugly may be harder to understand, since "charming," a term often used before 1881 to describe his work, has been applied by many later viewers to the *Little Dancer.* To appreciate that in 1881 its "ugliness" was its defining characteristic and to comprehend its troubling appeal involved an appreciation of the ways in which Degas' sculpture was controversial as no other previous work by him had been and to understand the complexity of its design and presentation.

★ ★ ★

The *Little Dancer* has long inhabited a realm apart from the topical: the timeless domain of the masterpiece. However, viewers in 1881 sensed that this arresting wax figure broached then-current, disturbing issues regarding the potential of youth – genetic determinism versus the influence of environment, family, and education – as well as the relationship between "high" art and popular culture. Such concerns remain as difficult and critical today as they were in 1881.

Fig. 45 *Criminal Physiognomy* (Paul Kirail), ca. 1880–81, pastel, 25¼ × 30 in. (64 × 76 cm), location unknown.

As the *Dictionnaire* entry on Degas suggests, we should begin by reconnecting the *Little Dancer* with the now all-but-forgotten pastel portraits (figs. 45 and 46) that were on view when the 1881 Impressionist exhibition was inaugurated on 2 April 1881 (the sculpture would join them only some two weeks after the show opened). The subjects of the pastels were notorious in 1881, so much a part of the popular imagination that, nine years later, the writer of the *Dictionnaire* entry on Degas presumed its readership was familiar with them. Abadie, Kirail, and Knobloch had figured in several sensational murders that preoccupied Paris for close to two years. Dubbed the "Abadie affair," it began early in 1879 with two brutal killings: of a grocer's boy in Saint-Mandé and of the Widow Joubert, owner

Fig. 46 *Criminal Physiognomies* (Emile Abadie, *left*; Michel Knobloch, *right*), ca. 1880–81, pastel, 18⅞ × 24¾ in. (48 × 63 cm), private collection.

of a magazine shop at 26, rue Fontaine, not far from Degas' apartment. These crimes were still unsolved in mid April, when the middle-aged proprietress of a disreputable tavern in Montreuil, on the outskirts of the city, was found stabbed to death, intensifying Parisians' dismay over the rise of crime.[5] The subsequent arrest of nineteen-year-old Emile Abadie (fig. 47) and sixteen-year-old Pierre Gille (fig. 48), and their confession to the Montreuil murder, did little to alleviate public anxiety. For the details they provided only fed the concern for national health that the recent defeat in the Franco–Prussian war had aggravated, underscoring the "moral gangrene" now thought to be infecting youths in the nation's capital.[6]

Sensitive to the societal pathologies that threatened national well-being, the new Republican leadership had begun to encourage a mode of criminal analysis based on scientific and medical models. Throughout the 1870s, and especially between 1879 and 1882, French as well as Italian anthropologists sought to extend the frontiers of criminology by building systematic classifications of criminal anatomy. Widely publicized, their findings suggested that crime is a manifestation of evolutionary atavism and that, in a very real sense, criminals are unevolved

Fig. 47 Police photograph of Emile Abadie, 1879, Archives de la préfecture de la police, Paris.

savages in a civilized world. It was purported that the innate tendency to moral degeneracy could be detected from atavistic signs in the shape of the skull, as well as in the form and disposition of facial features. This explanation of crime as biologically determined was, however, increasingly challenged by French anthropologists who placed greater responsibility for criminal behavior on environmental factors.[7] Raising the particularly vexing problem of the "premature corruption of barely formed characters," the "Abadie affair" resisted ready explanation by either of the two opposing theories.[8]

For those who supported the theory of "innate" criminality, Abadie's physiognomy possessed the tell-tale signs of a "bestial side," with its "low forehead, large and powerful jaw, prominent cheek bones, thick-lipped mouth, eyes by turn dull and menacing, [and] greenish complexion."[9] By contrast, the delicate features of the blonde, blue-eyed Gille unsettled observers precisely because he appeared so naturally "refined" and "upright." Even as practiced an observer as chief of police Gustave Macé so misread Gille's "frank countenance" as to initially presume him incapable of murder. "Here," cautioned critic Wolff, "physiognomists would waste their time in insisting that we read the man beneath the mask."[10]

Proponents of socially determined criminality likewise were thwarted by the case. Abadie's mother was a habitually unemployed seamstress, castigated by her neighbors as a flagrant "woman of loose morals."[11] Nonetheless, Abadie had had the benefits of the Catholic education that was being advanced as the moral antidote to crime by conservatives critical of the more strictly scientific solutions favored by Gambetta's Republicans.[12] Gille, the son of a manufacturer of artificial flowers, had enjoyed a more stable childhood and even some special educational opportunities. Yet both youths had demonstrated equally the "precocious depravity" that concerned social critics.[13] Abadie's criminal record dated back to 1876, when he was imprisoned for attacking his mother with a knife while he was drunk on absinthe. Gille had stolen 8,000 francs from his father's business, thereby bringing about its ruin. Together Abadie and Gille had recently organized a juvenile gang governed by fifty-three regulations. They subsequently carried out the premeditated robbery and murder of the tavern owner with a sang-froid evident in their impassive testimony to police.[14] Apparently feeling no remorse, they horrified observers with their "appalling cynicism."[15]

The "Abadie affair" thus became central to the current debate on juvenile crime. But what insured its celebrity was the way it engaged this discourse with another, that on the naturalist aesthetic in art and literature. On the one hand, the "Abadie affair" clearly addressed the "scientific" thesis central to Emile Zola's novels, that individual destiny is determined by the interaction of "heredity" (or genetics) and environment. Even more controversial was whether the "terrible realism" with which the naturalists, led by Zola, described sordid aspects of contemporary life had any redeeming social value or was simply sensationalist. The debate had been galvanized by the serialization of *L'Assommoir* in 1876. Zola had undertaken to produce, as he put it, "the first novel about the common people that does not lie but has [their] authentic smell." The result was as pungent as it was radically new. Set in a poor district on the northern edge of Paris, the novel tells the story, to quote Zola, of "the inevitable downfall of a working-class family in the polluted atmosphere of our urban areas." Chronicling the decline into abject poverty and dissolution of a laundress, Gervaise, *L'Assommoir* is memorable for the picture of brutality and degradation it powerfully and relentlessly draws. In addition to establishing Zola's reputation and leadership of

Fig. 48 Police photograph of Pierre Gille, 1879, Archives de la préfecture de la police, Paris.

the naturalist school of writing, the novel was an extraordinary success, its shocking revelations about aspects of contemporary life among the city's poor at once fascinating and repelling the public.[16]

The debate on naturalism sparked by *L'Assommoir* was rekindled in January 1879, when the stage version of Zola's novel premiered at the Théâtre de l'Ambigu, Paris, before a fashionable audience that included librettist Ludovic Halévy and quite possibly his close friend, Degas.[17] Journalists reported that, in the interest of steeping the production in naturalist "truth," the producers had gone to the "outlying [working-class] *quartiers*" to recruit "supernumeraries of the like one has never seen before on any stage."[18] This news assumed ominous significance with the subsequent revelation that both Abadie and Gille, themselves from such districts, had indeed been employed as extras in the production of *L'Assommoir*. In fact, it was in the wings of the Ambigu that Abadie and Gille had drafted their gang rules, recruited other bit players as members, and planned their crimes; and it was to the stage they had returned after murdering the tavern-keeper.[19] Opponents of naturalism seized upon this connection to denounce Zola's claim to a moral purpose: "To appear in *L'Assommoir* and commit murder," wrote *L'Evénement*, "is the height of naturalism."[20] This was certainly extreme. But even Zola's defenders recognized between *L'Assommoir* and the "Abadie affair" disquieting resemblances that raised questions about the relationship of art to life.

In effect, the story of the tavern-keeper, the "Bassangeaud woman," parallels that of Zola's laundress, Gervaise. Having had two illegitimate children when she was young, Madame Bassangeaud, in recent years, had become estranged from them. Moreover, she had become so promiscuous, as her addiction to absinthe worsened (Abadie was among her numerous lovers), that her husband of several years committed suicide the day before the trial to avoid the shame its revelations would bring.[21] Abadie had conceived his criminal exploits with a suspiciously theatrical flair for melodrama, writing his criminal statutes in what was now seen as "*L'Assommoir* style." Had he, as some now claimed, volunteered his services as an extra in *L'Assommoir* "to educate himself"?[22] Did naturalist art merely mirror life, or did it actively serve as a negative model? Certainly, in the "Abadie affair," art and life seemed to merge. When taken by the police to the scene of the crime, Abadie, it was reported, with high spirits "reenacted . . . the murder just as he might have rehearsed it before the Ambigu's stage manager." Evidence indicated that he had carried out the actual slaying with similar aplomb. Yet, while apparently oblivious to the consequences of his actions, Abadie was deeply affected by a murder scene in the theater rendition of *L'Assommoir*. Back at the Ambigu, just hours after killing his former lover, Abadie was so moved by the stabbing of the character Virginie that he had to leave the stage. But if art could seem more real than life, life now intruded upon art: it was reported that, ever since police chief Macé had begun spending evenings in the wings of the Ambigu seeking leads on the previous two murders, the supernumeraries, demoralized by mounting public suspicion directed at them, began to give dispirited performances.[23]

The trial of Abadie and Gille took place in August 1879. Both were found guilty of murdering the tavern-keeper and sentenced to death. The defense submitted an appeal – subsequently denied – and the press took sides. Liberals called for mercy, citing the potential for rehabilitating young people. Abadie's recently published memoirs, the apparently heartfelt "Story of a Man Condemned to Death," seemed to support such a claim. Conservatives argued conversely that the clear absence of morality in those so young revealed their unregeneracy; they

Fig. 49 Police photograph of Michel Knobloch, 1879, Archives de la préfecture de la police, Paris.

Fig. 50 Police photograph of Paul Kirail, 1876, Archives de la préfecture de la police, Paris.

demanded the youths' execution in order to make examples of them.[24] President Grévy's decision of November – to commute the sentences to "forced labor for life" in New Caledonia – was widely unpopular. Conservative writers such as Wolff became incensed, and even the general public expressed its disapproval of leniency to those "unceasingly in revolt against society."[25] Subsequent events reinforced this sentiment.

In December 1879, not long after Grévy's decision, Michel Knobloch (fig. 49), a nineteen-year-old with a history of five previous convictions, came forward and confessed to the murder of the grocer's boy. Implicating both Abadie and a fellow gang member, Paul Kirail (figs. 50 and 51), aged twenty, Knobloch's confession once again raised the perplexing question of the origins of criminality. Knobloch, evidently repentant, linked his criminal behavior to an unhappy childhood and later involvement with the "bad crowd" he had encountered at public dance halls, cafés-concerts, and theaters.[26] Having recently completed a jail sentence for theft, Kirail indicated his desire to reform by enlisting in the army and maintaining an exemplary record.[27] Interest in the problems posed by Kirail and Knobloch was, however, overshadowed by Abadie's confirmation of the worst suspicions about his criminality. Apparently guilty of a second murder, Abadie proved his earlier contrition false when, in May 1880, he released a document entitled "Proposal for the Reform of the Magistrature." Using the pseudonym "Robespierre the younger," he now displayed an implacable contempt for authority, attacking the magistrature in the name of "our young Republic" and "the people."[28] The text read, it was said, like a page from a "socialist newspaper," and seemed to many to bear out the current theory that linked recidivists with anarchists and Communards and that viewed them all as equally unregenerate.[29]

This latest outrage occurred just weeks after the close of the fifth Impressionist exhibition, in which Degas' *Little Dancer* had failed to appear. When the trial finally began, on 27 August 1880, Degas was in court, sketchbook in hand.[30] His presence there is testimony to a fascination that the events of the preceding months had no doubt intensified. Degas' keen interest in the sensational case was due in part to coincidence and to a web of personal connections with it. Just weeks before the first murder trial, the previous August, his close friend Ludovic Halévy, in the company of the artist's critical antagonist Wolff, toured the Parisian underworld – that of Abadie and his gang – with Macé, who, as head of the murder investigation, had become intimately acquainted with the teen-aged criminals. The usually blasé Halévy was shocked by the sordid gin halls, where even young children were subjected to the corrupting "odor of drunkenness and vice." This he confided to his journal and no doubt – along with other details – to Degas.[31] The subsequent connection of Abadie and his gang with the murder of the grocer's boy – and evidently with that of the owner of the magazine shop – brought the "Abadie affair" still closer home. Indeed, the death of the Widow Joubert had caused a great stir in Degas' neighborhood.[32] In contrast to the slaying of the tavern-keeper and the grocer's boy, it was vivid proof, if any were needed, that criminal activity was not confined to the locales that had arguably spawned it. Degas certainly must have often passed the widow's shop; he may even have been a customer. Yet another link between the artist and the "Abadie affair" was forged just weeks before the second trial, when an old friend of Degas, Paul Valpinçon, was named one of four alternate jurors for the August session of the criminal courts in which Abadie, Kirail, and Knobloch were to be tried.[33]

These personal connections to the "Abadie affair" no doubt stimulated and

Fig. 51 Police photograph of Paul Kirail, 1880, Archives de la préfecture de la police, Paris.

Fig. 52 *The Song of the Dog*, ca. 1876–77, transfer lithograph, 14 × 9¼ in. (35.5 × 23.5 cm), The Art Institute of Chicago.

were in turn fed by the artist's long-standing professional interest in issues it raised. For Degas, like his friend the writer Edmond Duranty, believed that modern art should aim to create images of modern life informed by the findings of science.[34] This goal would naturally have drawn the artist to a case that raised questions about the reliability of science, the effects of environment, and the moral purpose of art. Specifically, the theory of innate criminality now being invoked to explain the case was based upon the same notion of a "physiognomic science" that had long intrigued both Duranty and Degas. The developments in anthropology and evolutionary theory on which biological determinism rested were those that interested Degas' circle and had informed Duranty's recent study of physiognomy and gesture in paintings in the Musée du Louvre.[35] And, as works such as *The Song of the Dog* (fig. 52) attest, the artist had already drawn upon aspects of the new physiognomic "science" in his depictions of those very same haunts that the confessed murderer Knobloch now blamed for his criminality. Depicted in the midst of a café-concert performance, the singer Thérésa – as represented by Degas – exhibits the recessive chin, prominent nose and mouth, and low forehead typical of the artist's contemporary depictions of prostitutes. These physiognomic features were intended as legible signs, respectively, of inherent weakness, sensuality, and minimal intelligence.[36] The degree to which the character, if not the appearance, of a teen-aged murderer could have been shaped by exposure to environments such as Thérésa's was a question with a special relevance to Degas. Such places were after all the stuff of much of his art. Yet the artist's viewpoint in these establishments – such as the wings of the theater, where he might have brushed shoulders with an Abadie – was not that of a true participant, but rather that of a voyeur, a detached and worldly observer of the social scene at ease in places where he is not at home. In witnessing the trial, Degas extended this relationship into the criminal courts.

It is not surprising that this case, with its sensational pretrial findings publicized in the newspapers, was an event that attracted an avid audience. There were in fact two publics and a two-class system of access to the courtroom. At the back, outside the enclosure holding the twelve witness benches (see fig. 53, which shows only the first six witness benches), stood the largely working-class public that had queued for hours to secure the limited and highly contested standing-room spaces. The second audience, comprising the full range of Paris "society" – including aristocrats, well-known writers, actors and singers, and fashionable courtesans – gained entry by petitioning the presiding judge for an advance invitation that entitled one to a seat on a witness bench within the enclosure. As reformers never tired of arguing, the presence of the public, which was free, unlike the jury, to react immediately to testimony and, in the case of the "elegant" attendees, often given to the kind of ostentatious dress and self-display otherwise found at the Opéra, transformed a trial into theater; its stage was that space beyond the railing in front of the witness benches, with the magistrates in the center and, on either side and facing each other, the jury in shadow and the defendant bathed in the light that came through the clerestory windows (left and right, respectively, in fig. 53).[37]

Degas' courtroom sketches of the defendants (figs. 54–59) indicate that he sat in the front row of the witness benches, on the jury side. Like the jury, he apparently saw the defendants primarily in profile, since they responded almost exclusively to the officiating judge, or president, turning in their dock toward the bench.[38] Indeed the sketch that shows one of the defendants with his head leaning over the dock (fig. 57) suggests, by its straight-on vantage point, that Degas may

Fig. 53 Anon., *Criminal Courtroom at the Time of its Inauguration*, Musée Carnavalet, ARS NY/SPADEM, Paris.

have obtained special permission to sit with the journalists (one of whom, Jules Claretie, was an acquaintance) in the special press box, adjacent to that of the jury. From a position that was, in any event, privileged, the artist witnessed Knobloch's pathetic lies, Kirail's steadfast denial of guilt, and the shocking behavior with which Abadie repaid the system that had spared him death and now protected him from further punishment. Shielded, by a recent ruling, from capital punishment for a crime preceding that for which he had already received the death sentence, Abadie was freed from his earlier role as repentant. Attuned to the theatrical potential of the proceedings and his star billing, he now seized center stage, playing the untamable outsider by expressing his contempt for the judicial process and disturbing the trial. When the president stated, ironically, "You seem to feel you are being mocked by justice," Abadie replied unhesitatingly with a smile, "Completely, monsieur le Président."[39] This performance ended with the verdict of guilty for all three. Public outrage was not to be fully appeased. Abadie's sentence remained the same, and Kirail, due to extenuating circumstances, was sentenced to forced labor for life. And though Knobloch was given the death penalty, Grévy would again commute it. Indignation ran high.

Fig. 54 and *(facing page bottom)* fig. 57 *Michel Knobloch*, both 1880, black chalk, 6½ × 4¼ in. (16.4 × 10.7 cm), Notebook 33, pp. 15v and 16, private collection.

Given the current climate, Degas' decision to use his courtroom sketches as the basis for the pastel *Criminal Physiognomies* (figs. 45 and 46) he would show at the sixth Impressionist exhibition, scheduled to open eight months after the trial, was a gambit as unexpected as it was potentially dangerous to him as a professional. The artist had treated topical figures before, including entertainers such as Thérésa and the circus acrobat Mademoiselle La La, whom he had depicted hanging by her teeth from a rope suspended from the ceiling of the Cirque Fernando. But the subject of the criminals was loaded. By the fall of 1880, the controversy surrounding the "Abadie affair" was linked so directly to *L'Assommoir* that writers sometimes invoked the novel's characters when discussing Abadie. By contrast, the art Degas had exhibited to date had never been politicized in the same way as Zola's work. Despite the fact that the artist had exhibited images of laundresses in 1874, 1876, and 1879, it was with Daumier, rather than with the creator of

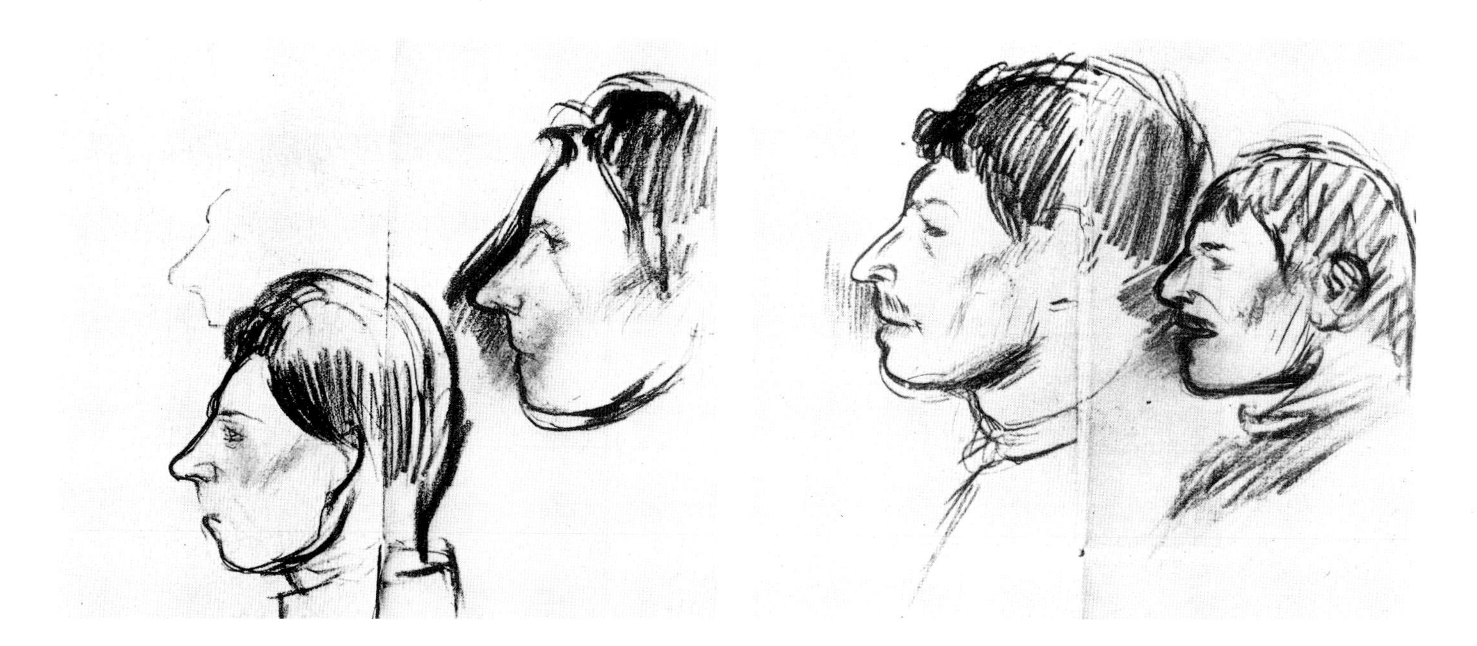

Fig. 55 *(above left)* *Michel Knobloch*, 1880, black chalk, 6½ × 8½ in. (16.4 × 21.4 cm), Notebook 33, p. 10v and 11, private collection.

Fig. 56 *(above right)* *Emile Abadie*, 1880, black chalk, 6½ × 8½ in. (16.4 × 21.4 cm), Notebook 33, p. 5v and 6, private collection.

Gervaise, that critics associated him, reserving such comments as "naturalist sketches in the manner of Zola" for the work of his follower Jean-Louis Forain.[40] Moreover, extensive media coverage had conferred on the criminals a celebrity that they clearly enjoyed and that social critics found reprehensible. The exploitive complicity they decried between publicity-hungry subjects and a sensation-seeking press had recently found a parallel in the world of art. At issue was the notoriety of the novel *Nana* – *L'Assommoir*'s sequel – detailing Gervaise's daughter's career as a courtesan. With great fanfare, it was serialized beginning in October 1879.[41] Did Degas – who, that same year, expressed to an interviewer his absolute "horror [of] publicity," repeatedly insisting, "We are not third-rate play-actors"[42] – really wish to appear to ride the same crest of notoriety as his subjects? Certainly, it could not have escaped his notice that some of the very same writers who had covered the "Abadie affair" – most notably Claretie and Wolff – had reviewed previous Impressionist exhibitions and would, in all likelihood, do so again. Nor could he have been unaware that Claretie, his longtime supporter, had described Abadie and Knobloch as "naturalist" criminals, insofar as they were malefactors without real passion, driven only by a vulgar cynicism.[43] As we have seen, the perception that Degas' depictions of modern life were detached had already earned him the reputation among critics as a somewhat jaded observer of the contemporary scene. By choosing to make and then exhibit the *Criminal Physiognomies,* he placed himself in an even more vulnerable position with respect to this charge.

Despite these clear risks, the type of criticism one might have anticipated failed to materialize, and the response to Degas' pastels was remarkably restrained. Most reviewers recognized the subjects as the defendants in the recent trial. Several who referred to them by name confused their identities. Nonetheless, almost all agreed with Gustave Geffroy on the "singular physiological assurance" with which Degas could "capture . . . these brutal foreheads and jaws, ignite flashes in these dead eyes, [and] convey flesh imprinted with . . . all the stains of vice."[44] No doubt conservative writers perceived Degas' subject as typical of naturalism's penchant for "disagreeable" themes.[45] Claretie and Wolff passed over the portraits altogether, with the latter decrying the artist's general attachment to things "ugly

Fig. 59 *(below)* *Michel Knobloch,* 1880, black chalk, 6½ × 4¼ in. (16.4 × 10.7 cm), Notebook 33, p. 7, private collection.

and horrible," and the former focusing on the empty glass case awaiting its "statuette."[46] Ironically, while the "terrifying realism" perceived in the pastel portraits failed to generate controversy, the "terrible realism" discerned in the sculpture the moment it went on view proved incendiary.[47]

A review by Louis Enault most clearly underscores the disparate forces at play in the response to Degas' pastels and his sculpture. In the same breath that the critic conceded the "force" and "energy" of the *Criminal Physiognomies,* he angrily dismissed the dancer as "quite simply hideous," adding, "Never has the misfortune of adolescence been more sadly represented."[48] To be sure, Degas' sculpture was by no means uniformly perceived in this way. But Enault's judgment would seem to have been more directly applicable to the criminals. In fact it was precisely the issues raised by the "Abadie affair" and their association with naturalism that informed the hostile reactions to the sculpture of the dancer.

The strong response of conservative critics to the work's "ugliness" confirms that it was the moral implications of this so-called homeliness that made the *Little Dancer*, as Mantz acknowledged, so very "disturbing." To such writers, she was a "flower of precocious depravity," presenting a "face marked by the hateful promise of every vice," her low forehead and lips "bearing the signs of a . . . profoundly heinous character."[49] Such phrases echo the language of articles about Abadie, Kirail, and Knobloch. In comparing the dancer to a "monkey" and an "Aztec" – both then regarded as synonymous with early stages of human evolution – the critic Elie de Mont underscored the atavism that biological determinists associated with innate criminality.[50] Self-absorbed, the *Little Dancer* seemed, like the criminals, "bestial," at once marked by base instincts and lacking the intelligence – or higher consciousness – to temper them.[51]

Invoking another aspect of the current debate on criminality, several reviewers alluded to the social pathology that linked the *Little Dancer* to deviants such as Abadie, Kirail, and Knobloch. In suggesting that she be preserved in a "bottle of spirits," de Mont evoked specimens like those currently on view at the Musée Dupuytren, Paris. It was to this display of human pathology, declared the hostile reviewer for *La France nouvelle,* that the dancer should be transported following the exhibition.[52] The portraits of celebrated murderers and their victims, as well as other figures illustrating various maladies, exhibited in glass cases in such museums, were frequently made of wax and incorporated actual clothing and wigs (figs. 60 and 61). The *Little Dancer* was also modeled in wax and, when exhibited in 1881, wore a wig of genuine hair and actual clothing. This prompted Henri Trianon to observe that Degas' "monster" was better suited to a "museum of zoology, anthropology, or physiology" than to a museum of art. He was alluding to installations like those in the large ethnographic exhibition in Paris of 1878 and the city's recently inaugurated Musée d'ethnographie du Trocadéro (fig. 62).[53] Clearly, the materials Degas employed in the *Little Dancer* not only achieved startling realism but endowed the figure with the quasi-scientific status of a specimen.

Why, then, did the audience of 1881 find the *Little Dancer* more threatening than images of criminals only recently at large? The "precocious depravity" reviewers saw in her was a future of prostitution. Hence the reported reaction of bourgeois fathers on first viewing Degas' sculpture: "Pray Heaven that my daughter doesn't become a *sauteuse.*"[54] The French word *sauteuse* means not only one who leaps (as it applies to the dance) but is also a slang expression for a whore, who jumps from man to man. The problems of unlicensed, and hence

Fig. 60 Wax mannequins of murderers and their victims, from the Musée Dupuytren, late nineteenth century, courtesy Roger-Viollet, Paris.

Fig. 58 *(facing page top)* *Emile Abadie,* 1880, black chalk, $6\frac{1}{2} \times 4\frac{1}{4}$ in. (16.4 × 10.7 cm), Notebook 33, p. 14, private collection.

Fig. 61 Wax mannequin showing female organs, from the Musée Dupuytren, late nineteenth century, courtesy Roger-Viollet, Paris.

uncontrolled, prostitution figured largely in the contemporary preoccupation with juvenile criminality.[55] As one commentator noted, "No social being is less protected than the young Parisian girl – by laws, regulations, and social customs."[56] Prone to vice by heredity – as the low forehead, flattened face, and protruding jaw were thought to reveal – the little dancer was involved in a profession that, it was believed, would inevitably lead to another. Nurtured in what one writer called the "depths of the dance schools," the little dancer, predicted a second, would soon ripen on the "theater's espaliers" into a "woman . . . for whom diplomats will make fools of themselves."[57]

The subject was by no means new to art or literature. For example, Degas' friend Halévy published a series of short stories between 1870 and 1880 featuring the "Cardinal family," a backstage mother and her two daughters, upwardly mobile young Opéra dancers. Though criticized as "salacious" in the *Grand Dictionnaire universel du XIXème siècle,* Halévy's light-hearted but pointed satires enjoyed enormous popularity. They appealed to Degas, who executed a series of illustrations of them (cats. 5 and 6), several of which he exhibited in 1877, at the third Impressionist exhibition, where they were admired by Claretie.[58] Very different in tone, however, was Zola's *Nana,* the latest text on the subject of venality and female availability in the theater's "pestilential atmosphere." *Nana* was currently in its stage production at the Théâtre de l'Ambigu. Indeed, it was because they saw the *Little Dancer* as a "little Nana" that the sculpture's detractors were so unsettled.[59] Like the young girl Zola had first introduced in *L'Assommoir,* the little dancer was clearly born of bad stock and subject to a corrupt environment. And like Gervaise's daughter at the end of the first novel, the dancer stood poised on the threshold of the life of depravity that became the subject of *Nana.*

Fig. 62 Wax mannequin of a native of Oceania, ca. 1880–95, formerly in the Musée d'ethnographie du Trocadéro, courtesy of the Photothèque, Musée de l'homme, Paris.

In Zola's *femme fatale,* Wolff and other conservatives perceived the same unconscious, malevolent force they discerned in Abadie and his gang.[60] Some of these same critics had earlier defended Zola's sordid depiction of working-class life in *L'Assommoir,* because they recognized the legitimacy of the writer's claim that his work embodied "morality in action."[61] However, in Nana's revenge on the upper classes for the deprivation of her youth, which took the form of sexual "reprisals," critics believed Zola's mission had finally been overwhelmed by his penchant for assaulting his reader with sensational and "nauseating details" of "every kind of disgrace." Chief among these was Nana's corruption of the established social order with the mores of backstage life, "where," fulminated Wolff, "nothing is left of station, birth, decency, or anything that governs the world." Because of what they perceived as its unflattering and cynical picture of contemporary France, Wolff and others repudiated *Nana* for not fulfilling the basic condition under which they could tolerate naturalism: that the ugliness depicted be justified by moral "instruction."[62]

Those who dismissed the *Little Dancer* as "hideous" considered her, like Nana, a "disgrace" to French society, similarly unredeemed by larger purpose. More thoughtful critics however detected profound meaning in the sculpture, as well as its signification of a major shift in Degas' work. Claretie, who discussed the figure by pairing it with the "gripping . . . profiles of murderers" he had previously passed over, concluded that Degas' brand of naturalism was at once "engaging [and] troubling." Mantz pushed this idea further. Seeing the dancer's "ugliness" as reflecting an "intention dictated by the spirit of a philosopher à la Baudelaire," the critic linked the maker of the "flower of precocious depravity" to the author of the *Fleurs du mal* (*Flowers of Evil*), who had famously declared ugliness an essential ingredient of beauty. Moreover, the *Little Dancer*'s ugliness was "instructive," the "intellectual result" of naturalism in the hands of an artist who it seemed was "without doubt a moralist."[63]

* * *

Degas a moralist? Did he mean the *Little Dancer* to be understood in this way? Critical responses do not, of course, constitute proof of artistic intention. But we shall see, in fashioning the *Criminal Physiognomies* and the *Little Dancer* and then exhibiting them together, that the artist appears quite consciously to have aimed to place his art at the intersection of several topical discourses. While naturalism was ostensibly the most critical of these, the reactions the pastels and sculpture engendered were determined by other, underlying concerns: the works each raised the specter of behavioral pathology in a classed society, and each did so with striking differences.

The threat posed by Abadie, Kirail, and Knobloch ultimately was contained by a judicial system that, on every level, Degas' *Criminal Physiognomies* can be seen to reinforce. In effect, the artist invested these pastel portraits with visual truths more ideological than perceptual. His strategy – one so blatant it could hardly have been unconscious – reveals itself in comparing the eight notebook sketches he made of the criminals in court with their police photographs (figs. 47, 49–51) and his subsequent pastel portraits (figs. 45 and 46). Quite simply – and unexpectedly – they are difficult to match up.

The high forehead, firm jaw, straight nose, and thin down-turned mouth identify the portrait on page sixteen of Degas' notebook (fig. 57) with the photograph of Knobloch (see fig. 49). On the facing page (fig. 54), Degas studied him in profile, but now slightly lowered the forehead and indicated potential adjustments to the nose and jawline. The two profiles on the verso of page ten and on page eleven (fig. 55) also depict Knobloch, with similar features and a crown of thick hair. In turn, the strong, thick nose, full lips, low forehead, and heavy eyebrows of the figure sketched on page fourteen (fig. 58) apparently indicate Abadie (see fig. 47).

The three remaining notebook sketches (figs. 56 and 59) are more difficult to match with the photographs. The short neck and absence of a part in the hair in the two profiles on the verso of page five and on page six (fig. 56) point to Abadie. However, the long, thin nose in the profile at the far left suggests Kirail (see figs. 50 and 51). Similarly, although the full hair of the portrait on page seven (fig. 59) suggests that it is another study of Knobloch, the blunt, stubbed nose and the indication of a mustache correspond to neither his photograph nor description in the police files.

These three problematic sketches are, however, quite easy to match up with the pastel portraits Degas made subsequently. Clearly, all relate to the double portrait (fig. 46): the sketch of the single profile (fig. 59) to the figure on the right; the two others (fig. 56) to that on the left. The figures in the pastel can in turn be identified by deduction. The portrait at the right must be of Knobloch, since the hair color bears out his nickname "le Roquin" ("Red"). Yet, following his sketchbook idea (fig. 54), Degas masked the resemblance by radically altering the nose, weakening the jaw, and lowering the forehead. The defendant in front of Knobloch, with the short, wide neck and low forehead, must be Abadie, although with smaller, more hooded eyes and looking considerably leaner and older than in his photograph. This identification is confirmed by a process of elimination; for the single figure in the second pastel (fig. 45), with his high neck, long nose, and short hair parted at left, could only be Kirail (see figs. 50 and 51).

The representational liberties Degas took with his subjects in the pastels indicate his interest in creating characterological portraits. For the artist adjusted the features of the murderers in ways that, according to contemporary indices of criminal anthropology, more readily yielded a "scientific," physiognomic indication of what was called their "moral mechanism."[64] Thus the weak, indecisive character Knobloch had revealed during his testimony was better expressed by a low forehead and weak chin; his new aquiline nose was a clue to his murderous tendencies.[65] Similarly, the changes Degas introduced into his portraits of Abadie and Kirail brought them in line with the journalistic accounts that described Abadie for one as possessing a "physiognomy as bestial and repulsive . . . as any human physiognomy can be."[66]

The adjustments Degas made had the soothing effect of negating the initially perplexing fact that, as we have seen, not every one of the defendants appeared clearly recognizable as a criminal type. Moreover, by making the three criminals appear older, the artist effectively reduced the disturbing contrast between their tender youth and their hardened viciousness. The title he chose for the works – *Criminal Physiognomies* – implicitly concedes the existence of a generic criminal type that can be classified visually: a biologically determined "race of Abadies and Knoblochs," as critics such as Claretie asserted.[67] Such efforts conspired to make the "Abadie affair" seem less troubling than it had in fact first appeared.

Similarly, Degas composed his portraits to assuage rather than exacerbate anxieties raised by the case. For he represented all three murderers securely within the embrace of the criminal system, in one instance seated behind the barrier enclosing the prisoner's dock (fig. 46) and in both accompanied by representatives

Fig. 63 *Head of a Man* (Emile Abadie), ca. 1880–81, pastel, 18⅛ × 23⅝ in. (46 × 60 cm), location unknown.

of the court (figs. 45 and 46). In addition, Degas depicted them in the strict profile view that both traditional and contemporary literature on physiognomy agreed provides the fullest reading of characterological information. It was precisely for this reason that criminologist Alphonse Bertillon was currently introducing profile views into police photography as part of the "anthropometric system" designed to make the identification of recidivists such as Abadie into a "science" and so to better control and limit criminal activity.[68]

In summary, the evidence provided by the two *Criminal Physiognomies* would seem to indicate that he sought to represent a highly topical and obviously naturalist subject in a manner that appeared to inscribe a position on the issues it raised. There was, by no means, unanimity in France regarding the validity of a theory of visibly stigmatized, "born criminals." While the larger scientific community might have preferred a sociological to a biological explanation for crime, the press, in reporting cases such as this, dwelt on visual characteristics, as did, among others, forensic psychiatrists and conservative critics like Wolff.[69] In presenting and classifying the criminals as he did, Degas adopted a journalistic approach to his subjects; he appears to have subscribed to the essentially conservative view of criminality as innate and visibly legible, to have appropriated the systems available for its physical and ideological containment, and ultimately to have reflected a widespread attitude to these specific perpetrators and their punishment. Implied judgment is particularly striking in a third pastel (fig. 63), which Degas made after his courtroom sketches (see fig. 58). Although this sheet in fact depicts Abadie leaning over the enclosure of the prisoner's dock, both the composition and the man's expression, his eyes half-closed and mouth slightly open, create the feeling of an execution – the murderer, his head on the guillotine block, receives the punishment that many regretted he had escaped.

Degas did not exhibit this pastel. In the two he showed, he in fact incorporated compositional elements that potentially preclude a strict reading of law and order: the cropped toque of the defense lawyer behind Knobloch (fig. 45) and the constable's epaulette in front of Abadie (fig. 46). The ambiguity of these forms troubled some reviewers. Critics for the right-wing periodicals *La France nouvelle* and *La Civilisation* wondered whether Degas might not himself be making light of justice.[70] Even Paul Cézanne's friend Antony Valabrègue found the meaning of these touches "somewhat difficult to understand" and "fantastic, in the manner of Edgar Allan Poe." His conclusion that they were intended to be "humorous" seems apt.[71] The juxtaposition of the tilted toque and the dominant, upright figure of Kirail, proudly looking in the other direction, alludes to the continuing arrogance of some of the defendants and the way in which they disrupted the proceedings, "making a game. . . of justice."[72] Similarly, the epaulette under Abadie's nose – which Elie de Mont interpreted as a mushroom – can also be seen as a bone and thus as an ironic reference to Abadie's reputed ferocity and primitive instincts. Yet while suggestively ironic, these compositional touches failed to seriously provoke the eighteen critics who commented on the criminal physiognomies or to dissuade them from admiring the "science" of Degas' representations.

In conceiving the *Little Dancer*, Degas adopted similar strategies. For his sculpture, he chose as model a young dancer whose background was not unlike that of Abadie and his gang: Marie van Goethem was the daughter of a laundress, and her sister was later to find work in the theater as an extra. The artist's intent to emphasize the biological connections between the dancer and the only slightly older juvenile criminals emerges clearly in drawings he made of her in preparation for his sculpture (see cats. 40 and 43). Here his experimentation with the facial features, making telling adjustments to the slope of her forehead and the jut of her jawbone, reveals the artist's desire to achieve a Neanderthal-like appearance (see cat. 43, lower right) and thereby to suggest a potentially "criminal" atavism. In so doing, Degas gave Abadie and his followers a younger sister. For the public in 1881, this could only have implied guilt by association.

It was the recognition of their affiliation that precipitated the outcry. While Degas' representations of Abadie, Kirail, and Knobloch raised questions about criminal responsibility, the "precocious decadence" of these three had nonetheless been contained, as Degas' compositions so artfully imply. A "little Nana" however was far more dangerous. For, as reviewers recognized, a career as a courtesan depended on complicity between "the depravity of the people" and "aristocratic corruption," a conspiracy between the upper and lower classes that shielded the Nanas from the law, allowing their "vices" to flourish unchecked.[73]

The threat to the ethical and social order that Nana and the *Little Dancer* symbolized was at the heart of the contemporary debate surrounding prostitution. At this time, discussion was particularly heated concerning the issue of regulationism, the "city-wide, police-administered system designed to control an officially tolerated population of prostitutes." On the one hand, abolitionists cited the tyrannies involved in a system of forced identification, whose collapse by 1880 seemed imminent in any event. On the other, neo-regulationists pointed to the need to stop the precipitous rise of "clandestine" prostitution, which they regarded as an invisible contagion that, if insufficiently checked, would endanger the entire society.[74]

Issues of visibility and containment were central to the neo-regulationist agenda. The regulationist apparatus sought to convert every *insoumise* – a prostitute working outside police control, either on the streets or, if more successful like Nana, kept by a series of powerful men – into a *soumise,* a prostitute under police control, registered as a resident of a brothel *(fille de maison)* or as an independent *(fille en carte).* Understandably, regulationists had long been eager to determine a distinctive set of physical characteristics linked to sexual deviancy that would identify the prostitute population. However, all attempts to classify prostitutes by elements of their physical appearance had basically failed, and therewith prospects for a theory linking sexual deviancy to physiological determinism. As chief of police Gustave Macé was later to note in a book based on his professional experiences, prostitutes looked like average women: "Not one of them was born for this line of work, and it is only out of need that they exercise this repugnant profession. Their moral corruption is rarely complete."[75]

Both in fashioning and exhibiting his *Little Dancer,* Degas played with and to the fears surrounding unregulated prostitution. First, his exhibit provocatively functioned as a kind of visual regulationism. His pastel portraits, obvious images of topical criminality, created a context in which the identity of the *Little Dancer* became highly and insistently readable. But while the threat was thus revealed, it was not removed. Unlike the images of dancers in Degas' paintings and works on paper, the figure is not part of a narrative that explains and delimits her. Quite the opposite. Freestanding, unnervingly lifelike, and set in the center of the gallery, the *Little Dancer* was disturbing precisely because the figure seems oblivious to what surrounds her and to the fact that she is, in a literal sense, out of context. For while upper-class males were accustomed to seek out illicit female companionship backstage at the Opéra (cats. 5 and 6), these same men would not expect to be confronted by one of them in the different social context of the art exhibition.

Here she was dangerous. Raising the specter of their complicity in her career, and doing so in mixed company that included proper bourgeois wives and daughters, the *Little Dancer* produced the intense anxiety reflected in the critics' railings about loosening morals and threats to the social order.

Degas' installation of the 1881 exhibition can be seen as theater. The *Criminal Physiognomies* were on view, as we noted above, when the exhibition opened, setting the stage for the subsequent appearance of the sculpture. When it arrived, Abadie and his cohorts, only recently the principles in a court drama, were overshadowed by the *Little Dancer.* "Displayed in prime position at the center of one of the galleries,"[76] she became a star and, like Zola's Nana, the center of controversy. Was this a case of brilliant stage management or rather simply an accident? Were the *Criminal Physiognomies* conceived as a foil? With the *Little Dancer,* was Degas courting a *succès de scandale,* or was his intention moralistic? In order to answer these questions, it is necessary to consider the artist's plans for the exhibition of the *Little Dancer,* as well as other works he made that are related to it.

The signs that Degas willfully inscribed on the faces of the criminals and, to a lesser extent, on that of the dancer raise the question of the degree to which he really embraced physiognomic science. In a series of monotypes made several years earlier of prostitutes in whorehouses, the artist had relied "on the predictability and prejudice of physiognomic codes and stereotypes," endowing the brothels' inhabitants with caricatured faces that, like Thérésa's (see fig. 52), underscore their animal – and potentially criminal – natures. Nevertheless, as Hollis Clayson convincingly demonstrated, Degas' monotypes were also "politically and aesthetically critical, . . . proposing that Parisian brothels were a brutalized and brutalizing ghetto." Rife with internal contradictions that suggest the artist's ambivalence regarding his subject, the monotypes deal with a "primitive form of sexual commerce" quite different from that in the world of *Nana.* In this regard, Degas' subject was, as Clayson observed, somewhat old-fashioned, bypassing the most recent and now predominant form of prostitution, the "stylized seduction" offered by clandestine trafficking, such as that practiced by Zola's protagonist.[77] By contrast Degas' *Little Dancer* can be seen as responsive to the social complexity he had avoided in the series of brothel monotypes. The young dancer's expression, which can also be read as proud, determined, even defiant, is ultimately too layered, too human, to illustrate a thesis postulating determinism based on the formative role of nature and/or nurture.

Duranty, whose views paralleled Degas' on many scores, remained skeptical that physiognomy would ever become a "true science" and questioned the notion that "hereditary appearance" necessarily indicated characterological make-up.[78] Indeed, Degas had long had personal reasons to question current notions of biological determinism and the racial rankings it was seen to justify. For, as has only recently been revealed, the artist had American relatives – two of his mother's first cousins, sons of her paternal uncle – who were "free men of color." Schooled in France, both Rillieux brothers had distinguished careers, particularly Norbert, an engineer whose inventions revolutionized the sugar industry. By the 1860s, he had left New Orleans to live in Paris, where he died at age eighty-nine in 1894. Given Degas' close ties to the New Orleans branch of his family, he must have known, or at least known about, his illustrious black cousins. Silence on this score suggests family embarrassment at miscegenation. Degas' failure to depict the black population of New Orleans, despite his attraction to it during his stay in Louisiana in 1872–73, might have been related to his own heightened sensitivity to issues of race.[79] Nonetheless, when, six years after his return from North

Fig. 64 *Schoolgirl*, ca. 1880–81, bronze, 10½ in. (26.6 cm), Virginia Museum of Fine Arts, Richmond, Virginia.

America, he depicted the mulatto acrobat Mademoiselle La La, Degas posed the figure suggestively and gave her outstretched arms dark, furlike shadows, seemingly hinting at her atavism.

But if the artist remained ambivalent on the subject of heredity, other works related to the *Little Dancer*, as well as the sculpture's display, indicate that he shared Duranty's belief that "the discipline of education" can control even "bad instincts."[80] The *Schoolgirl* (fig. 64), a sculptural idea contemporary with the *Little Dancer,* appears to embody this idea. That the two figures have similar faces links them in the same way that the dancer and the images of the criminals are related. The appearance of the schoolgirl suggests that the dancer's criminality was not inevitable and that, if educated properly, she might have quite a different future.

That education for young, lower-class women could indeed provide them with a way to avoid the economic traps that forced so many into prostitution was in fact a key concern for the French feminist movement in the late 1870s. Along with resolutions calling for "equal pay for equal work" and the abolition of state-regulated prostitution, the demand for equal education for both sexes had been part of the program of reforms issued by the First International Feminist Congress, held in Paris in July 1878.[81] This liberal feminist agenda was helped the following year, when sympathetic Republicans gained control of the senate and the presidency. The Camille Sée Law, passed in 1880, authorized the establishment of secondary schools for girls (albeit with a curriculum that would not prepare them for baccalaureate exams). Produced at this moment, Degas' two sculptures speak to and reflect the potential of adolescent females.

As Norma Broude showed, a direct link between Degas and the newly visible feminist movement in France is found in Diego Martelli, an Italian critic who was Degas' close friend and an enthusiastic supporter of the Impressionists. During the year Martelli spent in Paris, beginning in April 1878, he became involved in feminist issues, covering the Feminist Congress for an Italian newspaper. The ambivalence and anxiety his articles revealed were, during the course of his stay, transformed into committed support of the feminist program of social and legal reform, as an article on divorce laws, which he wrote after his return to Italy in April 1879, makes clear. Degas, whose intimacy with Martelli during his Paris stay is attested by the two major portraits he painted of him, was no doubt aware of his friend's evolving ideas regarding the illusions and hypocrisies of patriarchal authority.[82]

That Degas, at the very least, became sensitized to principles of feminism, can be discerned in changes he made at this time to his early painting *Young Spartan Girls Challenging the Boys.* In a public lecture on Impressionism given in Italy after he left Paris, Martelli referred to this composition. Describing its subject as "Spartan girls who challenge boys to the race that decided, in accordance with the law of those people, their submission," the critic declared that Degas had left the painting "unfinished" because he was too "modern in every respect" to deal with an historicizing subject that lacked the "pulse of real life." Martelli's observations – informed, it would seem, by the artist himself – apply to the canvas now in The Art Institute of Chicago (fig. 65), which is both unfinished and rooted in the classical tradition. His remarks, however, do not apply to the picture he was in fact discussing: a second version, now in the National Gallery, London (fig. 66). This is because, as X-rays corroborate, Degas reworked this painting, most importantly recasting the physiognomies of the youths so that they appear more like contemporary Parisians than antique statuary. He must have done this sometime between Martelli's departure, in April 1879, and the preparation of the catalogue

Fig. 65 *Young Spartans*, 1860, oil on canvas, 38½ × 55⅛ in. (97.8 × 140 cm), The Art Institute of Chicago, Charles H. and Mary F. S. Worcester Collection.

for the 1880 Impressionist exhibition, in which he revealed his intention to put this work on display.[83]

Degas carried out these revisions, Broude argued, as a result of the influence of Martelli on the subject of sexual inequality and precisely because he now discovered in this historical theme the "pulse of real life" that he had previously found lacking. He recognized that the unusual egalitarian training which, at least for a moment, allowed Spartan girls to compete on equal ground with boys, "might serve as a metaphor and as a reflection of the relationship betweeen the sexes in contemporary European society."[84] Knowing that Degas originally intended to show the painting in which he revised his early ideas along with the sculpture that embodied his most current thinking makes this argument all the more persuasive.

Pairing the *Little Dancer* with the *Young Spartans* would have created a scenario that might likewise have been accomplished had he shown it with the *Schoolgirl*. By juxtaposing his recent sculpture with his revised, early history painting, Degas would have provocatively emphasized the similarities and differences between his two depictions of adolescence by relying on analogies of form and content as a signaling device. The pose of the dancer relates to that of the little Spartan girl at the extreme left of the painting – an affiliation underscored by the wax model of the nude ballerina (fig. 72) that preceded the clothed version. Even more striking is the family resemblance between the "working-class mugs" that Degas gave to the Spartan youths (fig. 67) and the much discussed "bestial mugs" reviewers discerned in the *Little Dancer* and in the *Criminal Physiognomies*.

Moreover, there are telling parallels in their various activities. The young Spartans, evidently engaged in courtship rites, represent the future of a society that epitomized exemplary social ideals. In Plutarch, Degas had read that, to ensure the continued health of the race, Spartan adolescents exercised publicly in a state of nakedness that signified "complete probity, without any stimulation or corruption whatsoever."[85] By contrast, as determinists would have had it, Degas' young

Fig. 66 *Young Spartans*, 1860–62, reworked ca. 1880, oil on canvas, 42⅞ x 60⅝ in. (109 x 154 cm), National Gallery, London.

dancer, though clothed, participates in another, and very different, courtship ritual. The only discipline she experiences is found in the physical rigors of the dance class, which, in the end, will lead not only to her moral dissolution but to that of society at large. Yet the dancer's physical resemblance to the young Spartans suggests that their potential is in fact identical and that upbringing, not heredity, will prove to be the strongest determinant of their destinies.

However, Degas abandoned his plan to exhibit the *Little Dancer* along with the *Young Spartans*. Why he did so is impossible to determine exactly. Certainly, his decision the following year to exhibit the sculpture with the *Criminal Physiognomies* reflects a similar strategy of provocative counterpoint. But this time, the significance of one of the two elements – the criminals – was so overtly topical as virtually to ensure a legibility that an historical subject such as the *Young Spartans* could by no means guarantee. Moreover, the pairing Degas opted for in 1881 was less a study of contrast than of degree: putting the young dancer in the company of Abadie and his cohorts produced a picture of adolescence particularly disquieting to an audience that regarded the German victory of 1870 as the result of the superior education of Prussian youth. The moral and civic training at the heart of the new primary education developed by the Third Republic reflected the spirit of Zola's dictum that "France will be what the primary teacher makes it."[86] Degas' planned exhibition for 1880 suggested a similar point of view. The pairing that occurred in 1881 however was a more ambiguous and seemingly more pessimistic comment on contemporary French society. It was disturbing – and it could hardly be misconstrued to reflect the *philosophie gaie* that some had earlier detected in Degas' work.

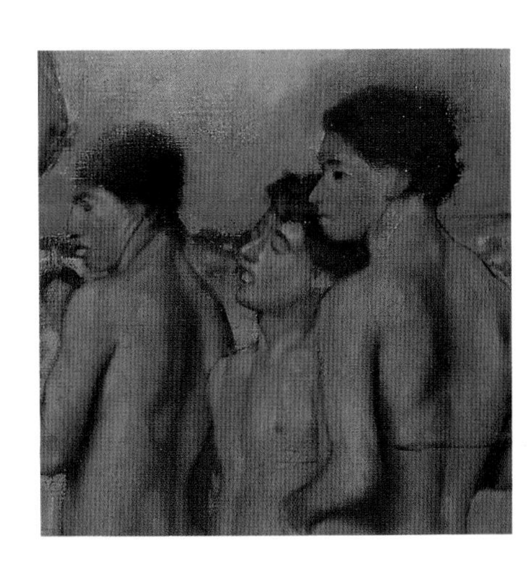

The shift in perception of Degas' art that the 1881 exhibition occasioned is revealed in one reviewer's observation that the artist had renounced the "little world of dancers," the backstage life that Degas had so often depicted and that was the focus of Halévy's *Famille Cardinal* stories.[87] Interestingly, Halévy was actively distancing himself from the tenor of this past production. Published in 1882, his new novel, *L'Abbé Constantin,* presented such a resolutely positive picture of family life that its author was described as having served up "angels in a sauce of virtue"; the book's great success in part derived from the public's fascination that this sentimental novel came from the pen of "the historian of the Cardinal family."[88] Degas' response to his friend's latest work was swift and cutting. As Halévy recorded in his journal, "My friend Degas is indignant about *L'Abbé Constantin,* nauseated would be more like it. He is disgusted with all that virtue, with all that elegance. He said insulting things to me this morning. [It seems] I must always do things like *Madame Cardinal,* dry little things, satirical, skeptical, ironic, without heart, without emotion."[89]

Degas' reaction is instructive with regard to his own ambitions. Criticized for his past production in the very terms that Halévy now applied to his own previous writing, the artist clearly disdained the kind of easy about-face by which his friend had attempted to start afresh. His current work also charted new territory. But to label it that of a "moralist," as did Mantz, was to simplify its expressive intent to the kind of before-and-after sermonizing of a pair of canvases, *Splendor* and *Misery,* that Ernst Ange Duez had shown, to considerable acclaim, at the Salon of 1874. Contrasting, in the first, an elegantly dressed prostitute in her prime, with, in the other, the aged, "hideous ragpicker" she will become, Duez fashioned what Mantz termed "a very moral diptych . . . strongly imbued with literature" – that is to say, highly legible as a narrative.[90] While Degas' eloquent pairing of the *Little Dancer* and *Criminal Physiognomies* may have made the sculpture appear more readable, the juxtaposition was more suggestive and complex. For although the meaning of the pastels seems relatively fixed, the *Little Dancer* took on different expressive meanings by virtue of the company it kept. At once a wry enactment of the formative influences of environment, the sculpture's quite literal ambitendency can be seen to reflect the artist's own. Although the work appears to respond to the issues of the day, it would be a mistake to "attempt to attribute to Degas himself anything more than the confusion and ambivalence that were probably felt by most of the men of his generation toward the feminist movement" or, for that matter, the range of other issues refracted in his art.[91] At the time he was crafting his *Little Dancer,* female behavior seemed less governable and female "morality" less stable than ever before. That his sculpture was perceived to touch upon these issues is clear from the anxiety and anger of the critics; and that Degas sought to provoke – challenging his male counterparts as his young Spartan girls did theirs – is highly likely as well.

In contrast to Halévy, Degas did not aspire to clarity, which in truth was not an element of the modern world he sought to represent. The "Abadie affair" – unnerving precisely because it seemed to blur the boundaries between life and art and threw into doubt neat scientific answers to messy questions – was an apt metaphor for the modern experience. Similarly, Degas' *Little Dancer* challenges the "truth" of our perceptions, our assumptions about the nature of class, and the validity of traditional aesthetic canons. At once thoughtful and disturbing, the sculpture, as exhibited in 1881, prompted contemporaries to reappraise Degas' treatment of modern life. As Gustave Geffroy concluded, the images of "boulevard corners and cafés, the backstages of theaters" that Degas had exhibited previously "indicate a thinker concerned with the [contrast between] the deceptive surfaces and seamy undersides of Parisian life."[92] With the *Criminal Physiognomies* and the *Little Dancer Aged Fourteen,* Degas stripped away much of the glitter of "la vie moderne," revealing more of its sinister aspects, as well as his own deep involvement with the issues of his time.

5 *LITTLE DANCER AGED FOURTEEN*: THE SEARCH FOR THE LOST *MODÈLE*

Arthur Beale

FOREWORD

My interest in and initial research on Degas sculpture began nearly three decades ago at Harvard University's Fogg Art Museum, where I was employed as a young conservator. Although my background was principally in the applied arts, I found myself in a teaching museum surrounded by graduate students in art history who expected to gain knowledge through our association. To my surprise and delight, I quickly discovered that my traditional training in how to make art, particularly sculpture, allowed me to make technical observations that were new and useful to my scholarly associates. In addition, as a conservator I had just learned in my apprenticeship training at the Fogg about the range of scientific tools available that could give depth to a technical examination producing factual data that enriched understanding of both object and artist. As my own interests began to focus on the conservation of three-dimensional objects, I increasingly found myself engaged in the projects and questions generated by the Ph.D. candidates whose thesis topics involved antiquities or decorative arts and sculpture. These ranged from ancient Greece to China to Europe and from 600 B.C. to the twentieth century. The student whose work engaged me the most and who had a significant influence on my future research endeavors was Charles Millard. His thesis, which was published in 1976 by Princeton University Press as a book entitled *The Sculpture of Edgar Degas,* remains today one of the definitive sources on the subject.

In the fall of 1971, I took a month-long "grand tour" to Europe to study nineteenth-century sculptors, their technologies, and foundry practice. During the first part of the trip in England and France, I was accompanied by Charles Millard, who was doing his own research, and in the second part in Italy, by the late David Rinne, who was my apprentice at the time. Both of these men helped compensate for my linguistic shortcomings. One of the highlights of the adventure was a visit to a remote mountain village in northern Italy, where Millard understood that the master foundryman Albino Palazzolo, who was largely responsible for the posthumous translation into bronze of Degas' sculpture, now lived in retirement. As luck would have it, David Rinne and I located him and had a brief conversation that was not as useful as I would have hoped, because of his advanced years and because of a very protective but charming son, Yvon, who occupied most of our time there. We did learn, however, that Yvon intended to publish a book on his father's work based in part on documents his father had from his years at the A. A. Hébrard foundry in Paris. He also indicated that his father had some of his own bronze casts of Degas sculpture with distinct

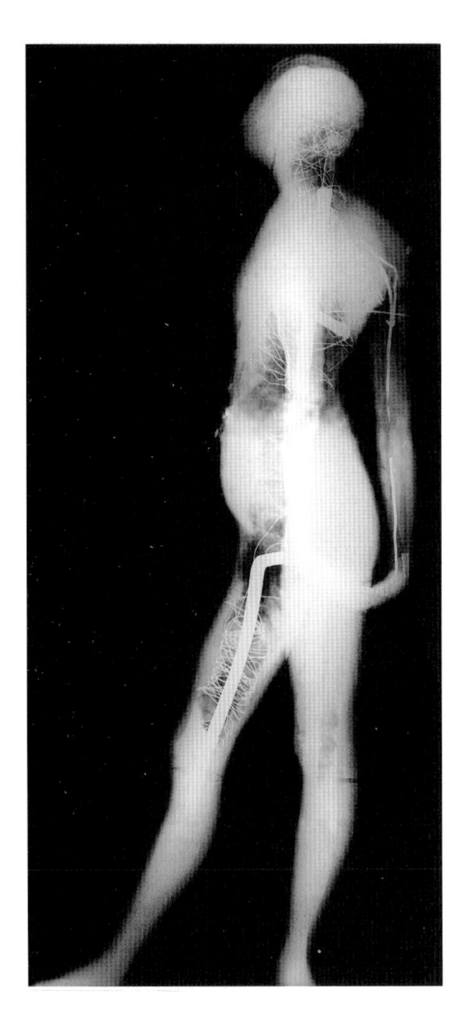

Fig. 68 X-radiograph of wax original *Little Dancer Aged Fourteen*, Collection of Mr. and Mrs. Paul Mellon, Upperville, Virginia.

markings.[1] Seven years later I was sent one of these for examination by a private collector.[2]

At Millard's suggestion, and with the permission and support of Paul Mellon and officials at the National Gallery of Art in Washington, in the spring of 1972, I undertook the first technical study of Degas' original sculptural models, including *Little Dancer Aged Fourteen*, which is principally made of wax (p. viii). Working with David Rinne, I made X-radiographs of a number of the original Degas sculptures in Mr. Mellon's Virginia home in order better to understand Degas' working methods and materials including armature constructions (fig. 68). Some of the observations I made in the course of this study were passed on to Charles Millard who, in turn, included them in his book. At the time we discussed doing a joint publication and then, as Millard noted in his preface, we decided that I would later publish the technical investigation separately. Career focus and other events forestalled that effort, but my research sporadically continued.

The next milestone in my career-long interest in Degas sculpture came in 1976, when the basement storeroom of the founder who employed Albino Palazzolo, A. A. Hébrard, yielded up its second treasure-trove. The first had been revealed in 1955 in the form of Degas' original wax and plasticine models, which were thought to have been destroyed at the time of the casting. They were sold to Paul Mellon through M. Knoedler and Co., Inc., the following year. As it turned out, only four sculptures seem to have been lost in the casting or during the two decades that preceded their reemergence. The second discovery to hit the art market after twenty-two more years passed was the existence of a complete set of unique bronze *modèles,* created by Palazzolo to protect the fragile originals by serving as a durable pattern from which to make molds for the subsequent bronze series of twenty-two each**,** lettered A through T or marked "HER" and "HER.D." These extraordinary bronzes were purchased in 1977 by Norton Simon from the Lefevre Gallery, London, for his museum in Pasadena, California. Charles Millard and I had the privilege of advising Simon on the purchase.

I had first learned of the existence of these bronzes seven years earlier when Millard excitedly related in a letter to me what he had learned from Mme. Hébrard and that she had shown him a number of bronze casts marked "modèle," part of a complete master set she had.[3] However, I did not realize the significance of these bronzes until my continuing research in nineteenth-century sculpture reproductive techniques revealed that the French foundries producing bronze multiples of the work of Jean-Baptiste Carpeaux and Antoine-Louis Barye, among others, also used durable, high quality bronze models as masters for production molds. I published this work in 1975 in a book edited by Jeanne L. Wasserman entitled *Metamorphoses in Nineteenth Century Sculpture*.

I was rewarded by Mr. Simon for my advice by the loan of the sculptures to the Fogg Art Museum for several months so that I could do an in-depth study and so they could be exhibited at the Fogg (fig. 69). As with my previous research efforts on Degas, serious publication proposals were generated but did not come to fruition. I did, however, share my findings with my art historical colleagues, Jeanne Wasserman and Patricia Failing, who incorporated some of them in their articles on the bronzes.[4] Later in 1977, Mr. Simon asked me to examine a bronze version of *Little Dancer Aged Fourteen* that, like his other purchases, was marked "modèle" (fig. 70). On a trip to California, I had the opportunity to examine this cast, along with several others of the same edition that belonged to private collectors in the Los Angeles area. For a number of years, I had been taking and

Fig. 69 Arthur Beale (right) and Clifford Craine comparing a bronze *modèle* from the Norton Simon Museum with a series cast.

comparing measurements, markings, and distinguishing features of as many of the *Little Dancer Aged Fourteen* bronze casts as I came in contact with in my travels as a conservator. This accumulated data told me that the Simon bronze was not the casting model for the others in the edition I had examined, because it was an average of 2% smaller in size than the rest. This percentage is close to the average size by which a bronze is expected to shrink upon cooling after being cast. In short, this means that the Simon *modèle,* instead of being 2% larger than the editions it supposedly spawned, as were the other *modèles* he purchased, was some 4% smaller than it should have been to be a bronze *modèle.* It seems that it was what is called a "surmoulage" or "after-cast," a second generation bronze not only smaller but also exhibiting a diminution of surface detail as a result of the foundry process. Where, then, was the *modèle* for the *Little Dancer Aged Fourteen*? I began to speculate that it was not to be found in bronze at all but, because of its large size, in plaster. Having already examined one of the two known plasters of the figure made by Albino Palazzolo,[5] the one purchased by Paul Mellon in 1968 from John Rewald, I was relatively sure that, because of the obvious manufacturing mold lines present, which would show in subsequent casts, it was not likely to have served as a *modèle.* Mr. and Mrs. Mellon gave this plaster to the National Gallery of Art in 1985, where I was able to examine it again recently with National Gallery of Art conservators Shelley Sturman and Daphne Barbour, who are technically studying this and other Degas sculptures which are promised gifts to the National Gallery by the Mellons. During the same trip, Mr. Mellon was kind enough to permit me to revisit the magnificent original wax in Virginia to make detailed observations and measurements.

By chance in 1982, while developing treatment proposals for ancient Greek vessels at Joslyn Art Museum in Omaha, Nebraska, I was also able to briefly examine the second known plaster, which had been given to the Museum in 1971 by M. Knoedler and Co., Inc., after having been on loan there since February of 1964.[6] For the reasons I will explain in the following essay, I felt that I had indeed found the lost *modèle* for Degas' *Little Dancer Aged Fourteen.* I am very grateful to

Joslyn Art Museum, not only to be able to study in depth their plaster cast, but also to have the opportunity to put in print at last some of my other findings gathered over the years about Degas' sculpture.

INTRODUCTION

Fig. 70 *Little Dancer Aged Fourteen*, bronze *modèle*, 39 in. (99 cm), Norton Simon Museum, Pasadena, California.

Much has been written about why Degas, an artist who principally worked in two-dimensional media, did sculpture. Unfortunately, whatever his reasons, what has survived in three dimensions from his hand was not intended for public display and had deteriorated significantly at the time of his death in 1917. The dealers Joseph Durand-Ruel and Ambroise Vollard inventoried Degas' possessions for his estate and found approximately 150 pieces, most of which were fragmentary.[7] An inventory was made of eighty sculptures.[8] Ultimately seventy-four sculptures were translated into bronze copies.[9] As a conservator I have read with interest the research that has appeared over the years that both documents and speculates upon how much restoration and modification occurred before the posthumous casts were made between 1919 and 1932. Several hands were involved, possibly including the sculptor Paul-Albert Bartholomé and foundryman Albino Palazzolo. Photo documentation taken at the end of 1917 into the first quarter of 1918, when compared to the later bronze versions, does reveal discernible alterations.[10] My own imperfect conversation with Mr. Palazzolo suggests their restoration and replication presented some serious challenges and called for creativity. I am sure that, as time goes on and the surviving fragile originals become more publicly accessible, Palazzolo's restorations undertaken before his mold-making started in 1919,[11] and Palazzolo's restorations before they went to Knoedler in 1955, will also be further scrutinized, as will their change from the time they entered the Mellon Collection and were cared for by conservator Joseph Ternbach and sculptor John McCarty.

So what is the importance of monitoring all this inevitable change over time? For a conservator who analyzes cause and effect, the goal is to preserve the integrity of the artists' original intent for as long as is materially possible. For the connoisseur, curator, or collector, it is to bring us as close as possible to the artist himself. It is for these very reasons that the plaster casts should be important to us. They are snapshots frozen in time in a relatively durable medium that keeps us in touch with Degas' original intent. Of course the wax original is primary; from the very hand of the artist! But it is principally made of fragile organic materials such as wax; what was once living hair, be it human or horse; fabric garments and slippers; and broken wooden paint brushes inside as supports (see fig. 68). Only the metal armature is made of an inorganic material, probably iron or perhaps a copper-based alloy, both of which are subject to corrosion. Despite its fragility, plaster in a dry environment is surprisingly stable. In fact, plaster sculptures from ancient Egypt have survived remarkably well. Beyond the structural stability of the plasters cast over metal armatures, their surface finishes, while containing natural organic resins that darken and become brittle over time, also contain mineral pigments and metal leaf that age quite slowly when combined together in a structure similar to what would be found in an easel painting. Experience has shown us that the most fragile part of the *Little Dancer* is her fabric tutu and hair ribbon. This is true of the original wax, the plasters, and the bronzes alike. I believe one would be hard pressed to find a version that had not had these elements replaced at some time in the last 65 to 116 years or so, which covers the span of their probable dates of manufacture. [12]

Quite simply put, if one looks for a stable sculptural medium that brings us through time close to the hand of Degas, then plaster meets the criterion. In addition, if my observations and conclusions are correct, the Joslyn Art Museum plaster cast (fig. 71) also possesses significant historic importance in that it represents the mother of the some twenty-three or more bronze casts of the sculpture now found world wide (cat. 45).

Fig. 71 *Little Dancer Aged Fourteen*, 1920–21, plaster and fabric, 39 in. (99 cm), Joslyn Art Museum, Omaha, Nebraska.

RELATED MATERIAL

It is well documented that *Little Dancer Aged Fourteen*, in its original wax form, was the only sculpture Degas publicly exhibited.[13] There is also now a growing body of evidence that Degas was exposed to sculptural techniques, including replication from one media to another, with the aid of sculptor friends and professional mold makers, and that at least three of his sculptures were translated into plaster during his lifetime. Both Charles Millard and Richard Kendall, in a recent publication, have found documentation that dates this casting to 1900.[14] One of these plasters, now in the Mellon Collection, appears to be all that records the original that was probably lost in the casting.[15] A second plaster from his lifetime seems to have emerged in 1996 in Paris.[16] The third, photographed and described by early authors, is still missing. Perhaps even stronger evidence of Degas' familiarity with casting, and even his use of it, is suggested by conservator Daphne Barbour in a 1995 article that describes the technical examination of Degas' *Nude Study for the Little Dancer Aged Fourteen* (fig. 72).[17] The study concludes that this wax was cast rather than modeled, as has been previously presumed. The technical evidence she presents is strong, including an X-radiograph of the plaster core and wood and metal core supports, the raised mold line on the exterior wax of the figure, and the analysis of the two mixtures of beeswax, one used in the arms, and the other in the rest of the figure. Joseph Ternbach in his December 1955 condition report on the same sculpture concludes that the "model was used for cast[ing]," I believe because of the prominent mold line he observed.[18] I am quite sure he is not referring to Palazzolo's mold making, because Ternbach does not mention it in any of his other condition reports on the sculptures, and those mold lines are not easily seen and, where evident, are negative cuts rather than raised positive lines.

From my own examination of the mold lines and the X-radiograph David Rinne and I made of the *Nude Study for the Little Dancer Aged Fourteen* in 1972, I would agree with Barbour's conclusion, and only suggest that the location of the armature and bubbles and air spaces seen in the core suggest that the core was poured in place inside a hollow wax cast. She also correctly points out that the arms are modeled over a wire armature with different wax and attached later, which is also evident in the X-radiographs (fig. 73). All of this represents some fairly complex casting and sculpting knowledge, inconsistent with what is seen in Degas' other sculptures. On the other hand, the mixture of wood and metal armature construction is more consistent, which leads me to conclude that Degas was probably working closely with a mold maker or sculptor to execute this piece. If this is true, then the documentary research would have this logically occur around 1900, when the three plaster casts were made.[19] Further supporting this thought is the fact that both the plasters and the wax seem to have been cast from piece molds, likely made of plaster themselves. I conclude this from the location

Fig. 72 *Nude Study for the Little Dancer Aged Fourteen*, ca. 1878–79 (reworked later), wax and plaster, 28½ in. (72 cm), National Gallery of Art, Washington, D.C. Collection of Mr. and Mrs. Paul Mellon.

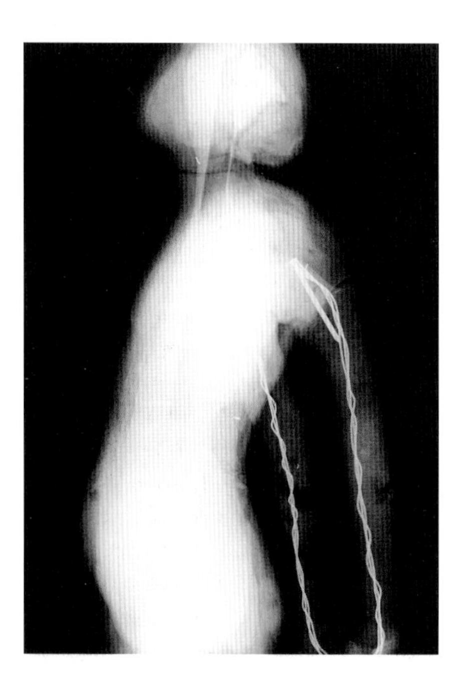

of the raised mold lines found on the casts. Millard has pointed out that the *Nude Study for the Little Dancer Aged Fourteen* is the only sculpture for which Degas had a base made in 1880, perhaps in preparation for showing it in the Impressionist exhibition in April of that year.[20] It is also his second largest sculpture to survive and, therefore, as Barbour suggests, one that had perhaps taken on a life of its own. Finally, I would note that a shift in the figure's proper right foot, that occurred after the plaster core and contiguous plaster base had been cast and hardened, changed the gesture of the dancer to one significantly different than the larger dressed version. Personally, I find the original position, as marked by a "wet" footprint on the top of the cast plaster base, as much more dynamic and balletlike, and wonder whether the change represents a damage immortalized in twenty-four or more bronze casts rather than the work of Degas (fig. 74).[21]

Until further technical studies or yet-to-be-located art-historical documentation is found, I feel that the evidence points to the *Nude Study* as the predecessor for the *Little Dancer Aged Fourteen*. The best evidence for this is usually hidden from view. The nude figure is quite anatomically correct while, when the dressed figure is seen without her tutu, it is clear that Degas had already resolved the stance and had no interest in modeling what would not normally be seen (fig. 20). Millard dates Degas' creation of this "study" to 1878–79, a possible full twenty years before his work with the mold makers.[22] This makes me convinced that the piece that has survived is a reworked wax cast of an earlier version now lost, as Barbour points out in her essay.[23]

CASTING METHODS

The challenges presented by translating into bronze a sculpture of very mixed media, among other reasons, seemed to have caused Hébrard and Palazzolo to wait to start the series of *Little Dancer Aged Fourteen*. In 1920 or shortly thereafter, with her hair bow and skirt removed, a cool setting flexible gelatin mold was made from the original wax. I believe the process was the same as has been related by Palazzolo in interviews and described before.[24] First, a protective coating such as shellac may have been put on parts of the wax original to facilitate later mold release.[25] Next, an even blanket of perhaps water-based clay was laid over the surface of the sculpture. A plaster "mother" or "retainer" mold was constructed in several sections on top of the clay. It appears to me that the original wooden base was also used in the mold making, because of damages and discolorations on the top of it that correspond to features seen on the plaster casts. The plaster retainer mold was removed, and then the clay on the surface of the sculpture, so that none remained to obscure detail. The plaster mold would then have been placed back over the original and bound together. The space formerly occupied by the clay was then replaced with a cool setting liquid gelatin mold designed not to melt the wax original (fig. 75). Once the gelatin solidified, the plaster retainer mold was removed and the flexible gelatin mold carefully cut away perpendicular to the original and, probably, corresponding to the separating joints in the plaster retainer mold. It is also possible that the gelatin mold was itself made in pieces to avoid the risky cutting near the soft original wax surface. At this point the original was no longer needed, except as a color guide. The gelatin mold would have been reassembled inside its plaster retainer, which would hold it in place, and would now be ready for casting. In the case of all but the *Little Dancer Aged Fourteen,* I believe that the gelatin mold was used to make an average of six hollow wax casts.

Fig. 74 Top of base of wax and plaster *Nude Study for the Little Dancer Aged Fourteen.*

Fig. 73 *(facing page bottom)* X-radiograph of section of wax and plaster *Nude Study for the Little Dancer Aged Fourteen.*

Fig. 75 Hébrard foundry workmen pouring gelatin into a mold, ca. 1920.

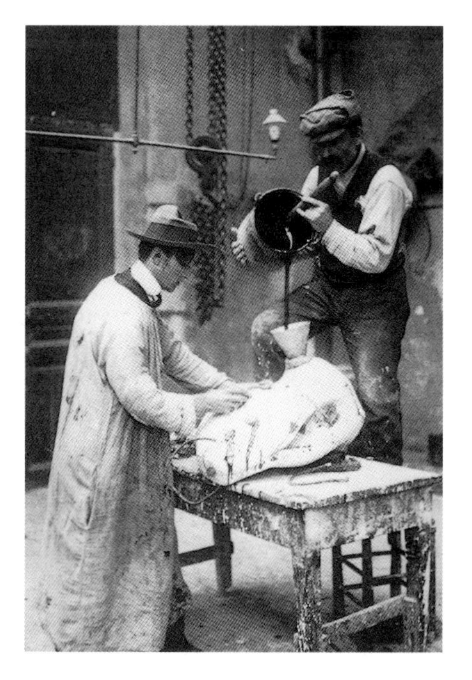

In order to make hollow bronze casts, cores of refractory material were also made, but will not be discussed here. These wax casts were then gated and vented with wax elements and then invested with a refractory mold material. The assemblage with the mold and core held in place by metal chaplets was then heated or "burnt out," hardening the investment and melting out the wax. Bronze was then poured into the space formerly occupied by the wax, allowed to cool, and the investment mold broken away. Finally, the now metal gates, vents, and chaplets were chased or cut away. What emerged was the bronze *modèle* set now owned by the Norton Simon Museum. The patination, or coloration, process will be discussed separately. In order to make the other twenty-two bronze copies, the process was repeated, but this time the bronze served as the model, instead of the fragile originals, which were made of wax, plasticine, or other materials.

On average, I believe that the gelatin molds made for each bronze of the series could be used up to six times to make the wax copies before losing shape or detail. I know this because, when I examined each Simon *modèle,* I counted the number of fine lines made on each bronze from a sharp knife, which was used to cut the flexible gelatin mold in half or more parts to free it from the surface. There were three to six sets of cut lines on each *modèle.* When divided by the total edition of twenty-two, I came up with an average of six. Traces of water-based clay, shellac, and gelatin mold residue were found inside many of the Simon *modèles,* further proving how they were used. I hypothesize that the incised inscriptions designating them as "*modèle*" and the particular number of each sculpture were added only after all the mold-making was complete, so these markings would not appear on the wax casts, and thus on the final series of bronzes. The letter marks A - T or HER or HER.D and the sculpture numbers 1 - 72 were later stamped or incised in each bronze of the series. The A. A. Hébrard stamp that appears in a rectangular box under the words *Cire Perdue,* or lost wax, was applied or reinforced in each wax cast, including the *modèle,* to assure legibility. Degas' signature was added by the Founder by a stamp impressed in wax and added when the *modèle* version was still in wax (fig. 76).

One of the most fascinating discoveries I made while examining the Simon bronzes was that, although they were measurably larger than the series by the expected percentage when compared, they also unexpectedly weighed less (see fig. 69). I believe the reason is that the *modèles* are finer casts with thin walls of consistent thickness. This set of bronzes, and particularly the wax casts made in the gelatin molds taken from the originals, were undoubtedly made by Albino Palazzolo himself.

The two exceptions to the casting and marking methods just described are the unnumbered sculpture entitled *Schoolgirl* (cat. 31), which has a different history from the other sculptures,[26] including when the bronze casts were made, and the *Little Dancer Aged Fourteen.* The departure point in the casting process of the series for the *Little Dancer Aged Fourteen,* I believe, came after the flexible gelatin mold was made from Degas' original wax. There are several possible reasons why Palazzolo and Hébrard might have decided on a plaster instead of a bronze model. The first would be to minimize the amount of sculptural detail that would be lost in the process of translation from one medium to another. Because of the properties of plaster, which hardens without loss of dimension or detail through a chemical process, unlike wax and bronze, which both shrink and loose dimension upon cooling and hardening, a plaster model would be the same size as the original with superior detail translated. The second possible reason for the choice of plaster would be that it would be far lighter to handle as a model, especially when

Fig. 76 Markings on *modèle* cast of bronze number 3, Norton Simon Museum, Pasadena, California.

Fig. 77 Detail of gelatin mold line on proper left arm of plaster *Little Dancer Aged Fourteen*, National Gallery of Art, Washington, D.C.

covered with a plaster retainer mold, which in itself would be heavy for that size of sculpture. The risk would be that a plaster model would not be as strong or as durable as a bronze one, but the answer to that would be to make several plasters from the same original gelatin mold in case one was damaged while making subsequent gelatin molds from it. As I mentioned above, perhaps as many as six wax casts for the series could be made in the gelatin molds before they would deteriorate. I believe that the National Gallery of Art plaster version of the *Little Dancer Aged Fourteen* was made in a slightly deteriorating gelatin mold, since the joints in the mold had begun to curl away from the retainer mold, leaving pronounced mold lines on the cast (fig. 77).[27]

TECHNICAL EVIDENCE

There is no question that the Joslyn Art Museum and the National Gallery of Art plasters of Degas' *Little Dancer Aged Fourteen* come from the same mold. Although the mold lines left from its manufacture on the Joslyn plaster are not as evident as those of the National Gallery's cast, they can be seen on close inspection and are found in exactly the same locations (figs. 78 and 79). The metal armature construction in each plaster cast as seen in X-radiograph is similar but not identical (figs. 80 and 81). The Joslyn armature is somewhat more complex, with shorter, less complete rods that are wired together at the center of the torso, and down one leg.[28] The armature in the National Gallery cast has one continuous rod from the base up the proper left leg to the top to the dancer's head. The same rod in the Joslyn cast is in two sections wired together in the chest area. Similarly, the armature that forms the shoulders into the arms is contiguous in the National Gallery cast and in two separate arm supports in the Joslyn cast. Daphne Barbour and I had the opportunity to examine each set of X-radiographs side by side at the National Gallery. We agreed that it appears that the Joslyn cast was made first, and that the problems of reinforcement encountered were then more easily solved in the simple armature construction of the National Gallery cast. Both casts have the appearance of having been poured solid with plaster; some casters apply a coat of plaster before the molds are closed and filled in order to avoid trapped air in detailed undercut areas of the sculpture's outer surface, while others get good results from pouring into a closed mold and rolling the plaster into place.

The greatest difference between the two plaster casts is found on their bases. Five tapered, one-half-inch recessed "keys" and prominent mold lines for a retainer, or mother, mold are found in the top of the Joslyn base (fig. 83), while the National Gallery base top is relatively smooth. It should be remembered that the base for *Little Dancer Aged Fourteen* is not important in the casting scheme devised by Palazzolo and Hébrard, since they only reproduced the figure in bronze and the base reproduction for each cast is usually made of wood. The cast plaster bases for each cast were probably created separately. The cast figure, with rod armatures protruding from the bottom of each foot, may have been cast first and then put in a form or mold for the base, which was then poured in place. The overall base dimensions of the Joslyn and National Gallery plasters are virtually identical, indicating they had the same model. Although they are 7⁄16 of an inch larger in width and ½ inch larger in depth and slightly higher than the wooden base on the Mellon wax, scratches and discoloration on the top of the original wooden base corresponds exactly to mold lines and features on the plaster bases. It does not, however, appear that the wooden base of the original has been cut

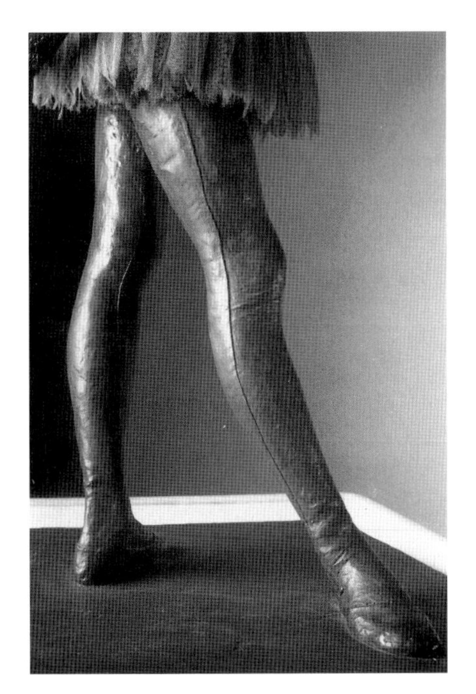

Fig. 78 Detail showing gelatin mold line on proper right leg of plaster *Little Dancer Aged Fourteen*, National Gallery of Art, Washington, D.C.

Fig. 79 Detail showing gelatin mold line on proper right leg of plaster *Little Dancer Aged Fourteen*, Joslyn Art Museum, Omaha, Nebraska.

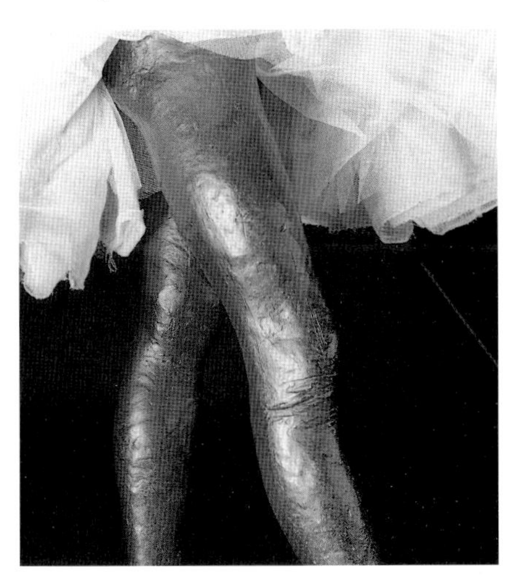

down. In fact, small brass nails are found every two to two-and-a-half inches apart near the top edge, where they probably once held a fabric drape during an early exhibition. It is therefore not clear why the plaster bases were made larger except that they were incidental to the making of subsequent gelatin molds, wax casts, and the resulting bronzes.

As previously mentioned, the top surfaces of the plaster bases have significant differences; but beyond the dimensions, they also have significant similarities. The National Gallery cast exhibits cast sculpture comb tool marks not seen on either the original wood or the Joslyn base. On the other hand, both cast plaster bases have two rough circular features in identical locations where plaster fill sprues or vents were cut off. Discolorations on the original wood base correspond in location to these features (see figs. 83–85). These base differences and similarities further suggest a manufacturing relationship but different functions of the casts. The Joslyn plaster base with its keyways was made to register now-missing plaster retainer molds that would have fitted over the entire figure when the gelatin mold was poured. I have reason to believe that the National Gallery cast may have been the color model for the bronze series.

First and foremost, the strongest technical evidence for these assertions lies in careful measurements. In many dimensions the plasters are identical. When ten measurements from the same locations are averaged, the Joslyn cast is approximately ½% larger than the National Gallery cast. This is not surprising if, as I have observed, the gelatin mold used to make the National Gallery cast appears to have been drying out, shrinking, and distorting when the plaster cast was made. Also unsurprising is the fact that the plasters are an average of 1% larger than the original Degas wax, given that they are quite heavily coated with shellac or varnish, metal leaf, and paint that add to their dimensions. Aging of the wax through drying and shrinkage over the better part of this century is also a factor that makes this percentage logical. When compared in their dimensions to the bronze casts, for which I maintain the Joslyn plaster is the model, the bronzes are about 3% smaller, or about 2% smaller than the wax original. Again, I would attribute the proportionally large size of the Joslyn plaster to its coatings, which might have been applied after its use as a *modèle*. This is reinforced by the fact that gelatin mold cut lines are not as clearly visible on the Joslyn plaster as they are on the Simon bronze *modèles*. I believe this is because some of them have been obscured by later overpaint and coatings, possibly to make the plaster cast more marketable. However, cut lines can be clearly seen, especially on the proper right knee of the dancer (see fig. 79). As a *modèle* the Joslyn plaster would not have had a tutu or hair ribbon, which would also have been added before exhibition and sale.

Albino Palazzolo, when asked why there were two plasters, replied on 23 February 1960 that "he produced himself two plasters that were cast on the original wax because the wax was too fragile to stand twelve repetitions in bronze." Mme. Hébrard was also asked about the plasters and seems to have reluctantly replied after a time that "the plasters were found in Degas' atelier."[29] I believe that Mme. Hébrard is referring to the small plaster casts found in Degas' studio after his death and not the larger plaster casts of the *Little Dancer Aged Fourteen*, about which the inquiry was made.

In correspondence with William A. McGonagle, Curator at Joslyn Art Museum, dated 1 July 1971, John Rewald writes, "I had thought that Hébrard had made these plaster casts in order to guide him with the bronze casting." Interestingly, he goes on to say "As I remember it, the cast that is now owned by

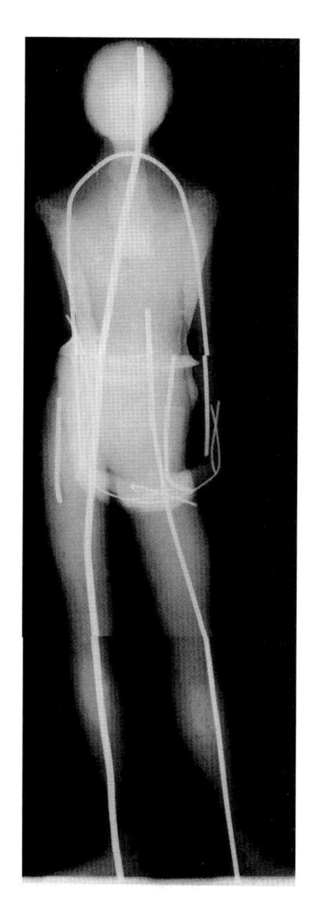

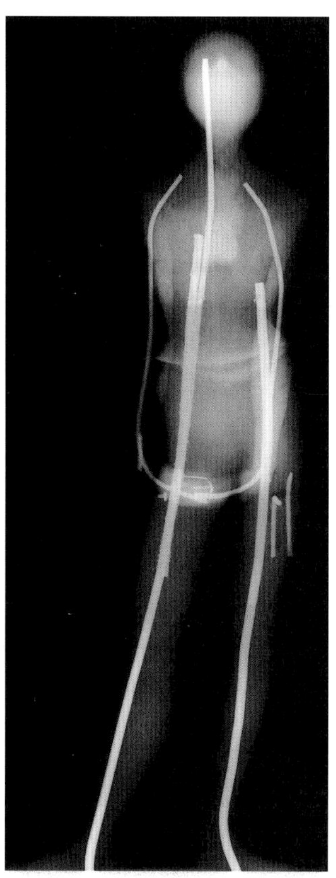

the Joslyn Art Museum was colored rather darkly, whereas the one that I obtained was considerably lighter in color and thus came closer to the bronze casts (which is the reason why I selected it)."[30]

Scientific analysis of pigment and coating samples taken from each plaster cast were conducted by Richard Newman, Research Scientist at the Museum of Fine Arts, Boston.[31] The results indicated that both casts were given an overall metallic quality with the use of ground brass metal leaf in an unidentified medium. An oil binder and lead white paint was found to be present in several of the samples taken from each cast. Samples analyzed from a pink slipper of each cast revealed the presence of red ochre, and bone black was also found to be common to both casts as a pigment. Dark brown layers are seen in cross-sections taken from the flesh areas on each cast. Although many more comparative samples and analyses would be needed for conclusive results, these preliminary findings suggest the material and techniques used to color each cast are very similar.

Although no scientific color measurements were done, the closeness in color of the plaster casts when compared to the original Degas wax is obvious. If Rewald was correct when he saw the two plasters side by side and perhaps with the wax original, and even next to one of the bronzes, and observed that the National Gallery plaster that he once owned was closer in color to the bronze casts than the Joslyn one, then perhaps he was identifying the color model (fig. 82).[31]

Among the most interesting and astonishing discoveries I made when examining the Degas' original sculptures in the Mellon home in 1972 and later confirmed in 1977, when I examined the Simon bronze *modèles,* had to do with color replication. Degas' originals were not only structurally fragile and altered over time, but drastically altered in color from environmental exposure and chemical change. What struck me most was the unevenness of the colors; top exposed surfaces were often very dark and altered while more protected under surfaces were much lighter and nearer their original color. My explanation is that most of the originals are formulas of wax or plasticine, both of which are soft sticky materials. Airborne dirt and heating soot fell on these top surfaces, stuck to them, and darkened them. I am also sure that natural light and heat induced chemical changes in the modeling materials. It is clear from Ternbach's examination and treatment records and my own observations that various natural resin coatings, including shellac, were used to facilitate mold removal or as a conservation measure. These coatings have darkened and discolored with age.

What I found most interesting is that when Palazzolo made the master bronze *modèles* to replicate faithfully the originals, he also meticulously replicated their aged, varied, and discolored finishes when he chemically patinated them. This must have been a very difficult and labor-intensive process. It is clear, when a *modèle* bronze is compared with a series bronze, that the complicated color variants and tones in the series casts are not as carefully or faithfully executed. The colors found on the bronze versions of the *Little Dancer Aged Fourteen* that I have seen are remarkably consistent and certainly had a color model. I have long suspected that some paint including pigment and binder was used in part to achieve the accurate and precisely placed colors, particularly of the bodice and slippers, on the bronze *Little Dancer Aged Fourteen*.[32]

Finally, another interesting but puzzling observation I made when examining the Simon bronze *modèles* was that the gelatin cut mold lines were sometimes under and sometimes on top of the chemical patinas. These chemical patinas on metal appear quite durable and should have been unaffected by the gelatin molds made on them. One possibility is that the cut lines seen under the patina were

Fig. 80 *(facing page top)* X-radiograph showing armature of plaster *Little Dancer Aged Fourteen*, National Gallery of Art, Washington, D.C.

Fig. 81 *(facing page bottom)* X-radiograph showing armature of plaster *Little Dancer Aged Fourteen*, Joslyn Art Museum, Omaha, Nebraska.

Fig. 82 *Little Dancer Aged Fourteen*, ca. 1920–21, plaster and fabric, 39 in. (99 cm), National Gallery of Art, Washington, D.C. Collection of Mr. and Mrs. Paul Mellon.

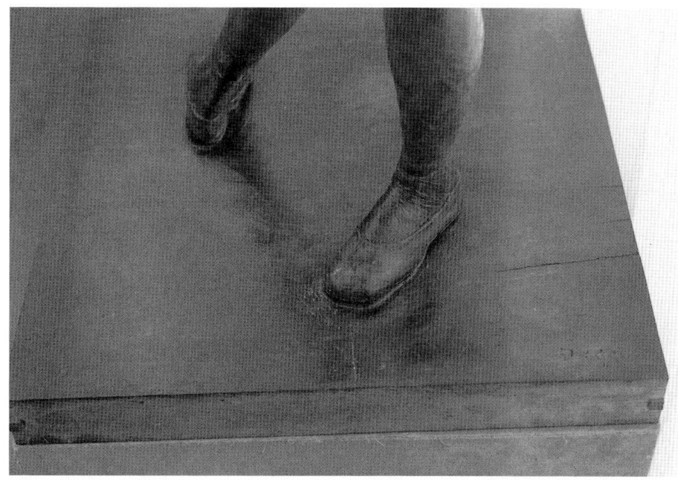

Fig. 83 *(above left)* "Keys" on the base of the plaster *Little Dancer Aged Fourteen*, Joslyn Art Museum, Omaha, Nebraska.

Fig. 84 *(above right)* Base of wax and fabric *Little Dancer Aged Fourteen*, Collection of Mr. and Mrs. Paul Mellon, Upperville, Virginia.

Fig. 85 Base of plaster *Little Dancer Aged Fourteen*, National Gallery of Art, Washington, D.C.

considered disfiguring and disguised as a restoration measure. I do not think, however, that the painted plaster surfaces would have fared as well with repeated gelatin molding. That is another reason why I believe that a second color model may have been made.

SUMMARY THOUGHTS

Time has taken its toll, not only on the dynamic, mysterious, and fragile sculptural works of Edgar Degas, but also on our ability to interpret them. An unusual number of hands have been involved in bringing this private art to wide public attention and acclaim. Serious questions have been asked about the propriety of this effort in light of its posthumous nature. Although it has not been my intent to fuel this debate, I hope that I have offered some information that will offer new perspectives. Most important, it should be clear that although bronze may be more noble and durable, it does not necessarily bring us closest to the artist. In the case of the plaster cast of Degas' *Little Dancer Aged Fourteen* in the collection of Joslyn Art Museum, we should come to a greater appreciation of how it fits into the complex process of replication and just how close it brings us to a great artist.

CATALOGUE

1 *Sketches of Dancers,* ca. 1876–77, brown ink with touches of blue ink on cream paper.

2 *Dance Rehearsal,* ca. 1875–76, oil on canvas.

3 *Ballet Dancer Adjusting Her Costume,* ca. 1875–76, pencil and chalk on pink paper.

4 *(facing page)* *Ballet Dancer with Arms Crossed,* ca. 1872, oil on canvas.

Degas

5 *In the Foyer,* ca. 1876–77, monotype.

6 *Pauline and Virginie Conversing with Admirers,* ca. 1876–77, monotype.

7 *Two Dancers,* 1880–81, pastel.

8 *The Ballet Class,* ca. 1880–81, oil on canvas.

9 *Two Dancers in a Rehearsal Room,* ca. 1877–78, aquatint, drypoint, and scraping on paper.

10 *(facing page)* *Dancer Tying Her Scarf,* ca. 1878–79, charcoal with white highlights.

Degas

11 *Ballet Girl in Repose,* ca. 1878–80, charcoal on cream colored paper.

12 *Little Girl Practicing at the Bar,* ca. 1878–80, charcoal and white chalk on pink paper.

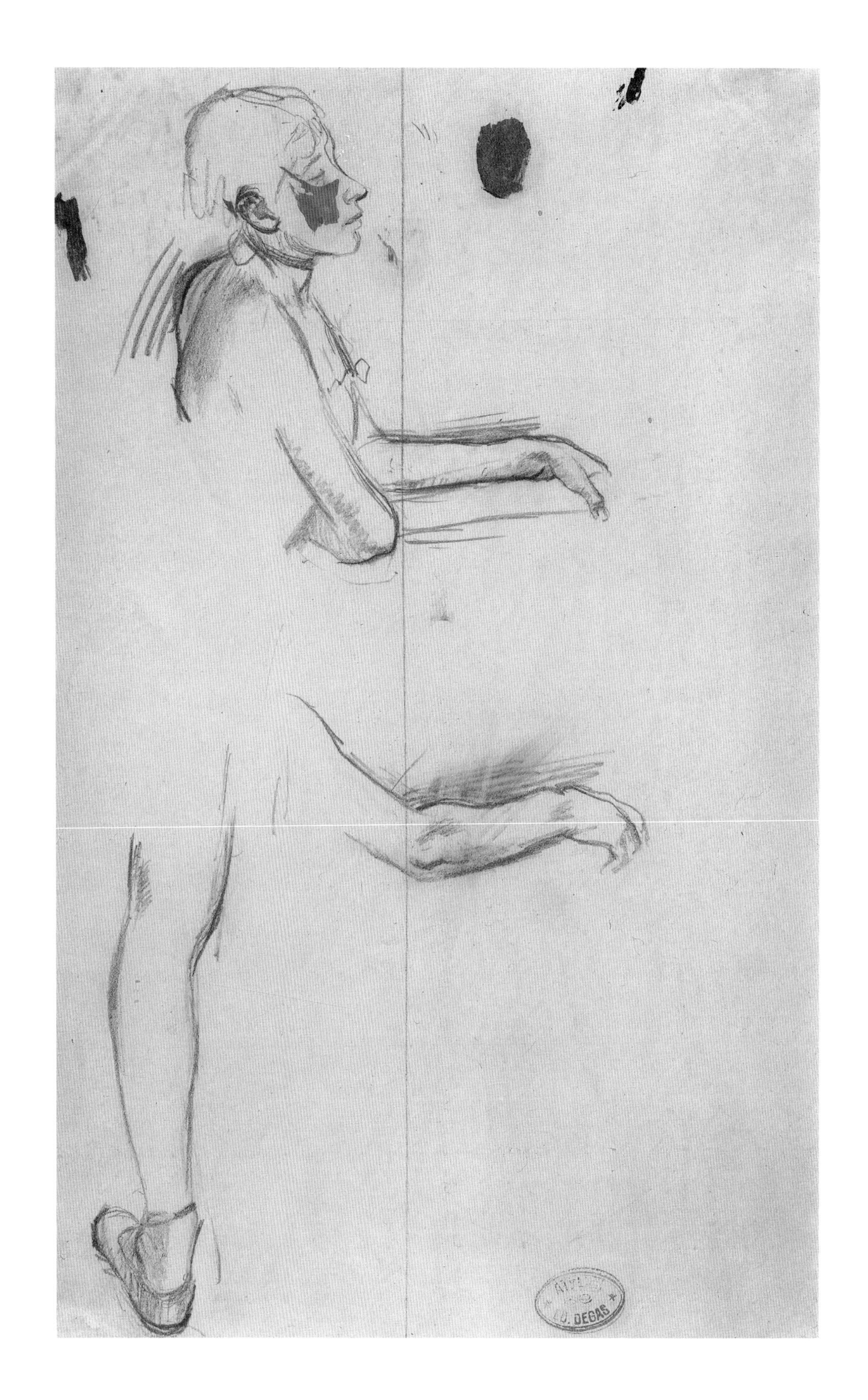

13 *Studies for Dancers at the Bar,* ca. 1876–77, pencil.

14 *Dancer Stretching at the Bar,* ca. 1877–80, pastel with stumping on ivory laid paper.

15 *The Dance Examination,* ca. 1879, pastel and charcoal on heavy gray wove paper.

16 *Dancer on Stage,* ca. 1877–80, pencil on paper.

17 *Actresses in Their Dressing Rooms,* ca. 1879–80, etching and aquatint.

18 *Dancers,* ca. 1878, lake pigment, gouache or essence.

19 *Dancers in the Wings*, ca. 1879–80, etching with aquatint.

20 *Entrance of the Masked Dancers,* ca. 1879–84, pastel on paper.

21 *On Stage III,* ca. 1876–77, softground etching, drypoint, and roulette.

22 *Three Ballet Dancers,* ca. 1876, monotype.

23 *In the Wings,* ca. 1878–80, lithograph.

24 *Dancer in Green,* ca. 1879, pastel on paper.

Degas

26 *Dancers (fan design),* ca. 1879–80, gouache (or distemper) with gold and charcoal on silk.

25 *(facing page)* *Dancer with a Fan,* ca. 1876–78, black chalk heightened with white on blue-gray paper.

Degas

28 *At the Theater: Woman with a Fan,* ca. 1878–80, lithograph.

27 (*facing page*) *Dancer with a Fan,* ca. 1879, pastel on paper.

29 *Dancing Lesson,* ca. 1880, oil on canvas.

30 *Dancer with a Fan,* ca. 1880, pastel on gray-green laid paper.

31 *Schoolgirl,* ca. 1880–81, bronze.

32 *Study of Three Dancers,* ca. 1880, charcoal and pastel on buff paper.

33 *Dancers,* ca. 1880, pastel with charcoal.

34a and b Notebook 29, Folios 25 and 41, ca. 1878–79, blue chalk on paper.

35 *Two Dancers*, ca. 1878–79, charcoal and white chalk on green commercially coated wove paper.

36 *Three Studies of a Nude Dancer,* ca. 1878–79, charcoal heightened with white chalk on gray wove paper.

37 *Dancer at Rest, Hands on Her Hips, Left Leg Forward,* ca. 1877–79, bronze.

38 *Study of a Nude Dancer,* ca. 1878–79 or later, black chalk and charcoal on mauve-pink laid paper.

39 *Nude Study for Little Dancer Aged Fourteen,* original version ca. 1878–79 (reworked later), bronze.

40 *Three Studies of a Dancer in Fourth Position,* ca. 1878–81, charcoal and pastel on grayish-tan laid paper.

41 *Three Studies of a Dancer,* ca. 1878–81, black chalk heightened with white on pink paper.

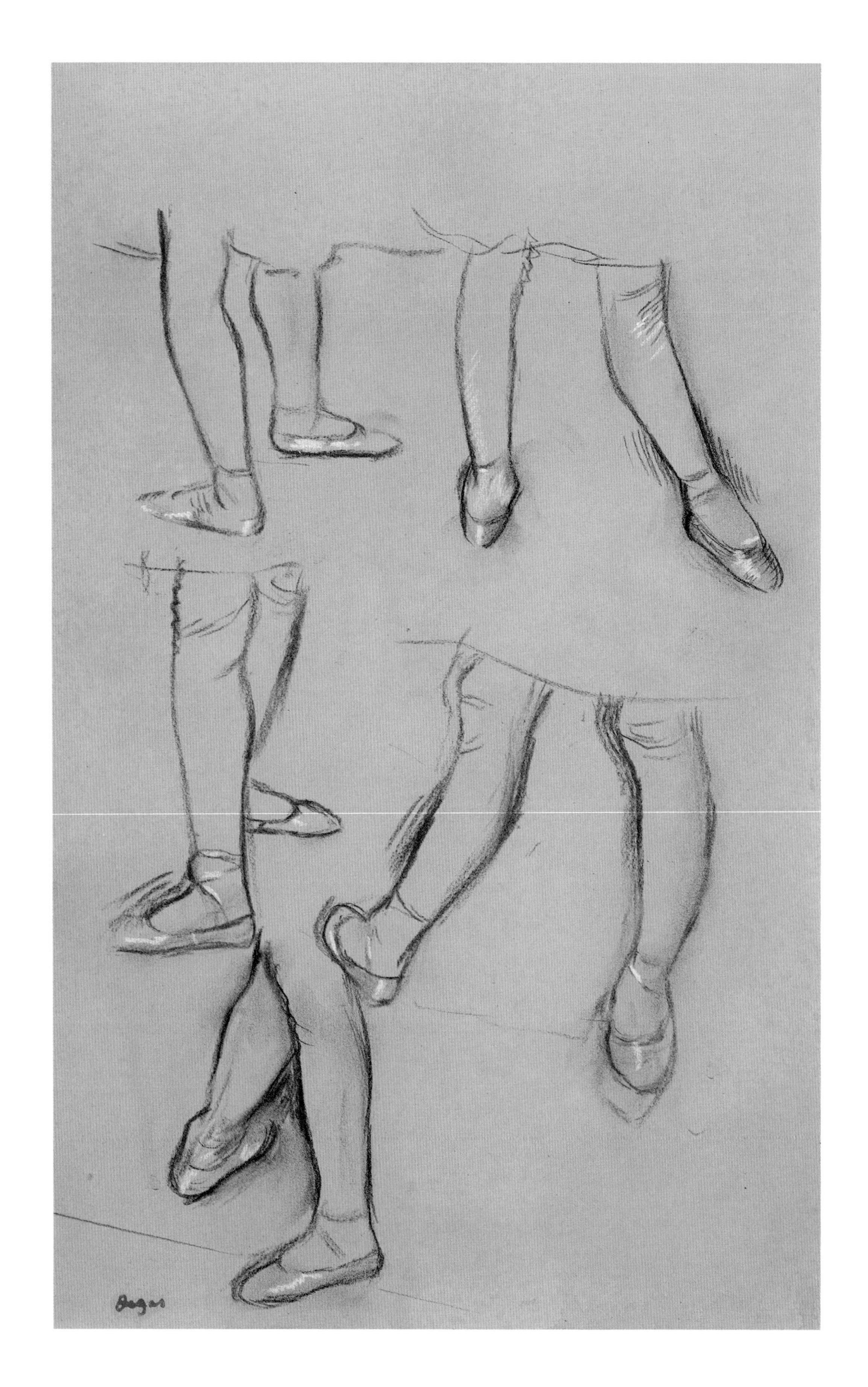

42 Studies for *Little Dancer Aged Fourteen,* ca. 1878–81, pencil, charcoal, and pastel on green paper.

43 *Four Studies of a Dancer,* ca. 1878–81, chalk and charcoal, heightened with gray wash and white, on buff wove paper.

44 *Little Dancer Aged Fourteen,* ca. 1921 or later, bronze and fabric.

45 *Little Dancer Aged Fourteen,* ca. 1920–21, plaster and fabric.

46 *Dancer Adjusting Her Dress*, ca. 1881–85, pastel on paper.

47 *Dancer Standing,* ca. 1885, charcoal and pastel on paper.

48 *Ballet Dancer Standing,* ca. 1885, black chalk heightened with white chalk and pastel on gray laid paper.

49 *Dancers,* ca. 1885, pastel.

50 *Dancer Ready to Dance, Right Leg Forward,* ca. 1882–95, bronze.

51 *Grand Arabesque, First Time,* ca. 1882–95, bronze.

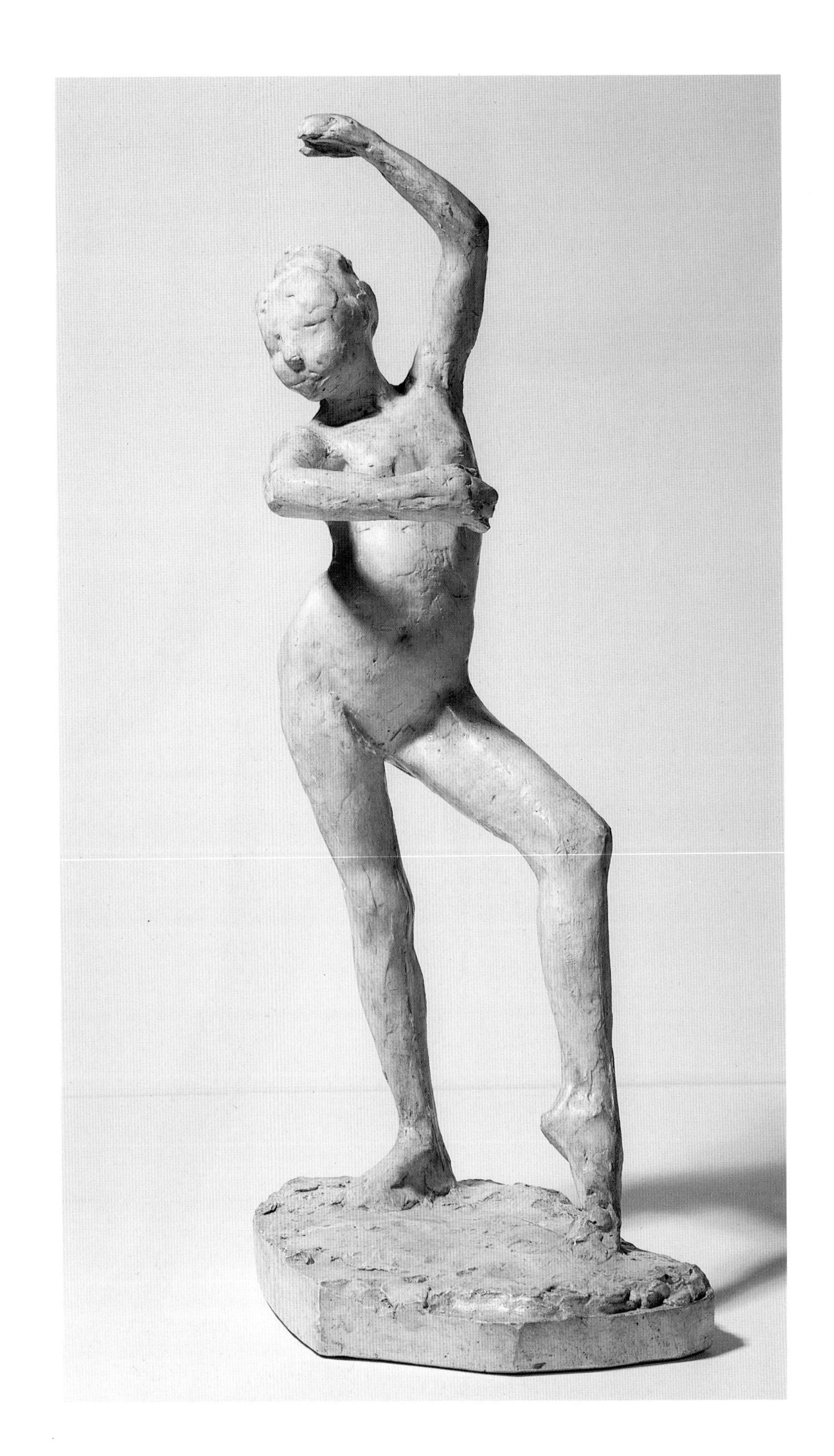

52 *Spanish Dance,* ca. 1920 or later, plaster.

53 *Dancer Moving Forward,* ca. 1882–95, bronze.

54 *Dancer Moving Forward, Arms Raised,* ca. 1882–95, bronze.

55 *Fourth Position Front, on the Left Leg,* ca. 1882–95, bronze.

56 *Dancer Looking at the Sole of Her Right Foot,* ca. 1900, plaster.

57 *Dancer Looking at the Sole of Her Right Foot,* ca. 1920 or later, bronze.

58 *Dancer at Rest, Hands Behind Her Back, Right Leg Forward,* ca. 1877–79, bronze.

59 *Dancer at Rest, Hands Behind Her Back, Right Leg Forward,* ca. 1885–95, bronze.

60 *Dancer at Rest,* ca. 1885–90, charcoal on paper.

61 *Dressed Dancer at Rest, Hands Behind Her Back, Right Leg Forward*, ca. 1895–1905, bronze.

62 *Dancer,* ca. 1897–1900, pastel and charcoal.

CHECKLIST OF WORKS IN THE EXHIBITION

Unless otherwise indicated, dates given for the sculptures are those of the wax and mixed-media originals.

References to the standard catalogues of works by Degas are indicated as follows: L. – Lemoisne 1946; R. – Rewald 1944; B.R. – Brame and Reff 1984; J. – Janis 1968; V. – Ventes I–IV; R.S. – Reed and Shapiro 1984.

A number of works will be shown at only one or two of the three exhibition venues. This is indicated by an abbreviation of the venue names following the appropriate entries: JAM (Joslyn Art Museum), CAI (Sterling and Francine Clark Art Institute), and BMA (The Baltimore Museum of Art).

1 *Sketches of Dancers* ca. 1876–77
brown ink with touches of blue ink on cream paper
7 7/8 × 9 7/8 in. (20.1 × 25 cm)
Fogg Art Museum, Harvard University Art Museums, Cambridge, Massachusetts, Bequest of Meta and Paul J. Sachs (1965.264)

2 *Dance Rehearsal* ca. 1875–76
oil on canvas
16 × 21 1/2 in. (40.5 × 54.5 cm)
Private Collection, courtesy The Phillips Collection, Washington, D.C.
L.362

3 *Ballet Dancer Adjusting Her Costume* ca. 1875–76
pencil and chalk on pink paper
15 1/2 × 10 1/4 in. (39.4 × 26 cm)
Detroit Institute of Arts, Bequest of John S. Newberry (65.145)
V.II, no. 332

BMA

4 *Ballet Dancer with Arms Crossed* ca. 1872
oil on canvas
24 1/8 × 19 7/8 in. (61.4 × 50.5 cm)
Museum of Fine Arts, Boston, Bequest of John T. Spaulding (48.534)
L.1025

5 *In the Foyer* ca. 1876–77
monotype
8 5/8 × 7 1/16 in. (21.9 × 17.9 cm)
André Bromberg, Paris
J.232

6 *Pauline and Virginie Conversing with Admirers* ca. 1876–77
monotype
8 1/2 × 6 3/8 in. (21.5 × 16.1 cm)
Fogg Art Museum, Harvard University Art Museums, Cambridge, Massachusetts, Bequest of Meta and Paul J. Sachs (M14295)
J.218

7 *Two Dancers* 1880–81
pastel
18 1/4 × 12 3/4 in. (46.4 cm × 32.4 cm)
Private collection
L.480

CAI

8 *The Ballet Class* ca. 1880–81
oil on canvas
32 1/8 × 30 1/8 in. (81.6 × 76.5 cm)
Philadelphia Museum of Art, Purchased with the W.P. Wilstach Fund (W 1937–002–001)
L.479

9a *Two Dancers in a Rehearsal Room* ca. 1877–78
aquatint, drypoint, and scraping on paper
6 3/8 × 4 9/16 in. (15.7 cm × 11.6 cm)
James A. Bergquist, Boston
R.S.33

JAM, BMA

9b *Two Dancers in a Rehearsal Room* ca. 1877–78
aquatint, drypoint, and scraping on paper
6 1/4 × 4 5/8 in. (15.9 × 11.8 cm)
Sterling and Francine Clark Art Institute, Williamstown, Massachusetts (1968.16)
R.S.33 [illustrated]

CAI

10 *Dancer Tying Her Scarf* ca. 1878–79
charcoal with white highlights
18 5/8 × 11 5/8 in. (47.5 × 30.2 cm)
The Hyde Collection, Glens Falls, New York (1971.63)
V.II, no. 351

JAM, CAI

11 *Ballet Girl in Repose* ca. 1878–80
charcoal on cream colored paper
9 13/16 × 11 9/16 in. (24.8 × 29.5 cm)
The Minneapolis Institute of Arts, Gift of Julius Boehler (26.10)
V.III, no. 109 (iii)

12 *Little Girl Practicing at the Bar* ca. 1878–80
charcoal and white chalk on pink paper
12 1/8 × 11 1/2 in. (31.1 × 29.2 cm)
The Metropolitan Museum of Art, New York, Bequest of Mrs. H.O. Havemeyer, 1929 (29.100.943)
Bought from the artist by H. O. Havemeyer

13 *Studies for Dancers at the Bar* ca. 1876–77
pencil
12 1/2 × 8 in. (31.8 × 20.3 cm)
The Jedlicka Family, Switzerland
Study for L.408

14 *Dancer Stretching at the Bar* ca. 1877–80
pastel with stumping on ivory laid paper
12 7/16 × 9 7/16 in. (31.8 × 24 cm)
The Art Institute of Chicago, Mr. & Mrs. Martin A. Ryerson Collection (1933.1229)
First owned by Ambroise Vollard

15 *The Dance Examination* ca. 1879
pastel and charcoal on heavy gray wove paper
24 5/16 × 18 5/16 in. (63.4 × 48.2 cm)
Denver Art Museum, Anonymous gift (1941.6)
L.576

JAM

16 *Dancer on Stage* ca. 1877–80
pencil on paper
$9\frac{3}{8} \times 6\frac{1}{4}$ in. (23.8 × 15.9 cm)
Hazlitt, Gooden and Fox, London
First owned by Ambroise Vollard

17 *Actresses in Their Dressing Rooms* ca. 1879–80
etching and aquatint
$4\frac{3}{4} \times 8\frac{3}{8}$ in. (12.1 × 21.3 cm)
Stanford University Museum of Art, Gift of Marion E. Fitzhugh and Dr. William M. Fitzhugh, Jr., in memory of their mother, Mary E. Fitzhugh (1963.5.13)
R.S.50 (fifth state)

18 *Dancers* ca. 1878
lake pigment, gouache or essence
$6\frac{7}{16} \times 4\frac{1}{2}$ in. (16.3 × 10.8 cm)
Yale University Art Gallery, New Haven, Connecticut, Collection of Frances and Ward Cheney, B.A. 1922 (1970.113.2)
L.482

BMA

19 *Dancers in the Wings* ca. 1879–80
etching with aquatint
$5\frac{1}{2} \times 4\frac{1}{8}$ in. (14.1 × 10.4 cm)
Sterling and Francine Clark Art Institute, Williamstown, Massachusetts (1962.30)
R.S.47 (seventh state)

20 *Entrance of the Masked Dancers* ca. 1879–84
pastel on paper
$19\frac{5}{16} \times 25\frac{7}{16}$ in. (49 cm × 64.7 cm)
Sterling and Francine Clark Art Institute, Williamstown, Massachusetts (1955.559)
L.527

CAI

21a *On Stage III* ca. 1876–77
softground etching, drypoint, and roulette
$3\frac{15}{16} \times 5$ in. (9.9 × 12.7 cm)
Joslyn Art Museum, Omaha, Museum purchase with funds provided by Michael and Gail Yanney in honor of Liz Stinson (1997.27)
R.S.24 (fourth state) [illustrated]

JAM

21b *On Stage III* ca. 1876–77
softground etching, drypoint, and roulette
$3\frac{15}{16} \times 4\frac{15}{16}$ in. (9.9 × 12.7 cm)
Sterling and Francine Clark Art Institute, Williamstown, Massachusetts (1962.32)
R.S.24 (third state)

CAI

21c *On Stage III* ca. 1876–77
softground etching, drypoint, and roulette
$3\frac{15}{16} \times 4\frac{15}{16}$ in (9.9 × 12.7 cm)
The Baltimore Museum of Art: George A. Lucas Collection (BMA 1996.48.1048)
R.S.24 (fifth state)

BMA

22 *Three Ballet Dancers* ca. 1876
monotype
$7\frac{3}{4} \times 16\frac{3}{8}$ in. (20 × 41.7 cm)
Sterling and Francine Clark Art Institute, Williamstown, Massachusetts (no. 1386)
J.9

23 *In the Wings* ca. 1878–80
lithograph
$10 \times 7\frac{1}{4}$ in. (25.5 cm × 19 cm)
Private collection, courtesy Ruth Ziegler Fine Arts, New York
R.S.38

JAM

24 *Dancer in Green* ca. 1879
pastel on paper
$19 \times 11\frac{1}{2}$ in. (48.3 × 29.2 cm)
New Orleans Museum of Art, Gift of Charles C. Henderson in memory of Nancy S. Henderson (74.282)
L.488

25 *Dancer with a Fan* ca. 1876–78
black chalk heightened with white on blue-gray paper
$18\frac{7}{8} \times 12\frac{3}{8}$ in. (48 × 31.5 cm)
Museum Boijmans Van Beuningen Rotterdam (F–II–222)
V.III, no. 339 (i)

JAM, CAI

26 *Dancers (fan design)* ca. 1879–80
gouache (or distemper) with gold and charcoal on silk
$13\frac{1}{8} \times 24\frac{3}{4}$ in. (33.3 × 62.8 cm)
The Baltimore Museum of Art: Fanny B. Thalheimer Memorial Fund (BMA 1963.9)
L.555

27 *Dancer with a Fan* ca. 1879
pastel on paper
$17\frac{3}{4} \times 11\frac{3}{8}$ in. (45 × 29 cm)
Private collection
L.545

28 *At the Theater: Woman with a Fan* ca. 1878–80
lithograph
$9\frac{1}{8} \times 7\frac{7}{8}$ in. (23.2 × 20 cm)
Museum of Fine Arts, Boston, Bequest of W.G. Russell Allen (60.260)
R.S.37

29 *Dancing Lesson* ca. 1880
oil on canvas
$15\frac{1}{2} \times 34\frac{13}{16}$ in. (39.4 × 88.4 cm)
Sterling and Francine Clark Art Institute, Williamstown, Massachusetts (no. 562)
L.820

30 *Dancer with a Fan* ca. 1880
pastel on gray-green laid paper
$24 \times 16\frac{1}{2}$ in. (61 × 41.9 cm)
The Metropolitan Museum of Art, New York, H.O. Havemeyer Collection, Bequest of Mrs. H.O. Havemeyer, 1929 (29.100.188)
L.823

JAM

31 *Schoolgirl* ca. 1880–81
bronze
$11 \times 4\frac{5}{8} \times 5\frac{3}{4}$ in.
(27.9 × 11.7 × 14.6 cm)
Virginia Museum of Fine Arts, Richmond, Virginia, Gift of Harry Brooks (no. 66.2)
R.LXXIV

32 *Study of Three Dancers* ca. 1880
charcoal and pastel on buff paper
$18\frac{3}{8} \times 20\frac{1}{8}$ in. (46.7 × 51.2 cm)
Private collection, Rochester, New York
L.579

33 *Dancers* ca. 1880
pastel with charcoal
$18\frac{3}{4} \times 24\frac{1}{2}$ in. (47.6 × 62.2 cm)
Private collection, courtesy Browse and Darby Gallery, London
V.III, no. 397

34a Notebook 29, Folio 25 ca. 1878–79
pencil on paper
$9\frac{7}{8} \times 14\frac{3}{8}$ in. (25.1 × 36.5 cm)
The Pierpont Morgan Library, New York, Thaw Collection(1985.47)

JAM, CAI

34b Notebook 29, Folio 41 ca. 1878–79
blue chalk on paper
$9\frac{7}{8} \times 14\frac{3}{8}$ in. (25.1 × 36.5 cm)
The Pierpont Morgan Library, New York, Thaw Collection(1985.47)

BMA

35 *Two Dancers* ca. 1878–79
charcoal and white chalk on green commercially coated wove paper
25⅛ × 19¼ in. (63.8 × 48.9 cm)
The Metropolitan Museum of Art, New York, H.O. Havemeyer Collection, Bequest of Mrs. H.O. Havemeyer, 1929 (29.100.189)
L.599

JAM

36 *Three Studies of a Nude Dancer* ca. 1878–79
charcoal heightened with white chalk on gray wove paper
18¹³⁄₁₆ × 24½ in. (47.7 × 62.3 cm)
Private collection, London
V.III, no. 386

37 *Dancer at Rest, Hands on Her Hips, Left Leg Forward* ca. 1877–79
bronze
14¾ in. (37.5 cm) high
Allen Memorial Art Museum, Oberlin College, Oberlin, Ohio, R.T. Miller, Jr. Fund 1955
R.XXI

38 *Study of a Nude Dancer* ca. 1878–79 or later
black chalk and charcoal on mauve-pink laid paper
18¹⁵⁄₁₆ × 12¹⁄₁₆ in. (48.1 × 30.6 cm)
Nasjonalgalleriet, Oslo (NG.K&H.B.15574)
V.IV, 287(a)

JAM

39 *Nude Study for Little Dancer Aged Fourteen*
original version ca. 1878–79 (reworked later)
bronze
28½ in. (72.4 cm) high
The Toledo Museum of Art, Toledo, Ohio, Purchased with funds from the Libbey Endowment, Gift of Edward Drummond Libbey (1950.246)
R.XIX

40 *Three Studies of a Dancer in Fourth Position*
ca. 1878–81
charcoal and pastel with stumping, touches of brush, and black wash on grayish-tan laid paper with blue fibers laid on gray wove paper
18⅞ × 24¼ in. (48 × 61.5 cm)
The Art Institute of Chicago, Bequest of Adele R. Levy (1962.703)
L.586 ter

41 *Three Studies of a Dancer* ca. 1878–81
black chalk heightened with white on pink paper
18⅛ × 24 in. (46 × 61 cm)
Private collection
L.586 bis

CAI

42 Studies for *Little Dancer Aged Fourteen*
ca. 1878–81
pencil, charcoal, and pastel on green paper
19 × 12 in. (48.5 × 30.5 cm)
Private collection, courtesy Thomas Gibson Fine Art Ltd., London
V.III, no. 149

43 *Four Studies of a Dancer* ca. 1878–81
chalk and charcoal, heightened with gray wash and white, on buff wove paper
19¼ × 12⅝ in. (48.9 × 32.1)
Musée du Louvre, Paris, Département des Arts Graphiques: Fonds du Musée d'Orsay
V.III, no. 341 (ii)

JAM

44a *Little Dancer Aged Fourteen* original wax
ca. 1878–81; bronze ca. 1921 or later
bronze and fabric
39 in. (99 cm) high
Sterling and Francine Clark Art Institute, Williamstown, Massachusetts (no. 45)
R.XX

JAM, CAI

44b *Little Dancer Aged Fourteen* original wax
ca. 1878–81; bronze ca. 1921 or later
bronze and fabric
38 in. (96.5 cm) high
The Baltimore Museum of Art: Alice Morawetz Bequest Fund (BMA 1943.1)
R.XX

BMA [illustrated back cover]

45 *Little Dancer Aged Fourteen* original wax ca. 1878–81; plaster ca. 1920–21
plaster and fabric
39 in. (99 cm) high
Joslyn Art Museum, Omaha, Nebraska, Gift of M. Knoedler & Co. (1971.271.a–b)
R.XX [illustrated text, front cover]

JAM

46 *Dancer Adjusting Her Dress* ca. 1881–85
pastel on paper
24¼ × 18¼ in. (61.5 × 46.3 cm)
Portland Art Museum, Portland, Oregon; Bequest of Winslow B. Ayer (35.42)
L.676

47 *Dancer Standing* ca. 1885
charcoal and pastel on paper
18⅝ × 15⅝ in. (47.3 × 39.6 cm)
Private collection
L.909

JAM, CAI

48 *Ballet Dancer Standing* ca. 1885
black chalk heightened with white chalk and pastel on gray laid paper
11⅞ × 9½ in. (30.3 × 24.1 cm)
The Baltimore Museum of Art: The Cone Collection, formed by Dr. Claribel Cone and Miss Etta Cone of Baltimore, Maryland (BMA1950.12.659)
V.II, no. 218 (i)

49 *Dancers* ca. 1885
pastel
18½ × 24⅜ in. (47 × 62 cm)
Private collection
V.III, no. 376

50 *Dancer Ready to Dance, Right Leg Forward*
ca. 1882–95
bronze
22 in. (55.5 cm) high
Sterling and Francine Clark Art Institute, Williamstown, Massachusetts (no. 48)
R.XLVI

51 *Grand Arabesque, First Time* ca. 1882–95
bronze
19 in. (48 cm) high
Sterling and Francine Clark Art Institute, Williamstown, Massachusetts (no. 46)
R.XXXV

52 *Spanish Dance* original wax ca. 1883–85; plaster ca. 1920 or later
plaster
18½ in. (47 cm) high
Private collection, MBS Co. (courtesy of Alex, Reid & Lefevre, Ltd., London)
R.XLVII

53 *Dancer Moving Forward* ca. 1882–95
bronze
25 × 12⅝ × 8¼ in. (63.5 × 32 × 21 cm)
Smith College Museum of Art, Northampton, Massachusetts (1965:29)
R.XXVI

54 *Dancer Moving Forward, Arms Raised*
ca. 1882–95
bronze
27¼ × 12⅜ × 12½ in.
(69.2 × 31.4 × 31.7 cm)
Hirshhorn Museum and Sculpture Garden, Smithsonian Institution, Washington, D.C. Gift of Joseph H. Hirshhorn, 1966 (HMSG1966.1298)
R.XXIV

55 *Fourth Position Front, on the Left Leg*
ca. 1882–95
bronze
22 9/16 × 12 3/8 × 13 1/4 in.
(57.3 × 31.4 × 33.6 cm)
The Baltimore Museum of Art: The Cone Collection, formed by Dr. Claribel Cone and Miss Etta Cone of Baltimore, Maryland (1950.413)
R.XLIV

56 *Dancer Looking at the Sole of Her Right Foot*
original wax ca. 1882–95; plaster ca. 1900
plaster
18 7/8 in. (48 cm) high
Private collection, MBS Co. (courtesy of Alex, Reid & Lefevre, Ltd., London)
R.XLV

57 *Dancer Looking at the Sole of Her Right Foot*
original wax ca. 1882–95; bronze ca. 1920 or later
bronze
18 × 8 9/16 × 7 3/8 in. (45.7 × 21.7 × 18.7 cm)
The Baltimore Museum of Art: The Cone Collection, formed by Dr. Claribel Cone and Miss Etta Cone of Baltimore, Maryland (BMA 1950.415)
R.XLV

58 *Dancer at Rest, Hands Behind Her Back, Right Leg Forward* ca. 1877–79
bronze
17 3/4 × 5 1/4 × 9 1/2 in.
(45.1 × 13.3 × 24.2 cm)
Brooklyn Museum of Art, Gift of Mr. and Mrs. Richard Rodgers (70.176.5)
R.XXI

59 *Dancer at Rest, Hands Behind Her Back, Right Leg Forward* ca. 1885–95
bronze
17 3/8 × 9 7/8 × 7 3/4 in.
(44.1 × 24.9 × 19.5 cm)
Hirshhorn Museum and Sculpture Garden, Smithsonian Institution, Washington, D.C. Gift of Joseph H. Hirshhorn, 1966
R.XXII

60 *Dancer at Rest* ca. 1885–90
charcoal on paper
14 × 9 in. (35.5 × 22.5 cm)
Janet Traeger Salz, Inc., New York
First owned by Jeanne Fevre

61 *Dressed Dancer at Rest, Hands Behind Her Back, Right Leg Forward* ca. 1895–1905
bronze
16 3/4 in. (42.5 cm) high
The Nathan and Marian Smooke Collection
R.LII

JAM

62 *Dancer* ca. 1897–1900
pastel and charcoal
22 × 17 3/4 in. (56 × 45 cm)
The Baltimore Museum of Art: The Cone Collection, formed by Dr. Claribel Cone and Miss Etta Cone of Baltimore, Maryland (BMA 1950.205)

BMA

NOTES

References to the standard catalogues of works by Degas are indicated as follows:
L. – Lemoisne 1946; R. – Rewald 1944; B.R. – Brame and Reff 1984; J. – Janis 1968; R.S. – Reed and Shapiro 1984.

CHAPTER I

1 See for example Reff, *Notebooks,* Notebook 6, p. 9; Notebook 8, pp. 26v, 28, and 29; Notebook 10, p. 27a; Notebook 13, pp. 51 and 77a; Notebook 14a, pp. 2–3; Notebook 18, p. 83; and Adriani, *Degas: Pastels, Oil Sketches, Drawings,* no. 30.
2 L.146; for a more complete discussion of the genesis of this painting, see Dumas, *Degas's "Mlle. Fiocre" in Context,* and Boggs, et al., *Degas,* pp. 133–37.
3 Zola, *Mon salon,* p. 165.
4 For Carpeaux's portrait, see Musée d'Orsay, *Catalogue sommaire,* p. 72; Degas' pleasure in a "reduction in terra-cotta of Carpeaux's *Fiocre*" which he would "touch and caress" in his near-blind last years is reported in Daniel Halévy, *Pays parisiens,* p. 72, though the phrasing leaves open the possibility that the work belonged to Halévy. A photograph of the Halévy salon in 1890 (see Loyrette, ed., *Entre le théâtre et l'histoire,* p. 153) appears to show such a bust.
5 R.II.
6 L.186.
7 Chesneau, "Au salon," p. 2, in Berson, *The New Painting* 1:19–20; Carjat, "L'Exposition du boulevard des Capucines," p. 3, in Berson, pp. 14–15; d'Hervilly, "L'exposition du boulevard des Capucines," p. 2, in Berson, pp. 23–24.
8 Burty, "Exposition de la société anonyme," p. 2, in Berson, pp. 36–38.
9 Zola, "Lettres de Paris," p. 1, in Berson, pp. 108–09; Flor, "Les Ateliers de Paris," p. 3, in Berson, pp. 280–81.
10 See for example L.186, L.294, and L.295.
11 Writing of *The Rehearsal of the Ballet on Stage* (L.400) (which is described in Boggs, et al., p. 227, as "Essence with traces of watercolour and pastel over pen-and-ink drawing on paper, mounted on canvas"), George Moore observed that it was "begun in watercolour, continued in gouache and afterwards completed in oils," to which a "finishing hand has been given in pen-and-ink"; see Moore, "Memories of Degas," p. 64. The best general account of Degas' techniques remains Rouart, *Degas à la recherche.*
12 Lemoisne, *Degas et son oeuvre,* 1:162.
13 L.297; Anon., *Art Journal* (1876): 211, cited in Pickvance, "Degas's Dancers," p. 258.
14 The three works, L.340, L.400, and L.498, are analyzed in Boggs, et al., pp. 225–30.
15 Chesneau, p. 2.
16 For this study, see Vente III, *Catalogue,* no.132 i; other links between *Rehearsal in the Ballet Foyer* and *Ballet Rehearsal on Stage* are their recognizable settings in the rue Le Peletier building, their predominantly monochrome palettes, and their conspicuous incorporation of linear under-drawing (in the former work, pen-and-ink were evidently used, as in the two companion pictures to *Ballet Rehearsal on Stage;* see note 14 above).
17 See for example L.496, L.625, L.900, L.905, L.909, L.1004, L.1012–19.
18 Browse, *Degas Dancers,* p. 56.
19 L.425.
20 House, *Impressionism for England,* p. 90.
21 For the identification of works representing these and other dancers, see Browse, pp. 60–62, 360–61, and Shackelford, *Degas: The Dancers,* p. 88. Shackelford links Nelly Franklin with cat. 10 in the present volume.
22 In his text (see note 23 below) Degas describes an encounter with Auguste Vaucorbeil (Director of the Opéra from 1879 to 1884), Louis Mérante (Maître de ballet at the Opéra from 1868 to 1886), and Madame Théodore, the instructor of the younger pupils. Degas was clearly on familiar terms with Jules Perrot, former dancer turned instructor, who featured in several of his pictures (see L.364–7, and Boggs, "Degas as a Portraitist," in Baumann and Karabelnik, eds., *Degas Portraits,* pp. 54–55.)
23 See Loyrette, "Degas à l'Opéra," in Musée d'Orsay, *Degas inédit,* pp. 46–63. For the *foyer de la danse,* see Kahane, *Le Foyer de la danse.* The letters are in Guérin, ed., *Degas Letters,* p. 66, and Degas' notes are in Lemoisne, p. 115; both seem to be datable to the late 1870s or very early 1880s on the basis of internal evidence in the notes (see Lemoisne's references 135 and 136) and the fact that letter no. 43 was sent from 19 bis, rue Fontaine St-Georges, the address of Degas' apartment until 1882.
24 For a description of the contents of Degas' studio in later years, see Lafond, *Degas,* p. 114.
25 Studies for this work are L.362 bis and L.376, Vente III, no. 132 i.
26 See Thomson, *The Private Degas,* p. 65.
27 Jeanniot, "Souvenirs sur Degas," pp. 153, 155.
28 L.602.
29 De Charry, "Les Indépendants," p. 3, in Berson, pp. 333–34; Ephrussi, "Exposition des artistes indépendants," p. 126, in Berson, pp. 336–37
30 Havemeyer, *Sixteen to Sixty,* p. 254; for the records of other visitors, see Kendall, *Degas: Beyond Impressionism,* pp. 32–33.
31 For Valadon's contacts with Degas, see Kendall, *Beyond Impressionism,* pp. 170–71.
32 Browse, p. 46; Guest, *Le Ballet de l'Opéra,* pp. 136–37; Kahane, p. 9. For many of the observations on the history and current practice of the ballet, as well as on Degas' depictions of the dance, I am deeply indebted to my discussions with Jill DeVonyar-Zansky.
33 Moffett, et al., *The New Painting,* p. 44.
34 See Chapter 2, note 51.
35 For a fine analysis of the making of this and other current ballet paintings, see Shackelford, chapter 2.
36 Coquiot, *Degas,* p. 79, and Smith, *Natural History,* pp. 16 and 33; the subject is discussed from a modern perspective in Kahane and Pinasa, *Le Tutu: petit guide.*
37 Coquiot, p. 74.
38 Un vieil abonné [Mahalin], *Ces Demoiselles de l'Opéra,* p. 48.
39 For the rue Le Peletier theater, see Gourret, *Histoire des salles,* pp. 141–62; details of the auditorium and dance foyer are visible in engravings reproduced in Gourret, pp. 156 and 160. The foyer was located in the adjoining eighteenth-century Hôtel de Choiseul, which accounts for the style of the room's interior. Degas' continued attachment to the building is noted in Browse, p. 67.
40 Vieil abonné, p. 273.
41 For the details of Marie van Goethem, see Reff, *The Artist's Mind,* p. 245, n. 18 and 19, and Millard, *The Sculpture of Edgar Degas,* pp. 8–9, n. 26. The dancer's name is variously spelled Goethen, Gutten, and Goeuthen.
42 Degas' entire professional life was spent in

various properties in this small quarter of Paris. In the late 1870s, he is recorded in the rue Blanche, the rue Frochot, the rue Lepic, and (around 1880) in the rue Fontaine St-Georges, the latter intersecting with the rue de Douai. The Halévys lived at no. 22, the van Goethems at no. 36.

43 Reff, *Notebooks*, Notebook 22, p. 11.

44 The possibility that Marie dissembled her age is considered in Boggs, et al., p. 347. In addition to the preparatory studies included in the present volume, one further drawing, *Three Studies of a Nude* (Vente III, no. 369), is at present unlocated.

45 Reff, *Notebooks*, Notebook 34, p. 2. The reference to Marie's hair is in Browse, p. 62, though the story is questioned in Millard, pp. 8–9, n. 26.

46 The unpublished Cassatt letter in question is cited in Millard, pp. 8–9, n. 26.

47 L.484; see Browse, notes to plates 160–65, and L.471–73, L.483, L.485–87.

48 Vieil abonné, p. 265; the appearance of a similar claim in a text of 1882, cited in Millard, pp. 8–9, n. 26, suggests that the 1887 description was plagiarized.

49 Browse, p. 62; the later career of one of the sisters, evidently Louise-Joséphine, is mentioned in Coquiot, p. 81, and the lives of all three girls are discussed in Millard, pp. 8–9, n. 26.

50 Berson, p. 326.

51 Saint-Léon, *De l'etat actuel*, p. 3. For Degas and Mauri, see Havemeyer, p. 246; Browse, pp. 62-63; Boggs, et al., pp. 456–57; Kahane, p. 12.

52 See Vizentini, *Derrière la toile*, and Vieil abonné.

53 Kahane, p. 13.

54 Saint-Léon, p. 9.

55 Vizentini, p. 27, gives the age as 5; Coquiot, p. 7, specifies 7; and Saint-Léon, p. 8, and Bernay, *La Danse au théâtre*, p. 99, agree on 8.

56 Both illustrations are taken from Claretie, "Paul Renouard." A very similar drawing to that depicted within the scene is reproduced in Vuillier, *La Danse*, p. 365.

57 Vizentini, p. 27.

58 Guest, pp. 123 and 99.

59 Blasis, *Traité elementaire*, pp. 101 and 21; Duval, *Terpsichore*, p. 12.

60 Smith, p. 19; Chesneau, *Le Statuaire J.-B. Carpeaux*, p. 113; a caricature of 1841 showing such exemplary dancers as Taglioni, Elssler, and Grisi (see Guest, p. 100) presents them as emaciated figures with spindly arms and legs.

61 Duval, pp. 43–44.

62 Further drawings of the same dancer are in Browse, pls. 76 and 78.

63 Kahane, p. 12, n. 7, pp. 42–43.

64 De Charry, p. 3; Mantz, "Oeuvres des artistes indépendants," p. 3, in Berson, pp. 356–59; de Villard, "Variétés," p. 2, in Berson, pp. 370–71.

65 Claretie, "La Vie à Paris," p. 3, in Berson, pp. 335–36; de Mont, "L'Exposition," p. 2, in Berson, pp. 360–62.

66 De Villard, p. 2; Claretie, "La Vie à Paris," p. 3; Huysmans, "L'Exposition des indépendants," pp. 225–57, in Berson, p. 349.

67 Ephrussi, p. 126.

68 Huysmans, in Berson, p. 349.

69 Vieil abonné, p. 26.

70 It should also be remembered that, in its original knee-length tutu, relatively little of the dancer's lower body would have been visible.

71 In Browse, p. 53, the position is described as "quatrième derrière."

72 Blasis, *The Art of Dancing*, p. 99 and pl. II, fig. 1; Bernay, p. 97.

73 Ephrussi, p. 126.

74 Sickert, "Degas," p. 184. The existence of similar poses in the recent paintings of Degas' contemporaries may point to other echoes or rivalries: see, for example, Whistler's *Harmony in Yellow and Gold: The Gold Girl – Connie Gilchrist* of 1876 and his *Harmony in Grey and Green: Miss Cicely Alexander* of 1876–77, and Renoir's *Madame Henriot "en travesti" (The Page)* of 1875–76.

75 Our Lady Correspondent, *Artist*, p. 153, in Flint, pp. 41–43; Ephrussi, p. 126.

76 Mantz, p. 1; Bertall, "Des peintres intransigeants," p. 2; Trianon, "Sixième exposition de peinture," p. 3, in Berson, pp. 366–69; de Mont, p. 2.

77 Mantz, p. 3.

78 Ephrussi, p. 126.

79 Kahane, p 12; in Lipton, *Looking into Degas*, pp. 89–91, the poverty of dancers above the level of "rats" is disputed.

80 For an account of the successes, see Vieil abonné, pp. 285–87.

81 Official attitudes to the situation are described in Kahane, p. 11.

82 Daly, cited in Kahane, p. 26.

83 Garnier, *Le Nouvel Opéra*, 1:53.

84 The caption reads: "Enfin, v'la z'une petite qui d'vient grande, a'doit bien déja commencer à gagner? – Oui, des puces!!!" The issue in question is numbered 293.

85 Cited in Kahane, p. 12.

86 Lipton, p. 89, Kahane, p. 6.

87 See Millet, "La Famille Mante," p. 109.

88 The two pastels are L.971–72; Browse, pp. 59–61.

89 See Browse, p. 61; Millet; Boggs, et. al., pp. 16–19.

90 Vizentini, pp. 31–34; Vieil abonné, p. 266.

91 Mallarmé, "The Impressionists and Edouard Manet," p. 121, in Berson, pp. 91–97; Claretie, "La Vie à Paris," p. 3; Vizentini, p. iv.

92 Ludovic Halévy, *La Famille Cardinal*, pp. 1–34.

93 Janis, *Degas Monotypes*, nos. 195–321. For further discussion of this sequence of prints, see Boggs, et al., pp. 280–84, and Kendall, "The Impromptu Print," in *Degas intime*.

94 For these and other *abonnés* at the time, see Loyrette, "Degas à l'Opéra," pp. 46–63; Vizentini, pp. 1–36; Vieil abonné, pp. 270–73.

95 De Charry, p. 3.

96 De Mont, p. 2; Mantz, p. 3; Trianon, p. 3; Our Lady Correspondent, p. 153.

97 Bertall, p. 1, in Berson, pp. 330–31.

CHAPTER 2

1 Claretie, "La Vie à Paris," p. 3.

2 Millard, p. 47.

3 For more detailed discussions of these issues, see Kendall, "Who Said Anything About Rodin," Kendall, *Beyond Impressionism*, pp. 31–38, and Kendall, *The Lost Plasters*.

4 Morisot, *Correspondence*, p. 181.

5 Fusco and Janson, *The Romantics to Rodin*, pp. 112–13.

6 For the Rouart collection, see Valéry, *Degas, Manet, Morisot*, pp. 8–10; Blanche, *Propos de peintre*, pp. 257–61; Distel, *Impressionism: The First Collectors*, pp. 177–93.

7 Pingeot, et al., *La Sculpture française*, cat. no. 144; Fusco and Janson, p. 112.

8 Blasis, *Traité elementaire*, p. 22; Duval, p. 33.

9 *Charivari*, 21 February 1846.

10 The Houdon bust is mentioned in Vieil abonné, pp. 270–71, and is visible in engravings reproduced in Kahane, nos. 2–4. The fan is B.R. no. 86.

11 The work is just visible in the turn-of-the-century postcard (fig. 5) toward the right-hand side of the Opéra facade. Its reception is discussed in Potts, "Dance, Politics and Sculpture," pp. 91–109, and de Margerie, *La "Danse" de Carpeaux*.

12 See Musée d'Orsay, *Catalogue*, p. 72.

13 Daniel Halévy, *Pays parisiens*, p. 72.

14 The very rare sculptures with dance themes listed in Salon catalogues of the period, such as *Un leçon de danse: satyrs* by A.-A. Pesne shown in 1881 (Salon 1881, *The Illustrated Catalogue*, no. 4195), almost invariably suggest a classical or literary subject. Similarly, dance sculptures by contemporaries such as Gérôme and Meissonier tend to have a pronounced historical character; see Ackerman, *Jean-Léon Gérôme*, cat. S21, and Durey, et al., *Ernest Meissonier*, nos. 155–56.

15 See Kendall, *Beyond Impressionism*, pp. 163–64.

16 The work is now in the Louvre, no. C.C.37.

17 Musée d'Orsay, *Catalogue*, p. 81.

18 For the encounters between Chapu and Degas in Italy, see Loyrette, *Degas*, pp. 91–100.

19 Baignières, "Le Salon de 1879," p. 148.

20 See Musée d'Orsay, *Catalogue*, pp. 144–45.

21 Mantz, "Salon de 1865," pp. 35–36.

22 The echo is clearer when the French title, *Chanteur florentin du quinzième siècle* is compared to its equivalent, *Petite danseuse de quatorze ans*.

23 Valéry, p. 42.

24 Fusco and Janson, p. 242.

25 Fevre, *Mon oncle Degas*, p. 36; for Dubois' *St John the Baptist*, see Musée d'Orsay, *Catalogue*, p. 146, and for Degas' version, see L.20 and related drawings.

26 Fusco and Janson, p. 118.

27 Gaborit, et al., *Sculptures en cire,* pp. 237–50. For Dubois' use of drawings, see Pingeot, *La Sculpture française,* p. 62.
28 Guillaume, "Le Salon de 1881," p. 673; Buisson, "Le Salon de 1881," pp. 211–12.
29 Baudelaire, *The Mirror of Art,* p. 121.
30 Ibid, pp. 121 and 288.
31 De Montaiglon, "La Sculpture," in Gonse, ed., *L'Art moderne,* p. 69.
32 Huysmans, in Berson, p. 349.
33 Huysmans, *L'Art moderne,* p. 90.
34 Ward-Jackson, "Reinvesting the Idol," p. 803.
35 Guillaume, "Le Salon de 1879," p. 920.
36 For Carpeaux, see Gaborit, pp. 189–94; for Guillaume, see Musée d'Orsay, *Catalogue,* pp. 168–73; for Dubois, see Gaborit, pp. 237–50.
37 In Duranty, *Le Pays des arts,* p. 163.
38 Gaborit, p. 17.
39 Ibid.
40 See the discussion of such artifacts in Chapter 3.
41 For Degas' awareness of Poussin and Moreau, see Kendall, *Beyond Impressionism,* p. 255; for Meissonier, see Durey, pp. 236–57; for Gauguin, see Gray, *Paul Gauguin,* especially cat. nos. 4 (ii), 6, 61, and 112; for Pissarro, see Thomson, "Camille Pissarro," pp. 25–28.
42 In 1880, fifteen were exhibited (see Salon 1880, *The Illustrated Catalogue*); the following year, the number was eighteen (see Salon 1881); the examples cited are 1880, no. 6192, and 1881, no. 4149.
43 Gaborit, p. 16.
44 The work is now in the Musée des Beaux-Arts, Lille. For Cuvelier, see Lami, *Dictionnaire* 1:470.
45 Degas' distress at the death of Cuvelier is recorded in Daniel Halévy, *Degas parle,* p. 157, and Morisot, p. 56. The works shown in 1878 are listed in *Exposition Universelle de 1878,* p. 90. They were referred to in Gamilly, "Les Beaux-arts," p. 94.
46 See Cooper, *Romantic Bronzes,* pl. 146, and Pyke, *Dictionary of Wax Modellers,* p. 50.
47 Gonse, "Musée Wicar," pp. 193–205; Blondel, "Les modelleurs en cire," pp. 493–504.
48 Reff, *The Artist's Mind,* pp. 246–47; Guérin, p. 63.
49 Claretie, *La Vie à Paris,* pp. 436–38.
50 Guillaume "Le Salon de 1879," p. 938. In Daniel Halévy, *Degas parle,* p. 62, it is revealed that Guillaume was the cousin of Degas' close friend, Henri Rouart.
51 For Dubois' *Eve,* see Gaborit, pp. 238–41.
52 RF 4311; for Cros' work in wax, see Gaborit, pp. 213–19.
53 Guillaume, "Le Salon de 1879," p. 929. Ringel added *d'Illzach* to his name after 1886; see Gaborit, p. 331.
54 An engraving of *Splendeur et misère* is in Chevillot, "Réalisme," p . 23. The portrait of Rollinat is in the Musée d'Art Moderne, Strasbourg; see Gaborit, pp. 331–32.
55 Blondel, p. 438.
56 Guillaume, "Le Salon de 1879," p. 925.
57 Gonse, *L'Art moderne,* p. 70.
58 Burty, "L'Exposition des artistes," p. 3, in Berson, pp. 209–10.
59 For the catalogue, see Berson, p. 260. Gauguin's sculpture is now in the Courtauld Collection; see Gray, no. 1, and House, p. 182. Several other sculptures by Gauguin were wholly or partly made in wax; see note 41 above.
60 Gray, nos. 3 and 4.
61 Though 74 works by the artist are now recognized, Joseph Durand-Ruel's memory of finding "about 150" pieces of sculpture in Degas' studio and apartment after his death is discussed in Millard, pp. 25–26. However, the inventory made of Degas' sculptures in January 1918 (perhaps after the ruinous examples had been discarded), now in the Durand-Ruel archive, lists only 80 items (see Pingeot, *Degas Sculptures,* pp. 192–93).
62 R.I; Reff, *The Artist's Mind,* pp. 249–56. The wax originals of all four works under discussion are reproduced in color in Luchs, "The Degas Waxes," pp. 178–211.
63 R.LXXIV; Reff, *Notebooks,* Notebook 34, pp. 13, 17, and 19.
64 R.XXI. A summary of the proposed dates is in Pingeot, *Degas Sculptures,* p. 162.
65 Luchs, p. 200.
66 Moore, p. 27; Jeanniot, p. 302; Whibley, "Modern Men," p. 603, in Flint, pp. 275–79. The practice of dressing wax maquettes in provisional costumes of fabric or paper was widespread. See, for example, *Le Souvenir* by Dubois, in Gaborit, pp. 242–44, and *Le Voyageur* and *Muse Dansante* by Meissonier, in Durey, nos. 151 and 155.
67 Boggs, et al., p. 349.
68 Barbour, "Degas's Little Dancer," pp. 28–32.
69 Elsen, *Pioneers,* p. 76.
70 Mantz, "Oeuvres des artistes indépendants," p. 3.
71 See Chapter 1, notes 41 and 44.
72 See Chapter 5.
73 The lost drawing is Vente III, no. 369.
74 Reff, *Notebooks,* Notebook 30, p. 56.
75 The possibility that Degas' abandonment of the figure with raised arms was linked in some way with the decision to "re-make" the arms in the *Nude Study* should perhaps be considered.
76 For recent discussions of the drawings, see Shackelford, chapter 3; Boggs, et al., pp. 346–49; Thomson, pp. 119–25; Callen, *The Spectacular Body,* pp. 21–29; Boggs, *Degas,* pp. 44–45.
77 In the notebook evidently in use at this time, Degas included some instructions for the *procédé bitterlin,* a process for the use of watercolor; see Reff, *Notebooks,* Notebook 30, pp. 89A and B.
78 The exceptionally weak, almost childish, depiction of legs at bottom left in the Louvre drawing is surely the work of another hand.
79 Doucet owned L.586 bis, Roger Marx L.586 ter; for the latter, see Marx, "Cartons d'artiste," pp. 321 and 324.
80 Pantazzi, "Fourteen-Year-Old Dancer," in Boggs et al., p. 343.
81 Reff, *Notebooks,* Notebook 34, p. 228. In Millard, p. 39 n. 64, it is also noted that a maker of dressed dolls shared the same address and may have contributed to the clothing of the sculpture.
82 Our Lady Correspondent, p. 153. The various kinds of shoes worn in rehearsal and performance, which included coarser practice varieties, are described in Vieil abonné, pp. 8–9.
83 Ephrussi, p. 126.
84 Mantz, "Oeuvres des artistes indépendants," p. 3; de Villard, p. 2; Huysmans, in Berson, p. 349; Our Lady Correspondent, p. 153.
85 Ephrussi, p. 126; Huysmans, in Berson, p. 349.
86 Huysmans, in Berson, p. 349; the wax is particularly thin and flaked on parts of the plait.
87 Havemeyer, p. 255. Havemeyer's testimony would also be consistent with the application of wax to the wig to facilitate the casting of the sculpture, a possibility that was being pursued by Degas around 1903.
88 The presence of wax on the bodice is specified in Huysmans, in Berson, p. 349.
89 Our Lady Correspondent, p. 153.
90 Ephrussi, p. 126; Degas' own view that the sculpture had "blackened" by 1903 is reported in Mathews, ed., *Cassatt and Her Circle,* p. 287. References to the coloring or painting of parts of the figure in Huysmans, *L'Art moderne,* and Whibley also appear to have been prompted by the hue of the wax or by confused memories of the sculpture.
91 Millard, p. 63, n. 36.
92 The dresses are said to have been made under the supervision of the artist's niece, Jeanne Fevre, who was familiar with the much-decayed wax figure from her period of residence in the artist's apartment in his last years. The shortness of the skirts appears to reflect the vestigial tutu on the wax, the tattered and much-trimmed condition of which is visible in a set of photographs taken in 1918 (see Pingeot, *Degas Sculptures,* p. 189). That this tutu was replaced on the wax original is clear from its present condition, but that the version recorded in 1918 was *already* a replacement is suggested in an undated newspaper clipping, evidently ca. 1924, in the Documentation of the Musée d'Orsay, where Adrien Hébrard claims "deux fois dèja depuis 1881 et du vivant même de Degas, il a fallu appeler l'habilleuse de Mlle Rosita Mauri pour renouveler, sans erreur, le costume de la statue." I am grateful to Theodore Reff for bringing this text to my attention.
93 Mantz, "Oeuvres des artistes indépendants," p. 3; Huysmans, in Berson, p. 349; Our Lady Correspondent, p. 153.
94 Mallarmé, in Berson, p. 96; Ludovic Halévy, *La Famille Cardinal,* p. 65.
95 See, for example, Montorgeuil, *Paris dansant,*

p. 213; for other contemporary accounts of dancers' dresses, see Vizentini, p. 26; Vieil abonné, pp. 7–8, 29, and 47; and Montorgeuil, p. 215. The most recent study of the subject is Kahane and Pinasa.

96 The wax in this area is more generalized, becoming progressively less articulated and "finished" between knee and hips.

97 The modern reconstruction of a "short" tutu for a bronze is described in Cassar, "The Making of a Replica Skirt." Longer (but not significantly "fuller") skirts have been added to bronzes at Baltimore (1979) and Rotterdam (1996). I am grateful to the staff of these institutions for supplying details of their projects. The first systematic attempt to reconstruct Degas' original tutu, based on his preparatory drawings and a study of the practice of the day, was initiated at Joslyn Art Museum in 1996 and followed by a similar venture at the Musée d'Orsay.

98 Goetschy, "Indépendants et impressionistes," p. 2, in Berson, pp. 282–85.

99 Lemoisne, "Les Statuettes," pp. 111–12; Vollard, *An Intimate Portrait,* p. 59. Contrary to Lemoisne's suggestion, Bartholomé had not yet embarked on his career as a sculptor at this time. For the possibility that Vollard's story applies to the *Nude Study,* see Rewald, *Degas, Works in Sculpture,* p. 7.

100 X, "Artistes indépendants," p. 109, in Berson, p. 372.

101 Dalligny, "Les Indépendants," p. 1, in Berson, pp. 335–36; Enault, "Chronique," p. 1, in Berson, p. 339.

CHAPTER 3

1 Huysmans, in Berson, pp. 348–55; de Mont, p. 2; Blanche, p.54.

2 Mantz, "Oeuvres des artistes indépendants," p. 3.

3 See Millard, pp. 119–26, Berson, and the present volume.

4 Our Lady Correspondent, p. 153.

5 De Charry, p. 3; Huysmans, in Berson, p. 349; de Villard, p. 2.

6 Whibley, in Flint, p. 277; Huysmans, in Berson, p. 349.

7 Ephrussi, p. 126; Louise, "Lettres familières," p. 3, in Berson, pp. 355–56; Mantz, "Oeuvres des artistes indépendants," p. 3; Huysmans, in Berson, p. 349; de Villard, p. 2; Bertall, p. 1.

8 Claretie, "Paul Renouard," p. 436; Soldi, "La Sculpture," p. 925; Fénéon, *Petit bottin,* unpag.

9 Moore, "Painter of Modern Life," p. 416, Relin, "La 'Danseuse de quatorze ans,'" p. 174; Manzi's print is reproduced as the frontispiece to Manson, *Edgar Degas;* Marx, pp. 321 and 324; Dewhurst, *Impressionist Painting,* p. 68.

10 It should be noted that no other single work of art by Degas had produced, or was to produce in his later life, such a volume of published response.

11 De Villard, p. 2.

12 Claretie, "La Vie à Paris," p. 3; Huysmans, in Berson, p. 349.

13 Whibley, in Flint, p. 278.

14 De Mont, p. 2; Our Lady Correspondent, p. 153. The word "aztèque" was popularly used for "runt" or "puny specimen."

15 Guitry, in M. Knoedler, *Edgar Degas;* Havemeyer, p. 255.

16 Our Lady Correspondent, p. 153; Mantz, "Oeuvres des artistes indépendants," p. 3; Moore, "Painter of Modern Life," p. 416.

17 Mantz, "Oeuvres des artistes indépendants," p. 3.

18 De Mont, p. 2.

19 Louise, p. 3; Our Lady Correspondent, p. 153; de Mont, p. 2. Some of these Parisian spectacles are discussed in Gaborit.

20 Mantz, "Oeuvres des artistes indépendants," p. 3.

21 Huysmans, in Berson, p. 349; de Charry, p. 3; Bertall, p. 1; Our Lady Correspondent, p. 153.

22 Ephrussi, p. 126.

23 Trianon, p. 2.

24 For a more complete discussion of these views, see Douglas Druick's essay in the present volume.

25 Claretie, "La Vie à Paris," p. 3; Louise, p. 3.

26 Claretie, "La Vie à Paris," p. 3.

27 De Mont, p. 2; de Charry, p. 3.

28 See Reff, "Unpublished Letters," pp. 87–88; Wissman, "Realists," in Moffett, p. 338.

29 Reff, "Unpublished Letters," p. 88.

30 Mantz, "Oeuvres des artistes indépendants," p. 3; Trianon, p. 2.

31 With the exception of the eighth Impressionist exhibition of 1886, this was Degas' last participation in a group show and the beginning of his perceived "withdrawal" from public displays. For the possibility that the "incomprehension of the crowd" encouraged this change of heart, see Kendall, *Beyond Impressionism,* pp. 39–40.

32 Mantz, "Oeuvres des artistes indépendants," p. 3.

33 Mantz, "Oeuvres des artistes indépendants," p. 3; de Mont, p. 2; Huysmans, in Berson, p. 349; Havemeyer, p. 254.

34 Reff, "Degas's Sculpture," amended and reprinted as chapter 6 in Reff, *The Artist's Mind.*

35 Millard; Relin; Pantazzi.

36 Boggs, et al., pp. 197–211.

37 Druick, "La Petite danseuse et les criminels"; Callen; Cassini, "Degas."

38 Pingeot, *Degas Sculptures;* Chevillot; Campbell, "Degas' Bronzes."

39 Blühm, pp. 42, 70, and 85.

40 For the catalogue entries in question, see Berson, pp. 260 and 326.

41 L.573. The possibility of some unexplained link between Duranty and Marie van Goethem and her family is suggested by the twice-repeated proximity of their names and addresses in Degas' notebooks (see Reff, *Notebooks,* Notebook 22, p. 211, and Notebook 32, p. 2) and the fact that in two of the supposed portraits of Marie (L.573 and L.479) she is shown reading a newspaper.

42 Moore, *Confessions,* p. 76.

43 See Tabary, *Duranty,* pp. 17–21.

44 The painting *Hommage à Delacroix* is in the Musée d'Orsay. For Duranty's wider activities, see Tabary, and Crouzet, *Un méconnu du réalisme.*

45 Bareau, *Manet By Himself,* p. 47; Moreau-Nélaton, *Manet raconté,* 1:103.

46 Duranty, "La Simple Vie," in Duranty, *Le Pays des arts,* pp. 322–49.

47 Ibid, p. 335.

48 See note 28 above.

49 Duranty, *Le Pays des arts,* p. 335.

50 The painting is L.271; the review is cited in Lemoisne, p. 62.

51 The three paintings are L.335, L.517, and L.660; Guérin, pp. 39, 61–62, 262–63; Duranty, "La Quatrième Exposition," pp. 126–28, in Berson, p. 219; Reff, "Unpublished Letters," p. 87, n. 4; Crouzet, pp. 393–94, 402.

52 Duranty, *La Nouvelle Peinture,* translated in Moffett, pp. 37–47; Rivière, *Monsieur Degas,* p. 60.

53 Moffett, pp. 42 and 44.

54 Ibid, p. 40.

55 Ibid, pp. 44–45.

56 Ibid, p. 44.

57 Ibid, p. 47.

58 Ibid, pp. 43–44.

59 Duranty's publications are listed in Tabary, pp. 181–224.

60 Exceptions are Reff, *Notebooks;* Relin, "La 'Danseuse de quatorze ans'"; Relin, "La 'Ballerina di quattordici anni,'" in Camesasca; Reff, "The Morbid Content of Degas' Sculpture."

61 De Villard, p. 2; Mantz, "Oeuvres des artistes indépendants," p. 3.

62 Ephrussi, p. 126.

63 Moore, *Confessions,* p. 416.

64 Mantz uses the phrase "poupées qui tournent aux vitrines des coiffures"; *Nouveau Petit Larousse,* ca. 1900, p. 817.

65 For doll manufacture, see Hillier, *Wax Dolls,* p. 131.

66 Lafond, p. 118.

67 Vollard, p. 22.

68 Reff, *Notebooks,* Notebook 34, p. 228.

69 For Morisot, see Higgonet, *Berthe Morisot's Images,* p. 77.

70 L.705, Metropolitan Museum of Art. The picture's association with Marie is proposed in Boggs, et al., p. 399. Similar hat stands can be seen in nineteenth-century engravings, such as those in Farwell, ed., *The Cult of Images,* nos. 113–14.

71 L.326, Fundaçao Calouste Gulbenkian, Lisbon.

72 In Reff, *Notebooks,* pp. 126–29, it is argued that the work was never exhibited; for the later use of the dummy or clothes stand see for example L.1423 bis. See also Hofmann.

73 Guérin, p. 127.
74 Jeanniot, p. 168.
75 Ibid, p. 292.
76 Raunay, "Degas," p. 470.
77 National Gallery, London.
78 L.89; see Kendall, *Images of Women*, p. 28.
79 Tabary, pp. 65–67, where the painter of the décor is identified as Hamon. A large painting of 1852 by Jean-Louis Hamon, *La Comédie humaine,* which depicts Punch and Judy in a fanciful historical setting, is in the Musée d'Orsay. For Sardou, see Reff, *Notebooks,* Notebook 29, p. 3.
80 Tabary, pp. 65–69; Crouzet, pp. 133–42.
81 Crouzet, p. 142.
82 Tabary, p. 68; Crouzet, p. 145.
83 Crouzet, pp. 152 and 150.
84 Tabary, p. 71.
85 Duranty, *Le Mariage de raison,* p. 3; Duranty, *Théâtre des Marionnettes,* p. 386.
86 Duranty, *Théâtre des Marionnettes,* pp. 321–23.
87 Ibid, p. 193.
88 Ibid.
89 The signatures of Coindre and Gillot appear on the larger drawings, presumably for the design and print execution respectively. Duranty, who was an accomplished draftsman, may have been more responsible for the smaller images.
90 The date of closure is given as 1867 by Tabary, but as 1869 by Crouzet. The incident in question is reported in Tabary, p. 69.
91 Silvestre, *Au pays,* p. 170; de Neuville, *L'Histoire anecdotique.*
92 Duranty's article of 1862 was republished in de Neuville, p. 85; see also Duranty, *Théâtre des Marionnettes.*
93 Duranty, "Daumier," p. 532. The exhibition was held at the Durand-Ruel galleries in 1878, a year before Daumier's death. For Daumier's sculptures, see Musée d'Orsay, *Catalogue,* pp. 118-24.
94 The lithograph is mentioned in Reff, *Manet,* p. 124. It is visible on Degas' wall in one of his own photographs; see Terrasse, *Degas et la photograhie,* p. 59.
95 Duranty, *Théâtre des Marionnettes,* p. 385.
96 Louise, p. 3.
97 Tabary, pp. 67–68.
98 Crouzet, p. 142, n. 49; *L'Exposition de Paris,* pp. 198–99.
99 Zola, *Au Bonheur des dames,* p. 23.
100 Huysmans, in Berson, p. 349.
101 Baudelaire, pp. 287, 290.
102 Zola, quoted in Brown, *Zola: A Life,* p. 129; Geffroy, *La Vie artistique,* p. 174.
103 Hillier, p. 9.
104 Strutt, ed., *The Crystal Palace,* p. 267.
105 *The Paris Exhibition of 1878,* 14 (24 May 1878): 243.
106 *Les Merveilles de l'Exposition,* p. 578.
107 Rambler, "Impressions," p. 198.
108 Ibid, p. 199.
109 Ibid.
110 De Ségur, *Les Malheurs,* p. 4.
111 Ibid, pp. 15–19.
112 Tallis, *The Crystal Palace,* 2:11. The reappearance of the Montanari figures in 1878 is recorded in Blondel, "Les Modelleurs," p. 439.
113 *The Paris Exhibition of 1878,* 15 (31 May 1878): 260.
114 De Montaiglon, "La Sculpture," in Gonse, *L'Art moderne,* p. 70.
115 Potts, "Dolls and Things," p. 358.
116 Ibid, p. 361.
117 "L'étiage," in Huysmans, *Croquis parisiens,* Rollinat, *Les Névroses,* p. 328, and see Chapter 2, note 54, above. See also Héran, "Art for the sake of the soul," in Blühm, pp. 93–102.
118 For Duranty's publications at this time, see Tabary, pp. 205–10; Duranty, "La Simple Vie."
119 Duranty, "Remarques sur le geste," "Notes sur l'art assyrien," and "Remarques à propos de l'art égyptien." For the earlier articles, see also Armstrong, *Odd Man Out,* ch. 2.
120 See for example Rhoné, "L'Egypte antique," and Blanc, *Grammaire.*
121 Reff, *Notebooks,* Notebook 18, pp. 85–86; Notebook 6, pp. 35, 69, 70; the paintings are L.82 and L.87.
122 Wilkinson, *Manners and Customs,* vol. 2, pl. xii; Reff, *Notebooks,* Notebook 18, p. 86.
123 L.532.
124 Fevre, p. 50.
125 L.869; see also Gordon, *Hélène Rouart.*
126 Guérin, p. 152.
127 See Humbert et al., *Egyptomania,* and Musée du Louvre, *L'Egyptomanie;* Claretie, "Paul Renouard," p. 450.
128 Daumier's composition appeared as a wood engraving by Peulot.
129 Both Long and Degas may have used the more popular edition of the book: detailed sources for *Love's Labours Lost,* for example, can be found in Wilkinson, *A Popular Account,* pp. 66, 79, 116, 196–97, and 237.
130 Havemeyer, p. 254.
131 Havemeyer, pp. 190, 299–30.
132 Guitry, in M. Knoedler.
133 Vollard, *Renoir,* pp. 38–39.
134 Gsell, "Edgar Degas," p. 374; for Hébrard, see the text referred to in Chapter 2, note 92. For the association between the *Little Dancer* and Egyptian art, as well as its morbid connotations, see also Reff, "Morbid Content," pp. 64–71.
135 See for example De Soria, *Histoire,* pp. 15–40, and Vuillier, pp. 1–3.
136 Blondel, p. 497.
137 See Gaborit, pp. 85–96.
138 Rougé, *Notice sommaire,* p. 80.
139 Whibley, p. 604.
140 Huysmans, in Berson, p. 349; Our Lady Correspondent, p. 157.
141 See Chapter 2, notes 90 and 91.
142 Confirmed in first-hand examinations; my thanks are due to Paul Mellon for generously granting access to the sculpture and to Beverly Carter for kindly helping with my requests.
143 Rougé, p. 79.
144 The photograph carries the date 1922, but the installation it records corresponds closely with the published descriptions of this room in the late nineteenth century; apart from Duranty's, see for example Rougé, p. 79. I am most grateful to Cristiane Ziegler and Catherine Bridonneau of the Départment des Antiquités Egyptiennes at the Louvre for their patient help with my inquiries on this matter and for arranging for me to examine *La Dame Nay* (see below).
145 X, p. 109; Bertall, p. 1; de Villard, p. 2. The phrase used by Bertall ("exposé en vedette") had a possible double meaning – that of a figure's appearance in a watchtower or a sentry box – which may have obliquely referred to the sculpture in its boxlike vitrine.
146 Claretie, "La Vie à Paris," p. 3.
147 Duranty, "Remarques à propos de l'art égyptien," 1 March 1878, pp. 224, 230.
148 Ibid, pp. 230–32, and 1 August 1879, p. 138.
149 Ibid, 1 October 1879, p. 324.
150 Blanc, p. 440.
151 Duranty, "Remarques à propos de l'art égyptien," 1 August 1879, p. 138.
152 Ibid, pp. 137–38.
153 Rougé, p. 80.
154 Duranty, "Remarques à propos de l'art égyptien," 1 March 1879, p. 210.
155 L.518, private collection.
156 Moffett, pp. 38 and 40.
157 Moore, "Memories of Degas," p. 28.
158 Duranty, "Remarques à propos de l'art égyptien," 1 August 1879, p. 135.
159 Ibid, 1 October 1879, p. 324.
160 Ibid, 1 March 1879, p. 221; Louvre inventory AF 554.
161 Mantz, "Oeuvres des artistes indépendants," p. 3.
162 Chevillot, p. 28.
163 The possibility that the implicitly dark skin of the model added a racial element to some of the critical reactions deserves to be considered. For this subject, see Le Norman-Romain, et al.
164 Sickert, p. 185.

CHAPTER 4

1 Silvestre, "Le Monde des arts," in Berson, *The New Painting,* pp. 140–41.
2 Wolff, "Les Indépendants"; for a review of Degas' submissions to the Impressionist exhibitions, see Tinterow and Norton, "Degas aux expositions impressionnistes," in *Degas inédit,* pp. 289–351.
3 Goetschy, "Indépendants et impressionnistes," in Berson, p. 282; A. E. [d'Echerac], *La Justice,* in Berson, p. 276. For Burty in 1874, "The Paris Exhibitions," in Berson, p. 10; for Burty in 1880, "Oeuvres des artistes indépendants," in Berson, p. 269. It was Paul Mantz, in his review of the 1881 exhibition, who noted the presence the previous year of the empty glass case for the *Little Dancer:*

"Oeuvres des artistes indépendants," in Berson, p. 358.

4 Larousse, *Grand Dictionnaire,* 17:1006–07, 2nd suppl. The review quoted in the entry was that by Mantz, "Oeuvres des artistes indépendants."

5 See, for example, the series of articles that appeared between January 1879 and September 1880 in *Le Figaro,* which at that time had the largest circulation of all the Paris conservative quotidiens. Also see articles by Othenin d'Haussonville on juvenile vagabonds and delinquents in *Revue des deux mondes:* "L'Enfance à Paris: La Vagabonds," 4 (1 June 1878): 598–627; "L'Enfance à Paris: La Mendicité," 5 (15 June 1878): 891–927; and "L'Enfance à Paris: Les Rendez-vous du crime – Les Jeunes Adultes et l'éducation correctionnelle," 6 (15 January 1879): 346–377. For a recent treatment of the subject see Robert A. Nye, *Crime, Madness and Politics in Modern France: The Medical Concept of National Decline* (Princeton, N. J., 1984), pp. 58ff.

6 D'Haussonville, as in "Les Rendez-vous du crime," p. 346.

7 Jacques Bertillon, "Fous ou criminals," *La Nature* (23 August 1879): 186–87. Also see Nye, especially pp. xii–xiii, 43–48, 63–170; Linda L. Clark, *Darwinism in France* (University, Ala., 1984), especially pp. 30–75; and Stephen Jay Gould, *The Mismeasure of Man* (New York and London, 1981).

8 D'Haussonville, "Les Rendez-vous du crime," p. 346. Also see M. Guérin, "Courrier du palais," *L'Univers illustré* (11 September 1880): "Abadie et Gilles ont éveillé l'attention des criminalistes qui se sont demandés comme et pour quelles causes on pouvait être perverti à un âge si tendre et ce qu'il y aurait à faire pour prévenir la corruption précoce des enfants jetés sur le dangereux pavé de Paris. . . ."

9 Marcel, "Gazette judiciaire: Cour d'assises de la Seine: Présidence de M. Mathieu de Vienne: La Bande Abadie, Gille et cie: Audience du 29 août 1879," *Paris journal,* 31 August 1879.

10 *Le Figaro,* 4 August 1879, p. 1, cols. 1–2.

11 Archives de la Seine, boîte D2u8, carton 89. This and the materials found in boîte D2u8, carton 99, and in boîte D2u8, carton 103, are the source of much of the information on the Abadie affair.

12 Clark, pp. 30ff. For the assertion that religion was the antidote to crime, see, for example, P. B., "L' Instruction et le crime," *Le Figaro,* 11 January 1880, p. 4, cols. 3–4. That this kind of "instruction" had failed Abadie was pointed out by journalists of the Republican left. See, for example, *Le National* (31 August 1879).

13 D'Haussonville, "Les Rendez-vous du crime," p. 348. Other journals echoed the same sentiment: "la débauche précoce" (*L'Univers illustré,* 9 August 1879); "la puérilité sinistre" (*Le Monde illustré,* 6 September 1879); "la corruption précoce" (*L'Univers illustré,* 11 September 1879); and "la perverse précosité" (*Paris journal,* 29 April 1879).

14 Archives de la Seine, boîte D2u8, carton 89. The "règlements de la bande Abadie" were widely printed in the daily newspapers. See "La Bande Abadie," *Paris journal,* 23 April 1879, and Jean de Paris, "Nouvelles diverses," *Le Figaro,* 11 June 1879, p. 2, cols. 4–5.

15 A common assessment. See, for example, Albert Bataille, "Gazette de tribunaux: cour d'assises: Les Assassins de Montreuil," *Le Figaro,* 30 August 1879, p. 3, col. 1.

16 Emile Zola, preface to English edition, *L'Assommoir* (first published in 1876), translated by L. W. Tancock, (Harmondsworth, Middlesex, England, 1970), p. 21.

17 "Les Carnets de Ludovic Halévy," *La Revue des deux mondes* (15 December 1937): 821 [entry for 20 January 1879].

18 Z. Z., "L'Assommoir à L'Ambigu," *Le Figaro,* 18 January 1879, p. 1, col. 5.

19 Details of this connection have been culled from articles in *Le Figaro, Le Temps, Paris journal, Le Monde illustré, L'Univers illustré, Le Journal illustré,* and *Le Voleur illustré,* as well as from the sources listed in note 11.

20 *L'Evénement,* 19 April 1879. Zola's response appeared in "Echos de Paris," *Le Voltaire,* 26 April 1879, p. 1.

21 De Paris, "Nouvelles diverses: Suicide de M. Banzengeaud [sic]," *Le Figaro,* 28 August 1879, p. 2, col. 3; "Faits divers," *Le Temps,* 29 August 1879, p. 3, col. 3; "Faits divers: Le suicide de M. Banzengeaud [sic]," *Paris journal,* 30 August 1879.

22 Pierre Quiroul, "A Propos de *L'Assommoir:* M. Emile Zola: inspirateur dramatique," *Le Figaro,* 6 September 1879, p. 1, col. 2. Albert Wolff remarked upon "La façon dont Abadie organise sa bande tient du roman, autant que du melodrame qu'il a étudié comme figurant dans les théâtres," in *Le Figaro,* 4 August 1879, p. 1, cols. 1–2. Also see Un Monsieur de l'Orchestre (pseud.), "La Soirée théâtrale," *Le Figaro,* 23 May 1879, for information on the recruiting and organization of the extras.

23 Un Monsieur de l'Orchestre, "La Soirée théâtrale,"; de Paris, "Nouvelles diverses: Les Assassins de Montreuil dans leur prison," *Le Figaro,* 26 May 1879, p. 2, col. 4.; and de Paris, "Nouvelles diverses: Le Crime de la rue Fontaine," *Le Figaro,* 28 May 1879, p. 5, col. 5.

24 Aristide Roger, *Le Journal illustré,* 16 November 1879: "Exécutera-t-on Gilles [sic] et Abadie? Ne les exécutera-t-on pas? Tel est le thème sur lequel, dans vingt journaux, la verve des chroniqeurs s'exerce chaque jour. Ces precoces scélérats sont indignes de pitié, dit l'un. . . . Ils sont si jeunes, répond l'autre. Ils ont été si mal élevés. . . ." Excerpts from Abadie's "Histoire d'un condamné a mort" appeared throughout the press in mid September 1879. Félicien Champsaur judged the work, with its professed moral aim to serve as a warning to others, a "cri du coeur, une émotion vraie," noting that "il y a un romancier naturaliste en Abadie"; see "Les Mémoires d'Abadie," *Le Figaro,* 18 September 1879, p. 1, cols. 1–3. In the same journal, however, Georges Grison called for death as the only effective deterrent to similar "monstres précoces"; see "L'Echelle de peines," *Le Figaro,* 10 September 1879, p. 2, col. 4.

25 Wolff decried the "fausse et dangereuse sensiblerie" with which the "carnaval humanitaire" elicited such undeserved pity, "Courrier de Paris," *Le Figaro,* 13 November 1879, p. l, cols. 1–3. For public opinion, see the police report of 14 November 1879 in Archives de la Préfecture de la Police, dossier Ba/1.612, Avril 1879, Assassinat de la femme Bassengeaud; and de Paris, "Nouvelles diverses: Le Recours en grâce des condamnés à mort," *Le Figaro,* 8 November 1879, p. 2, col. 2.

26 Archives de la Seine, boîte D2u8, carton 99. Also see "Gazette judiciaire: Les Assassins de Saint-Mandé – Affaire Lecercle," *Paris journal,* 28 April 1880, p. 3; and "Gazette des tribunaux: Cour d'assises: Abadie et sa bande. – L'assassinat de Julien Lecercle," *Le Figaro,* 29 August 1880, p. 2, col. 6, and p. 3, cols. 1–2.

27 The illegitimate son of a worker in a porcelain factory and also a former extra, Kirail had been arrested only once before meeting Abadie, with whom he was tried and convicted of theft in July 1879. See Archives de la Seine, boîte D2u8, cartons 99 and 103.

28 "Projet de réforme de la magistrature." Partial or whole reprints of this document appeared in the press during May 1880. See Grison, "L'Assassin Abadie et la réforme de la magistrature," *Le Figaro,* 29 May 1880, p. 2, cols. 1–4.

29 Grison, "L'Assassin Abadie"; Macé himself seems to have been a proponent of this view. Joseph Reinach, in his *Les Récidivistes* (Paris: Charpentier, 1882) quotes the former police chief to the effect that of every one hundred participants in the March 18 insurrection, twenty-five were recidivists and twenty-five were prostitutes. See Nye, pp. 73–74.

30 Degas' sketches, as well as the reviewers' comments (see, for example, Geffroy, "L'exposition des artistes indépendents," in Berson, p. 343), place Degas at the 1880 trial and reflect his first-hand experience of the court proceedings.

31 Ludovic Halévy, "Les Carnets de Ludovic Halévy" (entry for 29 July 1879), pp. 838–42. Macé discussed the "affaire Abadie" in *Mon musée criminel* (Paris, 1890), pp. 176–84.

32 De Paris, "Nouvelles diverses: L'Assassinat de la rue Fontaine: Obsèques de la victime," *Le Figaro,* 21 March 1879, p. 2, col. 4.

33 Archives de la Seine, boîte D2u9, carton 99, document 400. It is not clear whether Valpinçon actually served at the 1880 trial. Ten days before the opening of each session of the criminal courts *(Cour d'assises),* a jury list was drawn up of thirty-six *titulaires* and four *suppléants.* At the opening of the session, a jury

of twelve was chosen from the thirty-six *titulaires*. The *suppléants* formed part of this pool only if medical excuses, and so forth, brought the *titulaire* number to under thirty. For long sessions, however, two *jurés suppléants* were picked and required to attend the trial, but they had neither voice nor function unless a vacancy occurred. For the mechanics of jury selection and jury duty, see Larousse, "Jury," in *Grand Dictionnaire*, 4:1122–24.

34 On this subject, see Druick and Zegers, "Scientific Realism: 1873–1881," in Boggs, et al., pp. 197–211.

35 Degas's friend Comte Ludovic Lepic, an amateur anthropologist, had made "quelques restitutions de l'ancien homme et de l'ancien bête" for the Musée de Saint Germain (Duranty, "Le Salon de 1874."). In the summer of 1872, Berthe Morisot informed her sister that she was reading Darwin, probably *The Descent of Man*, translated into French that year. See Rouart, ed., *Correspondence of Berthe Morisot*, p. 90. Also see Duranty, "Remarques sur le geste dans quelques tableaux," January 1877; references to Darwin and allusions to *The Descent of Man* and *L'Expression des émotions chez l'homme et les animaux* on pp. 22, 33, 36, and 283.

36 For further discussion, see Druick and Zegers, pp. 205–06.

37 Katherine Fischer Taylor, *In the Theater of Criminal Justice: The Palais de Justice in Second Empire Paris* (Princeton, N. J., 1993), especially pp. 10, 12, 22–30, 34ff.

38 Ibid., p. 40.

39 Grison, "Fantaisies juridiques," *Le Figaro*, 1 September 1880, p. 4, col. 1.

40 Champsaur, "Les Mémoires d'Abadie"; on Forain, see François-Victor Fournel, "Les Oeuvres et les hommes: Courrier de théâtre, de la littérature et des arts," *Le Correspondant* (25 May 1879): 729–30, in Berson, p. 221.

41 On the criminals, see, for example, Wolff, "Courrier de Paris," and de Paris, "Nouvelles diverses," *Le Figaro*, 20 July 1880, p. 3, col. 3: "Ne trouvez-vous pas que décidément les voleurs et les assassins veulent trop prendre d'importance?. . . Ils savent qu'on s'occupe d'eux, et tous veulent devenir des hommes célèbres." On *Nana*, see, for example, Wolff, "Nana," *Le Figaro*, 12 October 1879, p. 1, col. 1: "Les murs de Paris sont couverts d'affiches annonçant la prochaine publication de *Nana* dans le feuilleton du *Voltaire*."

42 "Nous ne sommes pas des cabotins!" See Montjoyeux, "Chroniques parisiennes: Les Indépendants," *Le Gaulois*, 18 April 1879, p. 1, in Berson, p. 233.

43 Jules Claretie, "La Vie à Paris: Le Procès Knobloch et Abadie. – Souvenir de cour d'assises. – Un Assassin. – Les Fils de joie," *Le Temps*, 7 September 1880, p. 3, col. 3. Champsaur in "Les Mémoires d'Abadie," compared Abadie with *L'Assommoir*'s Lantier. The criminals thus confronted romantic criminal lore much as characters in Zola's *L'Assommoir* deconstructed the romantic myth of the hard-working man, as most recently embodied in Hugo's figure of Jean Valjean.

44 Geffroy, "L'Exposition des artistes indépendants."

45 Trianon, in Berson, p. 367.

46 Claretie, "La Vie à Paris," in Berson, p. 335; also Wolff, "Courrier de Paris," *Le Figaro*, 10 April 1881, p. 1, in Berson, p. 372.

47 Dalligny, "Les Indépendants," in Berson, p. 335; "Petite Chronique," *La Petite République française* (14 April 1881), in Berson, p. 364.

48 Enault, "Chronique," in Berson, p. 339.

49 Mantz, "Oeuvres des artistes indépendants."

50 De Mont, "L'Exposition du boulevard des Capucines," in Berson, pp. 361–62.

51 See, for example, Claretie, "La Vie à Paris"; Comtesse Louise, "Lettres familières," in Berson, p. 356; Mantz, "Oeuvres des artistes indépendants."

52 Louise.

53 Trianon. Despite the contemporary interest in polychrome sculpture and the use of wax as an artist's medium, the *Little Dancer* was a closer relative to the wax mannequins used in recent ethnographic displays than the salon entries of a Henri Cros or a Désiré Ringel. Critics stressed the "science" of Degas' rendering; see, for example, Silvestre, "Sixième Exposition," in Berson, pp. 365–66. In 1878 Duranty had been very critical of the mannequins' lack of verity. See Duranty, "Exposition des missions scientifiques," pp. 58–59.

54 "Fasse le ciel que ma fille ne devienne pas une sauteuse." See Mantz, "Oeuvres des artistes indépendants."

55 See, for example, Grison, "Fantaisies juridiques," *Le Figaro*, 1 September 1880, p. 4, cols. 1–2; and d'Haussonville, "La Vagabonds," "La Mendicité," and "Les Rendez-vous du crime." Also see Nye, pp. 158ff.

56 "Aucun être social n'est moins sauvegardé que la jeune fille parisienne – par les lois, les règlements et les moeurs." Ignotus, "Le Bilan du crime," *Le Figaro*, 18 August 1880, p. 1. For an analysis of preoccupation with prostitution and its reflection in the art of the period, see Clayson, *Painted Love*.

57 Trianon; see Mantz, "Oeuvres des artistes indépendants."

58 On the subject of Halévy's Cardinal family series and Degas, see Pantazzi, "Degas, Halévy, and the Cardinals," in Boggs, et al., pp. 280–84.

59 Wolff, "Courrier de Paris," *Le Figaro*, 4 August 1879: and "Nana," *Le Figaro*, 12 October 1879, p. 1, col. 3. See Louise: "une cire grandeur nature, représentant une petite Nana de quinze ans costumée en danseuse et devant que s'extasient les imbéciles."

60 As the figurants were "assassins de profession" (see Grison, "L'Echelle des peines," col. 5), so Nana "fait le mal par profession" (see Wolf, "Courrier de Paris").

61 Zola's preface to the first edition of *L'Assommoir*. For Wolff's review of *L'Assommoir*, see Wolff, "Emile Zola," *Le Figaro*, 23 January 1879, p. 1, col. 4; and "Courrier de Paris," *Le Figaro*, 21 November 1879, p. 1, cols. 1–2.

62 Wolff, "Courrier de Paris," *Le Figaro*, 21 November 1879, p. 1. col. 2. Wolff, "Nana."

63 Claretie added this observation to his article when it was reprinted in *La Vie à Paris*, pp. 148–51, in Berson, p. 335, n. 1. See Mantz, "Oeuvres des artistes indépendants."

64 "Rouage moraux" was the term used by Edmond Duranty in "Sur la Physionomie," *Revue libérale* (25 July 1867): 499–523.

65 Cesare Lombroso, "Introduction," in Gina Lombroso-Ferrero, *Criminal Man According to the Classification of Cesare Lombroso* (Montclair, N. J., 1972), especially p. 15: "The Nose: This is frequently twisted, upturned or of a flattened, negroid character in thieves; in murderers, on the contrary, it is often aquiline like the beak of a bird of prey."

66 Marcel, "Gazette judiciaire: Cour d'assises de la Seine: Présidence de M. Mathieu de Vienne: La Bande Abadie, Gille et cie: Audience du 29 août 1879," *Paris journal*, 31 August 1879.

67 Claretie, "La Vie à Paris: Le Procès Knobloch et Abadie," p. 3, col. 4.

68 Isabelle Sauvé-Astruc, "La Préfecture de police: Cent Ans de police scientifique: Une Grande Exposition à la mairie du Vème arrondissement," *Préfecture de police d'hier et d'aujourd'hui* (Exposition, Mairie du Vème arrondissement, 10–29 March 1987), pp. 11–20; see Nye, p. 58; also see Alphonse Bertillon's "L'Identité des récidivistes et la loi de relégation," in *Annales de démographie internationale* (1883).

69 On this subject, see Taylor, *Theater of Criminal Justice*, p. 130.

70 Louise; de Mont, "L'Exposition du boulevard des Capucines."

71 Valabrègue, "Beaux-Arts," in Berson, p. 369.

72 "Gazette des tribunaux: Cour d'assises de la Seine: Abadie et sa bande. – L'Assassinat du garçon épicier Lecercle," *Le Figaro*, 31 August 1880, p. 3, col. 4.

73 Adolphe Racot, "Paris au jour le jour," *Le Figaro*, 27 October 1879, p. 2, col. 4.

74 Clayson, *Painted Love*, pp. 10ff.

75 Gustave Macé, "La Police parisienne: le gibier de Saint Lazare," (Paris, 1888), pp. 258–59, in Clayson, p. 43.

76 Bertall, "Exposition," in Berson, p. 330.

77 Clayson, pp. 35, 40. See especially ch. 2, "In the Brothel," pp. 27ff.

78 Duranty, "Sur la Physionomie," pp. 508, 514, 518.

79 Benfey, "Degas and the Black World,"pp. 25–30.

80 Duranty, "Sur la Physionomie," pp. 508, 514, 518.

81 For the source for this information and the discussion of Degas, Martelli, and the feminist movement that follows, see Broude, "Edgar Degas and French Feminism."

82 Ibid.
83 For details, see ibid.
84 Ibid., pp. 641–43.
85 On this aspect of the picture's iconography, see Salus, "Degas' *Young Spartans Exercising,*" and quote from Plutarch, *Vies parallèles: Les Vies des hommes illustrés.*
86 Theodore Zeldin, *France, 1848–1945,* vol. 2 (Oxford, 1977), pp. 151, 177.
87 Dalligny, "Les Indépendants."
88 See the entry on "Abbé Constantin (L)" in Larousse, *Grand Dictionnaire,* 17:7, 2nd suppl.
89 Ludovic Halévy, "Les Carnets de Ludovic Halévy," in Norman Kleeblatt, ed., p. 114.
90 On the paintings by Duez, see Clayson, pp. 64 ff.
91 Broude, p. 658.
92 Geffroy, "L'Exposition des artistes indépendants."

CHAPTER 5

1 In personal correspondence with me dated 6 April 1970, Charles Millard related what he had learned from Albino Palazzolo's daughter, Lydia Palazzolo, who was living in Paris at the time. Among other things, she told him that when her father returned to Italy at age eighty-seven, he took with him several casts of Degas horses and dancers that he owned.
2 See note 21.
3 In a November 1955 *Art News* article (p.70), Jean Adhémar clearly mentions the bronze "master cast of each figurine" but mistakenly includes it in the count of the A–T lettered series.
4 Wasserman, "I Never Seem to Achieve Anything"; Failing, "The Degas Bronzes."
5 In a letter from Paris dated 21 March 1960 from George Bernice to E. Coe Kerr found in the Knoedler Gallery Library, an interview with Palazzolo is related in which he says that he made both plasters.
6 Records at Joslyn Art Museum indicate that Knoedler and Co., Inc., had purchased the plaster from Monsieur de Faucemberge in Paris in February 1956.
7 Cortissoz, "Degas."
8 Pingeot, *Degas Sculptures,* p. 25. The inventory itself is published on pp. 192–93.
9 Luchs, "The Degas Waxes," p. 180. See also Campbell, "Degas Bronzes," p. 10–48.
10 Some of these alterations are illustrated in Failing, "Cast in Bronze," pp. 136–41, and Barbour, "Degas's Wax Sculptures," pp. 798–805. Pingeot, *Degas Sculptures,* pp. 153–91, publishes the inventory photographs in their entirety. See also Pingeot, "The Casting of Degas' Sculptures," p. 62.
11 The date of 1919 is found in Rewald, *Degas, Works in Sculpture,* p. 14.
12 Sara Campbell at the Norton Simon Museum has not only developed a list of the past and present locations of all the known casts of Degas' sculpture, but also the dates that skirt replacements have been undertaken on the various casts of the *Little Dancer Aged Fourteen.* My first technical examination of the original was revealed from impressions left in the soft wax that the original hair bow had a coarser weave than the present one. Luchs, pp. 182–83, documents, "The figure received a new skirt, shorter and more curved than the original, around 1919." Impressions left in the soft wax of the back of the proper left leg of the original would suggest a low-count plain weave and perhaps confirm that the dancer once had a longer skirt. The best documentation of change is seen when the current version is compared to the 1917–18 photographs published by Pingeot in *Degas Sculptures,* p. 189. The current undergarment is a fabric of an open-meshed, netlike quality, and the outer part of the tutu the low-count plain weave. The skirt on the Joslyn cast was replaced in 1967 and again for this exhibition in 1997.
13 Millard, *The Sculpture of Edgar Degas,* p. 8.
14 Michel, "Degas et son Modèle," p. 628. In Degas' notebooks, he lists the addresses of mold makers at earlier dates, between 1865–68 and between 1870–82, but there is not yet evidence that they actually did work for him in these years. See Reff, *Notebooks,* vol. 1, Notebook 21.35, p. 109; Notebook 32.2, p. 138.
15 *Woman Rubbing Her Back With a Sponge, Torso* (Bronze No. 28).
16 Kendall, *The Lost Plasters.*
17 Barbour, "Degas's Little Dancer," pp. 28–32.
18 From records kept with the Mellon Collection, Upperville, Virginia.
19 Kendall, "Who Said Anything," p. 74.
20 Millard, p. 9.
21 I say twenty-four bronze casts because, in 1978, I examined an "extra" one marked in several places under the base with Albino Palazzolo's monogram (AP). It appears to have been put on the market by Yvon Palazzolo and sold by Sotheby's in December 1970, a little more than a year before I met him in Italy. Examination including comparative measurements with the Simon corresponding *modèle* proved it to be as represented. I also say "more" because in Sara Campbell's published inventory in *Apollo,* p. 38, more than one HER cast has surfaced. Although not related to this particular sculpture, another HER cast I examined turned out to be a *surmoulage* that probably used a later cast as a model.
22 Millard, pp. 8–9
23 Barbour, "Degas' Little Dancer," p. 32.
24 Adhémar, "Before the Degas Bronzes," p. 70.
25 Although scientific analysis has not yet confirmed the presence of shellac on the original sculptures, seen under ultraviolet light, some exhibit an orange fluorescence characteristic of shellac. Ternbach also mentions shellac coatings in some of his reports on the sculptures and suggests it was done by the foundry and perhaps even Degas himself. Ternbach also used shellac to preserve the sculptures.
26 Although the *Schoolgirl* was not cast in bronze as part of the original series, notes in the Knoedler gallery library indicate that three or more casts were made before Knoedlers had twenty more bronzes made in 1965. Alison Luchs reports that Mr. and Mrs. Mellon acquired the original wax sculpture in 1958, and I made an X-radiograph of it in 1972. The armature structure for this sculpture as revealed by the X-radiograph is quite different in that it looks professionally made, unlike the other Degas sculptures I studied, although at least one had a commercially made armature. An X-radiograph of this commercially made armature is illustrated in Sturman and Barbour, "The Materials," p. 51. In 1979, at Mr. Simon's request, I examined the bronze *modèle* for the *Schoolgirl* which, when compared to a series cast, was approximately 2% larger. Interestingly though, the word *"modèle"* had been inscribed in the wax cast of the *modèle* before being replaced by bronze, so that parts of this inscription can be seen in the series bronze casts unlike the Hébrard Degas bronze series done in the 1920s.
27 I am told by a master mold maker, Robert Shure of Skylight Studios, that the heat generated by the setting of the plaster casts accelerates the deterioration of a gelatin mold. Since these plasters appear to have been cast solid with plaster, a significant amount of heat from setting would have been generated. Shure also said that is why it is critical that the gelatin mold be removed quickly from a plaster once the plaster hardens, but before too much heat from setting is generated.
28 By testing with a magnet, ferrous metal was detected as the rod material in the Joslyn cast.
29 These are excerpts from a letter from George Bernice to E. Coe Kerr, Paris, 21 March 1960, found in the records of the Knoedler gallery library.
30 National Gallery of Art, Washington, D.C., Curatorial records file, *Little Dancer Fourteen Years Old,* 1985.64.62
31 Richard Newman writes in his report: "Samples were prepared as cross sections and examined by qualitative X-ray fluorescence in an electron beam microprobe. Some layers of the samples were also analyzed by FTIR microspecterometry. The FTIR analyses were carried out on separate pieces of material from the original samples, if possible. In some cases, since the entire sample was used for the cross section, layers were carefully scraped with a fine-tipped scalpel from the cross section for FTIR analysis."
32 I have also speculated that the Simon bronze surmoulage of the *Little Dancer Aged Fourteen Years Old* which is marked *"modèle"* might also have served as a color guide.
33 Melanie Rolfe at the Tate Gallery in London has undertaken analysis of the colorants in their bronze *Little Dancer Aged Fourteen,* but her work has not yet been published.

SELECTED BIBLIOGRAPHY

Ackerman, Gerald. *La vie et l'oeuvre de Jean-Léon Gérôme*. Paris, 1986.

Adhémar, Jean. "Before the Degas Bronzes." *Art News* (November 1955): 34–35, 70.

Adriani, Götz. *Degas: Pastels, Oil Sketches, Drawings*. London, 1985.

A. E. [Arthur d'Echerac]. *La Justice*, 5 April 1880, p. 2. Reprinted in Berson, vol. 1, p. 276.

Armstrong, Carol. *Odd Man Out: Readings of the Life and Work of Edgar Degas*. Chicago and London, 1991.

Baignières, Arthur. "Le Salon de 1879." *Gazette des Beaux-Arts* 20 (1879): 146–50.

Barbour, Daphne. "Degas's Wax Sculptures From the Inside Out." *Burlington Magazine* (December 1992): 785–805.

——. "Degas's Little Dancer: Not Just a Study in the Nude." *Art Journal* (Summer 1995): 28–32.

Bareau, Juliet. *Manet By Himself*. London, 1991.

Baudelaire, Charles. *The Mirror of Art*. Oxford, 1955.

Baumann, Felix, and Marianne Karabelnik, eds. *Degas Portraits*. Zurich, 1994.

Benfey, Christopher. "Degas and the Black World." *The New Republic* (21 October 1996).

Bernay, Berthe. *La Danse au théâtre*. Paris, 1890.

Berson, Ruth. *The New Painting: Impressionism 1874–1886*. 2 vols. San Francisco, 1996.

Bertall [pseud.]. "Exposition: Des peintres intransigeants et nihilistes, 36, boulevard des Capucines." *Paris journal,* 21 April 1881, pp. 1–2. Reprinted in Berson, vol. 1, pp. 330–31.

Blanc, Charles. *Grammaire des arts du dessin*. Paris, 1897.

Blanche, Jacques-Emile. *Propos de peintre: de David à Degas*. Paris, 1919.

Blasis, Charles. *Traité élémentaire, théorique et pratique de l'art de la danse*. Milan, 1820.

——. *The Art of Dancing, Comprising Its Theory and Practice and a History of Its Progress from the Earliest Times*. London, 1831.

Blondel, Spire. "Collections de M. Spitzer: les cires." *Gazette des Beaux-Arts* 24 (1881): 289–96.

——. "Les Modelleurs en cire." *Gazette des Beaux-Arts* 25 (1882): 493–504.

Blühm, Andreas, et al. *The Colour of Sculpture*. Amsterdam, 1996.

Boggs, Jean Sutherland. "Degas at the Museum: Works in the Philadelphia Museum of Art and John G. Johnson Col-lection." *Bulletin of the Philadelphia Museum of Art* 81, no. 346 (Spring 1985).

Boggs, Jean Sutherland, Douglas Druick, Henri Loyrette, Michael Pantazzi, and Gary Tinterow. *Degas*. Paris, Ottawa, and New York, 1988.

Boggs, Jean Sutherland. *Degas*. Chicago, 1996.

Bouillon, Jean-Paul. *La Promenade du critique influent*. Paris, 1990.

Brame, Philippe, and Theodore Reff. *Degas et son oeuvre: A Supplement*. New York, 1984.

Brettell, Richard, and Suzanne F. McCullagh. *Degas in the Art Institute of Chicago*. Chicago, 1984.

Broude, Norma. "Edgar Degas and French Feminism, ca. 1880: *The Young Spartans*, the Brothel Monotypes, and the Bathers Revisited." *The Art Bulletin* 70 (December 1988): 640–59.

Brown, Frederick. *Zola: A Life*. London, 1996.

Browse, Lillian. *Degas Dancers*. London, 1949.

Buisson, Jules. "Le Salon de 1881." *Gazette des Beaux-Arts* 24 (1881): 210–38.

Burty, Philippe. "Exposition de la société anonyme des artistes." *La République française,* 25 April 1874, p. 2. Reprinted in Berson, vol. 1, pp. 36–38.

——. "The Paris Exhibitions: Les Impressionnistes." *The Academy* (May 1874): 616. Reprinted in Berson, vol. 1, p. 10.

——. "L'Exposition des artistes indépendants." *La République française,* 16 April 1879, p. 3. Reprinted in Berson, vol. 1, pp. 209–10.

——. "Exposition des oeuvres des artistes indépendants." *La République française,* 10 April 1880, p. 2. Reprinted in Berson, vol. 1, p. 269.

Callen, Anthea. *The Spectacular Body: Science, Method and Meaning in the Work of Degas*. New Haven and London, 1995.

Camesasca, Ettore. *Degas Scultore*. Florence, 1986.

Campbell, Sara. "Degas' Bronzes." *Apollo* (August 1995): 6–48.

Carjat, Etienne. "L'Exposition du boulevard des Capucines." *Le Patriote français,* 27 April 1874, p. 3. Reprinted in Berson, vol. 1, pp. 14–15.

Cassar, May. "'Petite danseuse de quatorze ans': The Making of a Replica Skirt." Sainsbury Centre for Visual Arts, University of East Anglia, *Bulletin* 5 (Summer 1988).

Cassini, Tommaso. "Degas e l'espressione fisionomica." *Storia dell'Arte* 86 (1996): 114–29.

de Charry, Paul. "Les Indépendants." *Le Pays,* 22 April 1881, p. 3. Reprinted in Berson, vol. 1, pp. 333–34.

Chesneau, Ernest. "Au salon: avertissement préable." *Paris journal,* 8 May 1874, p. 2. Reprinted in Berson, vol. 1, pp. 19–20.

——. *Le Statuaire J.-B. Carpeaux, sa vie et son oeuvre*. Paris, 1880.

Chevillot, Catherine. "Réalisme optique et progrès esthétique: la fin d'un rève." *Revue de l'Art* 104 (1994): 22–29.

Claretie, Jules. "La Vie à Paris: les artistes indépendants." *Le Temps,* 5 April 1881, p. 3. Reprinted in Berson, vol. 1, pp. 335–36.

——. "M. Paul Renouard et l'Opéra." *Gazette des Beaux-Arts* 23 (1881): 435–55.

——. *La Vie à Paris*. Paris, 1881.

Clayson, Hollis. *Painted Love: Prostitution in French Art of the Impressionist Era*. New Haven and London, 1991.

Cooper, Jeremy. *Nineteenth-Century Romantic Bronzes: 1830–1913.* Boston, 1975.

Coquiot, Gustave. *Degas.* Paris, 1924.

Cortissoz, Royal. "Degas as He was Seen by His Model." *New York Tribune,* 19 October 1919, section IV, p. 9. Reprinted in "Degas: His Seventy-two Achievements as a Sculptor." *New York Herald Tribune,* 25 October 1925, section V, p. 8.

Crouzet, Marcel. *Un Méconnu du Réalisme: Duranty (1833–1880).* Paris, 1964.

Dalligny, Auguste. "Les Indépendants: sixième exposition." *Le Journal des arts,* 18 April 1881, p. 1. Reprinted in Berson, vol. 1, pp. 335–36.

Dewhurst, Wynford. *Impressionist Painting: Its Genesis and Development.* London, 1904.

Distel, Anne. *Impressionism: The First Collectors.* New York, 1990.

Druick, Douglas, and Peter Zegers. "Scientific Realism: 1873–1881." In Boggs, et al., pp. 197–211.

Druick, Douglas. "La Petite danseuse et les criminels: Degas moraliste?" In Musée d'Orsay, 1989, pp. 224–50.

Dumas, Ann. *Degas's "Mlle. Fiocre" in Context: A Study of "Portrait of Mlle. E. F. . .: à propos du ballet 'La Source.'"* Brooklyn, 1988.

Duranty, Edmond. *Théâtre des Marionnettes du jardin des Tuileries.* Paris, 1862, 1864 and 1880.

——. "La Simple Vie du peintre Louis Martin." *Le Siècle* (13–16 November 1872).

——. "Le Salon de 1874." *Le Musée universel* (1874) 4:194.

——. *La Nouvelle Peinture à propos du groupe d'artistes qui expose dans les galeries Durand-Ruel.* Paris, 1876. Translated and reprinted in Moffett, pp. 37–47.

——. "Promenades au Louvre. Remarques sur le geste dans quelques tableaux." *Gazette des Beaux-Arts* 15 (1 January 1877): 19–37; (1 February 1877): 172–80; (1 March 1877): 281–89.

——. "Notes sur l'art assyrien." *Revue de France* 26 (1 November 1877): 1–32.

——. "Exposition des missions scientifiques." *La Chronique des arts et de la curiosité* (23 February 1878): 58–59.

——. "Daumier." *Gazette des Beaux-Arts* 17 (1 May 1878): 429–43; 18 (1 June 1878): 528–44.

——. "Promenades au Louvre. Remarques à propos de l'art égyptien." *Gazette des Beaux-Arts* 17 (1 March 1878): 221–33; 19 (1 March 1879): 209–24; 20 (1 August 1879): 135–45; 20 (1 October 1879): 320–36.

——. "La Quatrième Exposition fait par un groupe d'artistes indépendents." *La Chronique des arts et de la curiosité* (19 April 1879): 126–28. Reprinted in Berson, vol. 1, pp. 218–19.

——. *Le Pays des arts.* Paris, 1881.

——. *Le Mariage de raison.* Paris, 1954.

Durey, Philippe, et al. *Ernest Meissonier.* Lyons, 1993.

Duval, Georges-J. *Terpsichore: petit guide à l'usage des amateurs de ballets par un abonné de l'Opéra, procédé d'une preface de Mlle. Rita Sangalli.* Paris, 1875.

Elsen, Albert E. *Pioneers of Modern Sculpture.* London, 1973.

Enault, Louis. "Chronique." *Moniteur des arts* (15 April 1881): 1. Reprinted in Berson, vol. 1, p. 339.

Ephrussi, Charles. "Exposition des artistes indépendants." *La Chronique des arts et de la curiosité* (16 April 1881): 126–27. Reprinted in Berson, vol. 1, pp. 336–37.

L'Exposition de Paris: Journal Hebdomadaire Illustré 25 (September 1878).

Exposition universelle de 1878 à Paris: catalogue officiel. Paris, 1878.

Failing, Patricia. "The Degas Bronzes Degas Never Knew." *Art News* (April 1979): 38–41.

——. "Cast in Bronze: the Degas Dilemma." *Art News* (January 1988): 138.

Farwell, Beatrice, ed. *The Cult of Images: Baudelaire and the 19th Century Media Explosion.* Santa Barbara, 1977.

Fénéon, Félix. *Petit bottin des lettres et des arts.* Paris, 1886.

Fevre, Jeanne. *Mon oncle Degas.* Geneva, 1949.

Flint, Kate, ed. *Impressionists in England: The Critical Reception.* London, 1984.

Flor, Charles. "Les Ateliers de Paris: les impressionnistes." *Le National* (16 April 1880): 2–3. Reprinted in Berson, vol. 1, pp. 280–81.

Fosca, François. "Degas sculpteur." *L'Art et les Artistes* III (1921): 373–74.

Fusco, Peter, and H. W. Janson. *The Romantics to Rodin: French Nineteenth-Century Sculpture from North American Collections.* Los Angeles, 1980.

Gaborit, Jean, et al. *Sculptures en cire de l'ancienne Egypte à l'art abstrait.* Paris, 1987.

Gamilly, Hector. "Les Beaux-arts: sculpture française." *L'Exposition de Paris: Journal Hebdomadaire Illustré* (22 June 1878): 91–95.

Garnier, Charles. *Le Nouvel Opéra.* Paris, 1894.

Geffroy, Gustave. *La Vie artistique,* 3rd series. Paris, 1894.

——. *La Sculpture au Louvre.* Paris, 1900.

Goetschy, Gustave. "Indépendants et impressionistes." *Le Voltaire,* 6 April 1880, p. 2. Reprinted in Berson, vol. 1, pp. 282–85.

Gonse, Louis, ed. *L'Art moderne à l'exposition de 1878.* Paris, 1879.

——. "Musée Wicar, objets d'art: la tête de cire." *Gazette des Beaux-Arts* 17 (1879): 193–205.

Gordon, Dillian. *Hélène Rouart in Her Father's Study.* London, 1984.

Gourret, Jean. *Histoire des salles de l'Opéra de Paris.* Paris, 1985.

Gray, Christopher. *Sculpture and Ceramics of Paul Gauguin.* New York, 1980.

Gsell, Paul. "Edgar Degas, statuaire." *La Renaissance de l'Art française et des industries de luxe* (December 1918): 373–78.

Guérin, Marcel, ed. *Degas Letters.* Oxford, 1947.

Guest, Ivor. *Le Ballet de l'Opéra de Paris.* Paris, 1976.

Guillaume, Eugène. "Le Salon de 1879: l'architecture et la sculpture." *Revue des Deux Mondes* (15 June 1879): 869–931.

——. "Le Salon de 1881: l'architecture et la sculpture." *Revue des Deux Mondes* (1 June 1881): 649–79.

Halévy, Daniel. *Pays parisiens.* Paris, 1929.

——. *Degas parle.* Paris, 1960.

Halévy, Ludovic. *La Famille Cardinal.* Paris, 1883.

——. "Les Carnets de Ludovic Halévy." Translated in Linda Nochlin, "Degas and the Dreyfus Affair: A Portrait of the Artist as an Anti-Semite." In Norman Kleeblatt, ed. *The Dreyfus Affair: Art, Truth and Justice.* Berkeley and Los Angeles, 1987.

Havemeyer, Louisine. *Sixteen to Sixty: Memoirs of a Collector.* New York, 1961.

Hertz, Henri. *Degas.* Paris, 1920.

d'Hervilly, Ernest. "L'Exposition du boulevard des Capucines." *Le Rappel,* 17 April 1874, p. 2. Reprinted in Berson, vol. 1. pp. 23–24.

Higgonet, Anne. *Berthe Morisot's Images of Women.* Cambridge and London, 1992.

Hillier, Mary. *The History of Wax Dolls.* London, 1985.

Hofmann, Werner. "Degas et la drame de la peinture." *Gazette des Beaux-Arts* 111 (1988): 119–22, 191.

House, John, et al. *Impressionism for England: Samuel Courtauld as Patron and Collector.* London, 1994.
Humbert, Jean-Marcel, et al. *Egyptomania: L'Egypt dans l'art occidental 1730–1930.* Paris, 1994.
Huysmans, Joris-Karl. *Croquis parisiens.* Paris, 1881.
——. "L'Exposition des indépendants en 1881." *L'Art moderne* (Paris, 1883): 225–57. Reprinted in Berson, vol. 1, pp. 348–55.
——. *L'Art moderne: Certains.* Paris, 1975.
Jamot, Paul. *Degas.* Paris, 1924.
Janis, Eugenia P. *Degas Monotypes: Essay, Catalogue and Checklist.* Cambridge, Mass., 1968.
Jeanniot, Georges. "Souvenirs sur Degas." *Revue Universelle* 55, no. 14 (15 October 1933): 152–74; 55, no. 14 (1 November 1933): 280–304.
Kahane, Martine. *Le Foyer de la danse.* Paris, 1988.
Kahane, Martine, and Delphine Pinasa. *Le Tutu: petit guide.* Paris, 1997.
Kendall, Richard. *Degas: Images of Women.* London, 1989.
——. "The Impromptu Print." *Degas intime.* Copenhagen, 1994.
——. "Who Said Anything About Rodin?" *Apollo* (August 1995): 72–77.
——. *Degas: Beyond Impressionism.* London, 1996.
——. *The Lost Plasters of Edgar Degas.* London and Paris, 1996.
Kendall, Richard, and Griselda Pollock, eds. *Dealing with Degas.* London, 1992.
Lafond, Paul. *Degas.* 2 vols. Paris, 1918–19.
Lami, Stanislas. *Dictionnaire des sculpteurs de l'école française au dix-neuvième siècle.* 4 vols. Paris, 1914–21.
Larousse, Pierre. *Grand Dictionnaire universel du XIXème siècle.* Paris, 1890.
Lemoisne, Paul-André. *Degas.* Paris, 1912.
——. "Les Statuettes de Degas." *Art et Décoration* (September–October 1919): 109–17.
——. *Degas et son oeuvre.* 4 vols. Paris, 1946–49.
Le Norman-Romain, Antoinette, et al. *La Sculpture ethnographique: de la "Vénus hottentote" à la "Tehura" de Gauguin.* Paris, 1994.
Lipton, Eunice. *Looking into Degas: Uneasy Images of Women and Modern Life.* Berkeley, 1987.
Louise, Comtesse. "Lettres familières sur l'art: Salon de 1881." *La France nouvelle* (1–2 May 1881): 2–3. Reprinted in Berson, vol. 1, pp. 355–56.
Loyrette, Henri. *Degas.* Paris, 1991.
——, ed. *Entre le théâtre et l'histoire: la famille Halévy.* Paris, 1996.
Luchs, Alison. "The Degas Waxes." In *Art for the Nation: Gifts in Honor of the 50th Anniversary of the National Gallery of Art.* Washington, D.C., 1991, pp. 178–211.
Mallarmé, Stéphane. "The Impressionists and Edouard Manet." *The Art Monthly Review and Photographic Portfolio* 1, no. 9 (30 September 1876): 117–22. Reprinted in Berson, vol. 1, pp. 91–97.
Manson, J. B. *The Life and Work of Edgar Degas.* London, 1927.
Mantz, Paul. "Salon de 1865." *Gazette des Beaux-Arts* 19 (1865): 35–49.
——. "Exposition des oeuvres des artistes indépendants." *Le Temps,* 23 April 1881, p. 3. Reprinted in Berson, vol. 1, pp. 356–59.
de Margerie, Laure. *La "Danse" de Carpeaux.* Paris, 1989.
Marx, Roger. "Cartons d'artiste: Degas." *L'Image* (October 1897): 320–25.
Mathews, Nancy Mowll, ed. *Cassatt and Her Circle: Selected Letters.* New York, 1984.
McMullen, Roy. *Degas: His Life, Times and Work.* London, 1985.
Les Merveilles de l'Exposition de 1878. Paris, 1879.
The Metropolitan Museum of Art. *Splendid Legacy: The Havemeyer Collection.* New York, 1993.
Michel, Alice. "Degas et son modèle." *Mercure de France* (16 February 1919): 457–78, 623–39.
Millard, Charles. *The Sculpture of Edgar Degas.* Princeton, 1976.
Millet, Joséphine. "La Famille Mante, une trichromie, Degas, l'Opéra." *Gazette des Beaux-Arts* 94 (1979): 105–12.
M. Knoedler and Co. *Edgar Degas: Original Wax Sculptures.* New York, 1955.
Moffett, Charles, et al. *The New Painting: Impressionism 1874–1886.* Geneva, 1986.
de Mont, Elie. "L'Exposition du boulevard des Capucines." *La Civilisation,* 21 April 1881, p. 2. Reprinted in Berson, vol. 1, pp. 360–62.
Montorgeuil, Georges. *Paris dansant.* Paris, 1898.
Moore, George. "The Painter of Modern Life." *Magazine of Art* 12 (1890): 416–25.
——. "Memories of Degas." *Burlington Magazine* (January 1918): 22–29; (February 1918): 63–65.
——. *Confessions of a Young Man.* London 1941.
Moreau-Nélaton, Etienne. *Manet raconté par lui-même.* 2 vols. Paris, 1926.
Morisot, Berthe. *The Correspondence of Berthe Morisot.* London, 1986.
Muehlig, Linda. *Degas and the Dance.* Northampton, 1979.
Musée du Louvre. *L'Egyptomanie à l'épreuve de l'archéologie.* Paris, 1996.
Musée d'Orsay. *Catalogue sommaire illustré des sculptures.* Paris, 1986.
——. *Degas inédit.* Paris, 1989.
de Neuville, Lemercier. *L'Histoire anecdotique des marionnettes modernes.* Paris, 1892.
Nepveu-Degas, Jean. *Huit sonnets d'Edgar Degas.* Paris, 1946.
Nouveau Petit Larousse. Paris, ca. 1900.
Our Lady Correspondent. *Artist* 2 (1 May 1881): 153. Reprinted in Flint, pp. 41–43.
Pantazzi, Michael. "Degas, Halévy, and the Cardinals." In Boggs, et al., pp. 280–84.
——. "The Little Fourteen-Year-Old Dancer." In Boggs, et al., pp. 342–46.
The Paris Exhibition of 1878: An Illustrated Weekly Review of Trade, Industry, Agriculture and Art (1878).
Pickvance, Ronald. "Degas's Dancers: 1872–6." *Burlington Magazine* (June 1963): 256–66.
Pingeot, Anne, et al. *La Sculpture française au XIXe siècle.* Paris, 1986.
Pingeot, Anne. *Degas Sculptures.* Paris, 1991.
——. "The Casting of Degas' Sculptures: Completing the Story." *Apollo* (August 1995).
Potts, Alex. "Dance, Politics and Sculpture." *Art History* 1, no. 1 (March 1987): 91–109.
——. "Dolls and Things: The Reification and Disintegration of Sculpture in Rodin and Rilke." In John Onians, ed. *Sight and Insight: Essays on Art and Culture in Honour of E. H. Gombrich at 85.* London, 1994.
Pyke, E. J. *A Biographical Dictionary of Wax Modellers.* Oxford, 1973.
Rambler, X. "Impressions d'un flaneur à l'exposition: les jouets." In *Paris Exhibition of 1878.*
Raunay, Jeanne. "Degas, souvenirs anecdotiques." *La Revue de France* (15 March 1931): 262–82; (1 April 1931): 469–83; (15 April 1931): 619–32.
Reed, Sue Welsh, and Barbara Shapiro. *Edgar Degas: The Painter as Printmaker.* Boston, 1984.

Reff, Theodore. "Some Unpublished Letters of Degas." *Art Bulletin* 50, no. 1 (March 1968): 87–93.
——. "More Unpublished Letters of Degas." *Art Bulletin* 51, no. 3 (September 1969): 281–89.
——. "Degas's Sculpture 1880–1884." *Art Quarterly* (Autumn 1970): 276–98.
——. *The Notebooks of Edgar Degas*. 2 vols. Oxford, 1976.
——. *Degas: The Artist's Mind*. New York, 1976.
——. *Manet and Modern Paris*. Washington, D.C., 1982.
——. "The Morbid Content of Degas' Sculpture." *Apollo* (August 1995): 64–71.
Relin, Lois. "La 'Danseuse de quatorze ans' de Degas, son tutu et sa perruque." *Gazette des Beaux-Arts* 104 (1984): 173–74.
——. "La 'Ballerina di quattordici anni', il suo tutù et la sua parrucca." In Camesasca.
Rewald, John. *Degas, Works in Sculpture: A Complete Catalogue*. New York, 1944.
Rhoné, Arthur. "L'Egypte antique." *Gazette des Beaux-Arts* 18 (1878): 441–66.
Rivière, Georges. *Monsieur Degas, bourgeois de Paris*. Paris, 1935.
Rollinat, Maurice. *Les Névroses*. Paris, 1883.
Rothenstein, William. *Men and Memories*. 2 vols. London, 1931–32.
Rouart, Denis. *Degas à la recherche de sa technique*. Paris, 1945.
——, ed. *The Correspondence of Berthe Morisot*. London, 1986.
Rougé, Emmanuel. *Notice sommaire des monuments égyptiens exposés dans les galeries du Musée du Louvre*. Paris, 1879.
Saint-Léon, Arthur. *De l'état actuel de la danse*. Lisbon, 1856.
Salon 1880. *The Illustrated Catalogue of the Paris Salon: 1880*. London, 1880.
Salon 1881. *The Illustrated Catalogue of the Paris Salon: 1881*. London, 1881.
de Ségur, Comtesse. *Les Malheurs de Sophie*. Paris, 1872.
Salus, Carol. "Degas' *Young Spartans Exercising*." *The Art Bulletin* 67 (September 1985): 501–06.
Shackelford, George. *Degas: The Dancers*. Washington, D.C., 1984.
Sickert, Walter. "Degas." *Burlington Magazine* (November 1917): 183–91.
Silvestre, Armand. "Le Monde des arts." *La Vie moderne* (1 May 1879): 52–53. Reprinted in Berson, vol. 1, pp. 140–41.
——. "Le Monde des arts: Sixième Exposition des artistes indépendents." *La Vie moderne* (16 April 1881): 250–51. Reprinted in Berson, vol. 1, pp. 365–66.
——. *Au pays des souvenirs*. Paris, 1892.
Smith, Albert. *The Natural History of the Ballet Girl*. London, 1847.
Soldi, Emile. "La Sculpture au Salon de 1882." *La Nouvelle revue* (15 June 1882): 925.
de Soria, Henri. *Histoire pittoresque de la danse*. Paris, 1897.
Strutt, J. G., ed. *The Crystal Palace and Its Contents, Being an Illustrated Cyclopaedia of the Great Exhibition of the Industry of all Nations*. London, 1851.
Sturman, Shelley, and Daphne Barbour. "The Materials of the Sculptor." *Apollo* (August 1995): 49–54.
Tabary, Louis Eduard. *Duranty: étude biographique et critique*. Paris, 1954.
Tallis, John. *Tallis's History and Description of the Crystal Palace and the Exhibition of the World's Industry in 1851*. 3 vols. London and New York, 1851.
Terrasse, Antoine. *Degas et la photographie*. Paris, 1983.
Thiébault-Sisson, François. "Degas sculpteur par lui-même." *Le Temps*, 23 May 1921.
Thomson, Richard. "The Sculpture of Camille Pissarro." *Source* 2, no. 4 (Summer 1983): 25–28.
——. *The Private Degas*. London, 1987.
——. *Degas: The Nudes*. London, 1988.
——. *Edgar Degas: Waiting*. Malibu, 1995.
Trianon, Henri. "Sixième exposition de peinture par un groupe d'artistes." *Le Constitutionnel*, 24 April 1881, pp. 2–3. Reprinted in Berson, vol. 1, pp. 366–69.
Valéry, Paul. *Degas, Manet, Morisot*. Princeton, 1960.
Vente I. *Catalogue des tableaux, pastels et dessins par Edgar Degas* . . . Paris, May 1918.
Vente II. *Catalogue des tableaux, pastels et dessins par Edgar Degas* . . . Paris, December 1918.
Vente III. *Catalogue des tableaux, pastels et dessins par Edgar Degas* . . . Paris, April 1919.
Vente IV. *Catalogue des tableaux, pastels et dessins par Edgar Degas* . . . Paris, July 1919.
Un vieil abonné [Paul Mahalin]. *Ces demoiselles de l'Opéra*. Paris, 1887.
de Villard, Nina. "Variétés: exposition des artistes indépendants." *Le Courrier du Soir*, 27 April 1881, p. 2. Reprinted in Berson, vol. 1, pp. 370–71.
Vizentini, Albert. *Derrière la toile*. Paris, 1868.
Vollard, Ambroise. *Renoir: An Intimate Record*. New York, 1925.
——. *Degas: An Intimate Portrait*. New York, 1937.
Vuillier, Gaston. *La Danse*. Paris, 1898.
Ward-Jackson, Philip. "Reinvesting the Idol: J. K. Huysmans and Sculpture." *Burlington Magazine* (December 1996): 801–08.
Wasserman, Jeanne L., ed. *Metamorphoses in Nineteenth Century Sculpture*. 1976.
——. "I Never Seem to Achieve Anything with My Blasted Sculpture." *Harvard Magazine* (November–December 1977): 36–43.
Whibley, Charles. "Modern Men: Degas." *National Observer* (31 October 1891): 603–04. Reprinted in Flint, pp. 275–79.
Wilkinson, J. Gardner. *Manners and Customs of the Ancient Egyptians*. 3 vols. London, 1837.
——. *A Popular Account of the Ancient Egyptians*. 2 vols. London, 1854.
Wolff, Albert. "Les Indépendants." *Le Figaro*, 11 April 1879, p. 1. Reprinted in Berson, vol. 1, p. 251.
——. "Courrier de Paris." *Le Figaro*, 10 April 1881, p. 1. Reprinted in Berson, vol. 1, p. 372.
X. "Exposition des artistes indépendants." *La Chronique des arts et de la curiosité* (2 April 1881): 109–10. Reprinted in Berson, vol. 1, p. 372.
Zola, Emile. "Lettres de Paris: autre correspondance." *Le Sémaphore de Marseille*, 30 April–1 May 1876, p. 1. Reprinted in Berson, vol. 1, pp. 108–09.
——. *Au bonheur des dames*. Paris, 1883. Reprint, Paris, 1994.
——. *Mon salon: Manet: écrits sur l'art*. Paris, 1970.

LENDERS TO THE EXHIBITION

Allen Memorial Art Museum, Oberlin College, Oberlin, Ohio
André Bromberg, Paris
The Art Institute of Chicago, Chicago, Illinois
The Baltimore Museum of Art, Baltimore, Maryland
James A. Bergquist, Boston, Massachusetts
Brooklyn Museum of Art, Brooklyn, New York
Sterling and Francine Clark Art Institute, Williamstown, Massachusetts
Denver Art Museum, Denver, Colorado
The Detroit Institute of Arts, Detroit, Michigan
Fogg Art Museum, Harvard University Art Museums, Cambridge, Massachusetts
Hazlitt, Gooden and Fox, London
Hirshhorn Museum and Sculpture Garden, Smithsonian Institution, Washington, D.C.
The Hyde Collection, Glens Falls, New York
Janet Traeger Salz, Inc., New York
The Jedlicka Family, Switzerland
Joslyn Art Museum, Omaha, Nebraska
The Metropolitan Museum of Art, New York, New York
The Minneapolis Institute of Arts, Minneapolis, Minnesota
Musée du Louvre, Département des Arts Graphiques: Fond du Musée d'Orsay, Paris
Museum Boijmans Van Beuningen, Rotterdam, The Netherlands
Museum of Fine Arts, Boston, Massachusetts
Nasjonalgalleriet, Oslo, Norway
New Orleans Museum of Art, New Orleans, Louisiana
Philadelphia Museum of Art, Philadelphia, Pennsylvania
The Pierpont Morgan Library, New York, New York
Portland Art Museum, Portland, Oregon
Private collections in Denmark, London, Switzerland, and the United States
Smith College Museum of Art, Northampton, Massachusetts
The Nathan and Marian Smooke Collection
Stanford University Museum of Art, Stanford, California
The Toledo Museum of Art, Toledo, Ohio
Virginia Museum of Fine Arts, Richmond, Virginia
Yale University Art Gallery, New Haven, Connecticut

INDEX